in 1963, a group of Republican congressmen felt the need for a careful and scholarly reexamination of the foreign and domestic problems affecting the tranquillity
of the United States. At the first meeting of
this unofficial committee of legislators, it
was decided that men of outstanding academic stature be requested to submit papers
for discussion. No requirements of party
affiliation or specific philosophic affiliation
were set, and it was agreed that these
papers were to be study (not position)
papers.

"*The Conservative Papers,* therefore, are
not necessarily papers *by* conservatives. . . .
They do not define *the* conservative position. But they represent the sort of thinking
that those of us who call ourselves conservatives respect. In that sense, they should
provide a more meaningful insight into
conservatism than any of the often doctrinaire works which, from all angles of the
political spectrum, bombard us with castigations or glorifications of what warring
factions regard as conservative."

THE CONSERVATIVE PAPERS

THE CONSERVATIVE PAPERS

WITH AN INTRODUCTION BY
Representative Melvin R. Laird

Chicago
QUADRANGLE BOOKS

The Challenge to Western Civilization by Charles Malik is a condensation and fusion of various addresses, including: Passing to the Offensive, a commencement address delivered in June of 1961 at Seattle University; Some Urgent Tasks, an address given at the John Carroll Society in Washington, D.C. on October 18, 1961; Will the Future Redeem the Past, delivered at Colonial Williamsburg in June of 1960; and The Renewal and Doom of Civilization, a commencement address delivered at American University in June of 1961.

The Essentials of Solidarity in the Western Alliance by Henry A. Kissinger is an adaptation of two articles: "Nato's Nuclear Dilemma," published by The Reporter, March 28, 1963 (Copyright 1963 by the Reporter Magazine Company); and "Strains in the Alliance," which appeared in the October 1962 issue of Foreign Affairs (Copyright 1962 by the Council on Foreign Relations, Inc., New York).

Do Deficits Matter? by Raymond J. Saulnier is based on a Mead Lecture under the same title given at Trinity College, Hartford, Connecticut, April 4, 1963.

Inflation by Gottfried Haberler was adapted from his Inflation: Its Causes and Cures, published by the American Enterprise Institute for Public Policy Research (rev. ed.) June 1961, and reprinted by permission of the American Enterprise Institute. Copyright © 1960, 1961 by the American Enterprise Association.

Labor Union Power by Edward H. Chamberlin is adapted from an address delivered by Mr. Chamberlin to the American Mining Congress at its 1962 Metal Mining and Industrial Minerals Convention and Exposition in San Francisco, California, September 23–27, 1962.

Library of Congress Catalog Card Number 64–11731

First published 1964
by Anchor Books
and by QUADRANGLE BOOKS, Inc.,
180 North Wacker Drive, Chicago 6

CONTENTS

INTRODUCTION

by Representative Melvin R. Laird (Wisconsin)

Early in 1963, a group of Republican congressmen felt the need for a careful and scholarly re-examination of the foreign and domestic problems affecting the tranquillity of the United States. The group was made up of substantially the same men who had in 1960 prepared a report and brought together a corollary collection of papers on American strength and strategy—perhaps the most closely reasoned analysis of the nation's defense posture yet attempted.

I was fortunate to be able to serve as "chairman" of the *ad hoc* committee which sponsored *The Conservative Papers*. It included congressional experts in various political and economic fields:

Gerald R. Ford of Michigan, Thomas B. Curtis of Missouri, Peter Frelinghuysen, Jr. of New Jersey, John J. Rhodes of Arizona, Glenard P. Lipscomb of California, Charles E. Goodell of New York, Clark Mac-Gregor of Minnesota, and Robert Taft, Jr. of Ohio.

At the first meeting of this unofficial committee of legislators, it was decided that men of outstanding academic stature be requested to submit papers for discussion. No requirements of party affiliation or specific philosophic affiliation were set.

At our first meeting, also, it was decided to enlist the professional editorial assistance of two men who had worked on our earlier Strength and Strategy report, Ralph de Toledano and Karl Hess. To them, and to my legislative assistant, William J. Baroody, Jr., must go the credit for the final preparation of the collection for publication.

It was generally agreed that these papers must, within

the realm of human fallibility, eschew any policy recommendations. They were, in short, to be study (not position) papers. Obviously, the academic authors would offer some conclusions, whether explicitly or otherwise. But the main thrust of their work would be to the presentation of facts and the illumination of politico-economic questions.

The Conservative Papers, therefore, are not necessarily papers *by* conservatives. They are papers which might spark a conservative-liberal debate in the dignified and solid terms in which such a confrontation should be couched. They do not define *the* conservative position. But they represent the sort of thinking that those of us who call ourselves conservatives respect. In that sense, they should provide a more meaningful insight into conservatism than any of the often doctrinaire works which, from all angles of the political spectrum, bombard us with castigations or glorifications of what warring factions regard as conservative.

Labels, we are sure, would not preoccupy the men who wrote these papers. Each is a scholar, and I would assume that the *ad hoc* committee would have some difficulty in categorizing him. Each, in his own conscience, surely can define his political position. But each seeks truths that cannot be neatly packaged for the shelves of the political supermarkets. Those are the kinds of truths and thinking that this particular group of congressmen, who strive to be principled, constructive, and creative conservatives, set out to get. We believe that we succeeded—and that this published collection will as a *gestalt* make a significant contribution to American political thinking.

Despite our objections to frequently misunderstood political labels, however, the title of this compendium was inevitable, suggested by an earlier though obversely oriented collection: *The Liberal Papers*.

We are pleased by the differences in these two collections, and we are confident that they will draw a neat distinction which makes an important point about conservatism. *The Liberal Papers* seemed to seek a severance from the mainstream of our traditions and our thought. They were startlingly, eagerly "new" in every approach—

and obviously impatient of older disciplines, older logic, older aspirations. In the precise sense of the word, they offered a radical doctrine. *The Conservative Papers* explore not only what we seek, but what we have and what we are. What programs they do discuss, they discuss on the basis of principles. Perhaps that is the most important orientation of all in dealing with the term conservative: principles come first; programs follow and are based on those principles—not vice versa.

For instance, there is nowhere in these papers a detailed, programmatic study of defense policy. As legislators, we are involved in such discussions daily. What we sought here were papers which, as in Dr. Malik's, would bring some significant thinking (and if the word is not too old-fashioned, some inspiration) to bear on the question of the goals and objectives without which a defense program must remain simply a mechanical contrivance and a pile of military hardware wondrous in cost and complexity but less than meaningful in human terms or viable in the context of national survival. The engineers, for instance, can design missiles. Unless a consensus is reached on the use of those missiles, on the values they are poised to defend and upon which the fateful judgments to launch or not to launch must be based, they become an encumbrance rather than a shield.

Many of the papers, however, may seem overly economic in approach and thus suggest a more programmatic collection. It is our view that those who attempt a divorce between politics and economics, a major weakness of today's politicalized thinking, do their principles an ill service. Our thinking in including several, rather than just one economic paper, was that their various subject areas provided good bridges between principle and application without becoming litanies of policy proposals.

But do we, who requested and studied the papers, draw any firm conclusions from them?

Yes we do. We feel that these papers bolster, with studied wisdom, certain principles which we hold to be the basic unifying ingredients of the conservative position:

That man's nature basically is spiritual, not mechanistic;

that the individual's right and capacity to govern himself and set his own goals must be the primary objective of government as it seeks to establish system while avoiding despotism; that limitation of government's power is everywhere of the first order so that the individual's power may be enhanced; that there are values beyond history and above mere mortality.

In all these papers we see respect for those principles and respect also for the long past in which they became organic, and the longer future in which they will further evolve. Conservatives work today to build a new tomorrow upon the foundation of the past. What they seek to conserve is the best of what we have and the freedom to achieve the best of what the future proposes. These papers have helped us in the realization of the task. We hope they will help others.

To say that no one of us agrees with every word of every paper would be to state, we hope, the obvious. We sought no conformity of thought and we ended with none. Each of us has picked each paragraph apart in his own mind and conscience. The reader must do the same. In so doing, we frankly hope and deeply believe that the conservative position—which may be adduced from such works as these —will come to be known more accurately as the American position.

Melvin R. Laird

NOTE: Because of its unique dedication to studies in those fields to which these papers are addressed, the Hoover Institution on War, Revolution, and Peace, Stanford University, will be the recipient of the royalties earned by this book.

THE CONSERVATIVE PAPERS

THE CHALLENGE TO WESTERN CIVILIZATION

by Dr. Charles Malik

Charles Habib Malik, Ph.D., LL.D., Sc.D., Litt.D., Phil.D., H.L.D.: Distinguished Professor of Philosophy at the American University of Beirut, Beirut, Lebanon; former President of the General Assembly, the Security Council, and the Economic and Social Council of the United Nations; former Chairman of the Commission on Human Rights of the United Nations; former Ambassador of Lebanon to the United States; and former University Professor at the American University in Washington, D.C.

Communism started from zero forty-three years ago, and today it rigidly controls one third of mankind and has penetrated and softened up in varying degrees the remaining two thirds: was this phenomenal development inevitable? The victory of Communism in the late forties in China means that the largest compactly homogeneous mass of humanity, numbering some six hundred million people, is now the sworn enemy of everything free and Western: was this development inevitable? The Korean War, despite all its heroic exertions, ended in a draw: was this outcome inevitable? In Southeast Asia there has occurred during the last ten years an advance of Communism and a retreat of freedom: was this advance and retreat inevitable? Whereas international Communism was effectively absent from the Middle East ten or fifteen years ago, and in the consideration of Middle Eastern problems Communism was treated as though it did not exist, international Communism enters decisively today into the determination of every Middle Eastern problem: was this development inevitable? Whereas ten or fifteen years ago Communism was effectively absent from Latin America, today it is visibly present: was this development inevitable? The Communist Party, receiving orders directly from Moscow, is certainly more active and influential today in Asia and Africa than ten years ago, and responsible United States officials have said that the Communists have markedly intensified their activity in the United States: was this penetration inevitable?

Backing international Communism as its embodiment and vehicle is the most superbly organized international political party in history, the Communist Party, with the most advanced techniques of intellectual, social, economic, and political penetration and subversion ever devised: was the impotence of the West in developing any comparable counterforce inevitable? Backing international Communism materially is the Soviet Union, which appears to command atomic and nuclear weapons in abundance, whereas ten or fifteen years ago the United States had a monopoly of these weapons: was this decline in Western relative strength inevitable?

The visible struggle appears to occur all on this side of the iron and bamboo curtains: in Europe, in the Middle East, in Southeast Asia, in the Far East, in Latin America; and when people expect a crisis to break out tomorrow, they do not expect it in Albania or Rumania or Russia or China but in the home of freedom. Freedom then is on the defensive and not Communism: is it fated that the West should be always on the defensive, always reacting? The West today appears gladly to welcome neutralism in areas in which it would not have countenanced this phenomenon a decade ago: is this constant retreat of Western influence inevitable? In the nascent nationalism of Asia and Africa, which is otherwise a natural and good thing, there is an admixture in varying degrees of anti-Westernism, if not pro-Communism that leads to anti-Westernism: was this spread of anti-Westernism as a concomitant of the growth of nationalism inevitable? In the very nations that have attained the dignity of political freedom and independence other dimensions of freedom have been severely curtailed, namely, personal freedom, intellectual freedom, social freedom, spiritual freedom: was this contraction of the domain of freedom inevitable? Communism has been more persistent and effective in presenting to the Asian and African mind a well thought out interpretation of existence, the Marxist-Leninist ideology, than any outlook that has been forthcoming from the West: was this timidity in the articulation of the ideology of freedom inevitable?

The simple fact that the free world has not succeeded in forty years in pushing back the tide of Communism by one inch from where it really got political control leaves the strong impression that we are here dealing with an irresistible and irreversible thrust which will inevitably inherit and transform in its own image all the kingdoms and cultures of the earth: is this creeping tide of Communism completely irreversible? Perhaps the most distressing fact is the self-satisfaction and self-congratulation that prevails in the West; the softness, the laxity, the lack of determination and decisiveness, the general decadence, the uncritical readiness to settle for "peaceful coexistence": are we then face to face with some ineluctable judgment of fate or God?

I

In terms of the ultimate world struggle, how are we to assess the net performance of the immediate past? International Communism is today on an over-all basis relatively stronger than ten or fifteen years ago, and the free world is relatively weaker; there is a marked over-all advance by the one and a corresponding over-all retreat by the other. In history it is impossible at any moment to work out a neat, final balance sheet, for at no moment "in history" does history come to an end. It all depends then on the future. The future could redeem the past or it could confirm it. But it will redeem nothing unless the question of the inevitability or otherwise of the developments of the immediate past is first squarely and honestly faced. For either you believe that these things were inevitable or you believe that they could have been helped.

If you believe that they were inevitable—the outcome
of the struggle in China, in Korea, in Indochina; the Communist penetration of Asia, Africa, the Middle East, and
Latin America; the absence of any effective counteracting
force to the Communist Party; the relative decline in Western influence and Western economic and military strength
—that all these developments of the nineteen-fifties *could
not have been helped, then you are already a Marxist.* For
Marx, Lenin, and Khrushchev hold firmly (and Khrushchev repeats it every day) that the iron laws of history
are precisely such that whatever happens, Communism
will come out on top. Therefore, to them, and to you, if
you believe in the inevitability of these developments (that
is, if you refuse to assume moral responsibility for them),
the Communist advance and the Western retreat did not
come about by accident: the universe was such, history
was such, the nature of human society and its development was such, the economic, social, and political situa-
tions in Asia, Africa, Europe, and America were such, that
the advance and the retreat *had to take place.* I warn you
therefore against declining to assume full moral-historical
responsibility for what happened during the last two decades; for if you do so you are already a Marxist, and
Marxian Communism will have already won in your soul.

The only hope, therefore, is to believe that nothing of
what transpired was inevitable and that everything could
have been prevented or reversed. Only on the basis of
radical moral responsibility can you overcome the fatalism
of the cosmologists and the determinism of the dialectical
materialists. The future will never redeem the past, and
we will only pass from one fiasco to another, from one
pathetic drift to another, unless in contemplating the past
we can put our finger with certainty on such and such an
act and such and such a decision and such and such a
person and honestly say that this act or decision or person *could have been different* and therewith the course of
events would have taken a radically different turn.

What must be done in the immediate future to reverse
the trend of the immediate past?

Four conditions are absolutely *sine qua non:* unity

among the Western Allies, deeper understanding and statesmanlike assistance toward the peoples of Asia and Africa, winning the technological competition especially in the matter of armaments, and winning the economic competition in productivity. If the Atlantic world breaks up, whether from internal friction or external pressure, there will be complete disarray in the free world and little will be left to oppose effectively the onward march of Communism anywhere. If the Asians and Africans are not understood on the deepest possible level, and if the Communists prove that they are more friendly and helpful to them, then Asia and Africa will gradually fall to their wiles. If the Communists do better in the technological revolution, especially with respect to weapons, then all will be lost. If the West does not outproduce them both quantitatively and qualitatively, then the rest of the world will be sucked into their system.

Nothing is half as important today as that the spiritual unity of Europe, America, and the Mediterranean world be understood and affirmed. By any standard of measurement, the material and human resources of North and South America, of Western Europe, of Japan, of Australasia, and of as much of Africa (and there is no reason why all of Africa should not be included) and Asia as may be persuaded to co-operate can be so marshaled and coordinated as to outdo the Communist domain in any field of human endeavor by a ratio of at least five to one. It is all therefore a question of vision, will, overcoming the softness of life, and inducing the necessary unified effort. The free world has nobody and nothing to blame but itself if it cannot so order its house as to beat the Communists decisively in every realm.

The West should stand firm at all costs against any further expansion of Communism. But merely holding the line is patently not enough. This was the error of the doctrine of containment. It is a passive, defensive, unchallenging policy, and such a policy, except as a necessary first step, is doomed to failure; first, because this is a dynamic universe; second, because we are dealing with the most aggressive enemy, who will always swirl around and underneath and above all our containing devices; third, because a merely defensive or containing attitude means we are so lazy and self-satisfied that all we wish is to get away with our own skins, and without vision and concern for the rest of the world, we will sooner or later find that others, including our erstwhile friends, have no concern for us; and fourth, because we cannot be true to our own freedom if we do not wish and work for freedom for others.

It is interesting to note the sort of qualifications that responsible leaders sometimes use for "peace." The Communist spokesmen employ peace without qualification; by which they mean that they should be allowed to carry out their international proletarian revolution "in peace." But the spokesmen of the West speak of peace "with justice and freedom." This is a correct qualification from the Western point of view: peace without justice and freedom is no peace. But which of the two qualifications do they drop when they wish to use only one? They usually drop freedom and leave justice. This to me is wrong. It could betray an unconscious readiness to sacrifice freedom for what is sentimentally called justice. Both are certainly necessary, but freedom is more fundamental. Freedom creates justice but not conversely; for justice could be something mechanical without the ultimate freedom of the spirit which demands and creates and recognizes and enforces justice. The West can only be true to itself if it says, "I am prepared to settle for peace with freedom and justice," and if it wants to use only one of the two, "I am prepared to settle for peace with freedom."

It follows that an active policy of liberation is of the essence of any sound Western program for the coming years. When the late John Foster Dulles spoke of liberation shortly after he became Secretary of State, was there a Communist or fellow-traveling or Olympian or softheaded or pacifist or appeasing voice in the world that did not attack him? This synchronization of all these voices against anyone who would dare stand up and actively challenge Communism is one of the strange phenomena of this age. It measures the success of international Communism in intimidating and softening up the free world.

But only a believing, active, sustained, and bold looking forward to a free Eastern Europe, a free Russia, and a free China is worthy of the magnitude of the gigantic world struggle. A radical distinction must be made between the great peoples of these countries and their Communist governments. Policies should be devised and pursued in conformity with this distinction. The flame of freedom must be kept burning in the soul of the oppressed. The hope of liberation must never be allowed to fade away from their hearts. As free peoples they have an honorable and equal place in the company of the free. Their energies will be given the freest scope. Their spiritual and cultural contributions to the whole world are awaited and welcomed. With vision and leadership the West should be able to promise them greater material benefits than they have been able to achieve under Communism; benefits which they themselves would acquire by their own free exertions. But they should be promised much more: they should be assured of the freedom to criticize, the freedom to think, the freedom to create, the freedom to live, the freedom to work, the freedom to choose and turn out their own governments, the freedom to lead on the basis of merit in a world freed of the poison of mistrust, subversion, and intrigue.

The Communists never tire of assuring the rest of the world that "peaceful coexistence" means only that they will realize their unalterable aim of communizing the world without war, and that where they do not succeed in this, they will keep in mind the possibility of non-peaceful means. They are therefore absolutely determined to dominate the world with or without war. What they are saying behind all this jargon is that the international Communist movement wants to overthrow every existing government, regime, system, outlook, religion, and philosophy, and bring the whole world, all human thought, aspiration, action, and organization under its absolute control. This is their declared, unchanged, and unchanging objective.

I have yet to hear one Western leader who, assured to his face that he is doomed and will be "buried," can muster enough courage and conviction, if not to use the vulgar phrase "bury" with respect to Communism itself, at least to use some such civilized expression as that the days of Communism are numbered and that Communism will one day be completely forgotten. When Mr. Khrushchev assures Western leaders that their children or at most their grandchildren will all be Communist, I have yet to hear one Western leader who assures Mr. Khrushchev with the same gusto that his children or at least his grandchildren will live to regret and be thoroughly ashamed of the fact that their fathers or grandfathers were ever Communist. And whereas international Communism believes and acts on the belief that the days of everything non-Communist are numbered, my deepest fear is that Western leadership believes no such thing with respect to Communism. My fear is that the softening-up process has reached such an advanced state that all now believe that Communism is here to stay and that therefore the utmost they can do is to manage somehow to "coexist" with it. The deepest crisis of the West is the crisis of faith in its own values. Whereas Communism believes that non-Communist values must be eliminated from the face of the earth, and acts on this belief, the West no longer believes that Communist values themselves are doomed to utter destruction and oblivion and therefore no longer acts on this belief. I am yet to meet or know of one important Western leader who entertains a dynamic vision for the Communist realm which includes the certainty that the children of present-day Communists will have completely repudiated Communism and will have adopted the fundamental values of freedom. Let the West face up to this advanced state of decay in its own soul.

II

There are five fronts in which it is necessary today to pass to the offensive—the front of Communism, the front of neutralism, the front of those who are engaged in undermining the unity of the Western world, the front of materialism, and the front of what I would term the least common denominator. The center of the first two fronts lies outside the Western world, the center of the last two fronts lies inside the Western world, and the center of the third front exists at once inside and outside.

Morally and spiritually the Communists put you and me on the defensive; they make us feel guilty, and we supinely accept the terms of their debate. They talk in terms of "capitalism," "imperialism," "colonialism," "monopolies," "profits," "exploitation," "means of production"—all purely economic, purely materialistic terms. And how do we engage ourselves in debate with them? We usually answer that the exploiting capitalism of the nineteenth century no longer exists, that imperialism has been liquidated, that monopolies are now owned by the people, and that, as to profits, everybody now shares in them. It is evident that there is about this response a pathetic air of apology, a ring of feebleness, a sickly note of timidity, and those who make it clearly suffer from a guilty conscience. When we thus accept to be drawn into debate with the Communists on their own terms we confirm them in the feeling that they were right; it is as though we were telling them, "You are right in your attack; we are sorry for our past ways; but behold, we have now corrected them."

This will not do. The Communists should be answered, not apologetically, not as though they were right, but in terms taking them completely off their guard. They should be answered in human, moral, and spiritual terms.

It is most important that the Communists be put on the defensive. It is most important that the total arsenal of political, moral, and spiritual values be brought to bear upon this struggle. Naturally, if we do not believe in the primacy of these political, personal, moral, and spiritual values, we will not bring them up at all, or we will bring them up tongue-in-cheek. But to keep on talking only in their materialistic terms, to accept timidly their universe of discourse, to be constantly on the defensive vis-à-vis their onslaught, is already to have been vanquished by them.

One is not seeking to win a game of words and arguments: it is history and destiny that are at stake. I would certainly settle for losing the argument of words, provided I win the contest of history. The pathos of the situation today is that the argument reflects the contest. It is most important therefore to develop and execute policies and actions that will put the Communists and their friends historically on the defensive. Those who believe in man and his freedom, who know truth, and who trust in God, the guarantor of all freedom and all truth, must therefore pass to the offensive, not only of thought and conviction, but of that real, decisive, historical action that will cause the Communists to take to their heels.

Those who, for whatever reason, wish to remain outside the gigantic world struggle between Communism and freedom have every right to expect the rest of the world to respect their freedom.

As a matter of fact, real neutralism, implying real freedom of choice and real independence of judgment, is a triumph for the idea of freedom. The free world can only welcome it.

But a neutralist, rightly asking that his will be respected, has no right himself to impose his will on others. By his own logic, he must not object if others choose not to be neutral in this great struggle. Himself refusing to take a stand, the neutralist must respect those who do. A neutralist who is all the time working to extend the domain of neutralism, especially if this extension happens to be at the expense of only one side, is obviously not neutral.

Nor will one who really wishes to—and can—stay outside the struggle, play one side against the other. A neutralist in that case identifies his interests with the division of the world. He flourishes so long as there is tension; as soon as tension relaxes, he ceases to reap much value from his neutralism. Below a certain degree of tension, and above a certain degree of tension when the pressure increases considerably on the neutralist to take a stand, neutralism ceases to be profitable. *A neutralist, beginning by wanting to serve peace and understanding, could easily develop vested interests in the absence of peace and the absence of understanding.*

Then there is a neutralism that is, in fact, a Communist front. In a life-or-death struggle this kind of neutralism cannot be tolerated.

There are people and forces, inside and outside the

Western world, whose effect is to undermine whatever unity there is in that world. I am not thinking of the Communists, whose very purpose is to conspire in that direction. I am thinking of the softheaded, the duped, the tired, the frightened, the sentimental, the superficial, the unauthentic, and the perfectly innocent who mean well. If these people have their way, freedom will finally fall by sheer division and default. An offensive must, therefore, be mounted on this front.

England cannot be separated from Europe. Therefore, a determined effort must be made to heal the breach between the so-called inner six and outer seven.

France is an integral pillar of the West, and Western civilization is unthinkable apart from French culture. Therefore, France does not deserve an unequal treatment, and every force that tends to weaken or embitter or humiliate France must be resisted.

Germany must not be so slighted and intrigued against as to begin to think of neutralism as an alternative. Therefore, Berlin must not be abandoned, and those who desire a weak Germany must not prevail.

Japan is vital to every balance in the Far East. Therefore, relations with Japan should be deepened further, in the service of freedom and man.

Latin America must not be allowed to drift toward neutralism and anti-Americanism. Therefore, far-reaching measures must be devised and prosecuted with a view to ridding the Western Hemisphere of the Communist virus and promoting the friendliest relations between Latin and Anglo-Saxon on the basis of their common civilization.

The United States cannot go it alone in the modern world. Therefore isolationism in all its subtle shades should not have the last word, and America should embark on a bold, new policy of developing still more intimate relations with all her friends.

I include many things under the front of materialism: the quest after money and material gain, the all-consuming passion for economic security, greed and covetousness, trusting only our senses and what they deliver. I also include the fundamental spiritual attitude which denies real order in the nature of things, which denies that there is a real objective higher and a real objective lower, which instead derives the higher integrally from the lower, which obliterates the dimension of rank, excellence, quality, depth, and which, therefore, knows no rest, no grace, and no ultimate peace.

But there is a higher and a lower in the nature of things. An animal is higher than a stone, and man is higher than an animal. And in man his moment of understanding is higher than his moment of bodily desire, and perhaps his love is even higher than his understanding.

Nothing is more needed today than a mighty spiritual offensive which will put the material in its place and restore to the spiritual its original primacy and pre-eminence. Man, it seems, can never learn this lesson; he must always invert the right order of values and put the lower things first.

This does not mean that I scorn or spurn or sneer at the wonderful products of industry. On the contrary, I look upon science and industry as among the most important benefactors of mankind and upon their products as among the greatest monuments of the creative mind and spirit of man. And I will always wish and work, not only for me to enjoy the marvelous products of industry but also for others to enjoy them. The concept of economic and social justice is an absolutely valid concept. But he who does not know how man may become so ensnared and infatuated by these things as to lose the original, sharp edge of his soul, has still much to learn.

Those who believe in man and his freedom, who know truth, and who trust in God cannot allow the creative sources of their being to be sapped by softness and materialism. Nor can they rise to the historic demands of the hour in meeting the challenge of Communism, in helping the uncommitted world, and in effecting the needed Western unity, except on the basis of the primacy of the mind and spirit. They must, therefore, rebel against the tyranny of the lower and reinstall the higher on its legitimate throne.

The question of the least common denominator is the

distressing phenomenon of people without an enduring backbone. Because diverse points of view in this age are mingling and challenging each other on every turn, people with a weak backbone soon take on the color of those who surround them. Let a Communist meet a man from the free world, and soon the atmosphere is one of class struggle and pure economics.

Men of real backbone will never betray their fundamental convictions. They will never allow other points of view to dull or flatten their souls. They will at least remain silent, and silence often speaks a volume of words. God allows you to see the truth: it is possible to sacrifice yourself for it without asking or expecting anything in return.

In this age of softness, appeasement, and compromise, it is most essential that we pass to the offensive of holding fast to the deepest we know. Nothing is more tragic than that those who believe in man and his freedom, who know truth, and who trust in God should, in the intensity of the challenge, forget their principles or water down their beliefs. When the soul thus loses its integrity, none can respect it any more. Nor can it in the end respect itself.

The law of freedom does not require that all points of view should merge into a blur. All that is necessary is an order of mutual respect. Above all change and compromise, one point of view should remain immovable and grounded as on a rock. When the darkness lifts, that which is held by the rock will lift all men unto itself. And its immovability will itself cause the darkness to lift.

III

What is pre-eminently at stake in Mediterranean-Western civilization today is its human and universal elements. It is man who is denied; it is the affirmation that there is nothing that binds and cements all men into one family that is the prime danger; it is the fragmentation of humanity into endless exclusivisms, whether national or cultural or racial or economic, that poses the deepest challenge. Western civilization is doomed until, jolted out of its complacency, self-satisfaction, and sense of apartness, it rediscovers and reaffirms what is genuinely human and universal in its own soul. This means not only economic and technical sharing with Asia, Africa, and Latin America, but intellectual, moral, and spiritual sharing. What is supremely good must be good for all. Those who keep on repeating, as though they discovered a transcendental wisdom, that their ideas, their way of life, their civilization, is "not for export," but only their industrial products, do not know that they are thereby digging the grave of their civilization and the grave of their way of life.

A civilization in which the human and universal has atrophied can relate itself to others only through force, and force is not an enduring mode of relation, and it can always be broken by force. I am not speaking of diplomacy and propaganda; I am thinking of a whole philosophy of history. I am saying that a civilization is doomed if it is not creatively conscious of something universal and human it can and must give; and I am saying that Western civilization need not be doomed, because no civilization conceived and developed the human and universal more than it did.

Most certainly it is not a question of "imposing" anything on anybody; what is genuinely human and universal is never imposed; it is awaited, welcomed, and embraced. What is non-universal in your civilization you keep to yourselves; nobody wants it.

The Communists have a message. It affects the whole of human life. It provides a total interpretation. They are not afraid to say, this is good and that is bad. They are not afraid to shock and challenge the received customs and habits and ideas. They believe in something. The West does not want to shock and challenge; it is civilized; it is afraid lest it offend. Its trouble, therefore, may lie precisely in the fact that the content of its belief is very thin. For that which you really believe to be true and human and universal you will want to share with others; you cannot keep it under a bushel. The question is whether there is a profound part of your being that you honestly feel you must share with others. The question is whether you honestly feel that you are not complete or happy so long as others are humanly incomplete, that you are not self-sufficient so long as others are miserable or subhuman, a prey to every superstition and every dark fear.

The self-sufficiency of the Anglo-Saxon world, its age-old protectedness by seas and oceans, is its greatest present spiritual trial. It has not needed the rest of humanity. But the world has suddenly become physically one, and minds and ideas are much more critically and instantaneously and perpetually interacting with one another. Only he, therefore, who feels with humanity, who is at one with all conditions of men, who is insufficient and incomplete without them, who is not protected and separated from them, can help them and lead them and love them and be loved by them. The incompleteness of the Communist until he completes himself in others is what gives him the dynamism, the vision, the appeal in the eyes of Asia, Africa, or Latin America.

IV

The West contains the greatest concentration by far of science, technology, and industry in the world. These things are rooted in a cumulative tradition that extends for thousands of years. They are also self-perpetuating. They represent much more than mere mechanical technique: they represent a fundamental theoretical attitude of a whole culture toward nature, man, history, an attitude that cannot be transplanted to other cultures overnight. With Germany and Japan securely on the Western side, and with science and technology developing as they are in the West, there is no reason to believe that any comparable concentration will arise anywhere else in the world for at least another century. In the space of a century of scientific and technological superiority in which the mind is truly alerted to the ultimate issues of destiny, much indeed can be assured.

This is so far as science and nature and the harnessing of nature's forces are concerned. What about man and culture and history? The dimension of history is now more fully disclosed to the inquiring mind than ever before. And, incidentally, it is the canons of Western scholarship itself that have opened this majestic dimension of the past—not only of the Western past, but of every past. It is almost literally true that the past, in its fundamental structure, is now a completely open book. One need not fear that there is anything important still hidden that will, when uncovered one day, truly astound the world. There will be endless refinements, but the basic contributions are all known. Let every living culture, therefore, display its full achievements. In the total array of cultures and civilizations that can thus be fathomed, Western civilization, rooted as it is in Greece, Rome, the Near East, the Mediterranean, and Western Europe, stands out as something quite unique. In its unbroken continuity for four thousand years or more, in the creative principles of thought and feeling it established, in the patient disclosure of the mystery of God which it has inherited and which it can never disown, in the incomparable products of beauty and reflection and worship and political wisdom and collective endeavor which it has deposited, it need not feel any sense of inferiority with respect to any other civilization whatsoever. In fact, all other civilizations have learned and continue to learn from it, far more than it has any need to learn from them. This is its distinctive universal and humane character; namely, its preoccupation with truth, the truth that is valid for all; and its concentration upon man as the origin, center, and end of everything. He who, placing himself above any petty political or diplomatic considerations in order to see the truth in itself and for its own sake, penetrates to the depths of achievement of Western civilization, has no doubt whatever about its infinite sources of strength. The only question is whether those of its children who have been initiated into its deepest mysteries are going to prove worthy of what they have received and known.

The total forces of the West have not been fully committed. *This is most important.* Should the occasion arise for the total commitment of these forces, who can predict the outcome? Every time it has happened in the past, the West emerged finally victorious. Let the West *as a whole* really feel the pinch, and then I doubt whether anything can stand in its way. Having regard to its infinite potentialities of mind, morals, and material and to the creative potency of freedom, I do not have the slightest doubt that the enemies of God, man, and freedom will not have the last word—no matter how much suffering the resistance and destruction of them will entail.

There is a remarkable awakening in America as to the issues and dangers involved. This has never happened before in peacetime. People seem to me to be ready for any eventuality: they only ask to be told what is expected of them. It is quite possible that in many respects the people are ahead of their leaders. I feel that in a matter of days, if not hours, they could be galvanized into the most heroic action. A civilization that is thus alert and ready cannot be said to be nearing its end.

This raises the question of co-ordination. The greatest danger is unco-ordinated individualism, the frittering away of effort, the non-convergence of energy and interest onto a single point, onto a unitary outcome. People are excited; they sense the danger; they want to join in some common effort; they crave to know what that common effort is; but so far nobody has told them, nobody has summoned them to a supreme effort for the common good. A man demanding that he be shown the way, yet appearing to wait indefinitely without anybody showing him the way, soon develops a terrible inner frustration. If Western civilization goes down, it will be only because its leadership has failed to show it the way. There is no impersonal law of growth and decay here at work whatsoever. There is the very personal moral failure of the leaders to show the way. *And a real way out most certainly there is.* The actual, ready potentialities of this civilization, in every sphere, are so tremendous, so overpowering, that with the proper co-ordination and the right voice of leadership it can rise to any challenge. The greatest danger today is that either this leadership is not forthcoming or its voice will come too late.

THE ESSENTIALS OF SOLIDARITY
IN THE WESTERN ALLIANCE

by Henry A. Kissinger

Henry A. Kissinger is a member of the faculty of the Center for International Affairs at Harvard University, and Director of the Defense Studies Program. Among his books are *Nuclear Weapons and Foreign Policy* (1957) and *The Necessity for Choice: Prospects of American Foreign Policy* (1961).

In a major address on July 4, 1962, President Kennedy called for a partnership between the United States and Europe. With the passage of the Trade Bill, this "great design" seems to have come a step closer. To many, the Atlantic Community beckons as the great hope of the 1960's. The possibility of establishing a vital Atlantic system is indeed one of the great opportunities of our time. It may well be that to future historians it will appear the distinctive feature of our decade, far transcending in importance the crises which form the headlines of the day.

Yet the luster of the ultimate goal should not hide the obstacles in the way. Too often, there is a tendency to speak of an inevitable development of greater cohesion in the West. The fact is, however, that the West's opportunity has come at a time of serious internal division. This paper attempts to demonstrate how U.S. policies with respect to the German problem and NATO nuclear matters—the most vital issues confronting the Western Alliance—have exacerbated the divisions of the West and to suggest what measures are necessary to achieve greater solidarity within the Western Alliance.

The German Problem

The perspective of nations differs with their obligations, their geography, their history, and their power. No alliance can perfectly reconcile the goals of all of its members, particularly if one ally has world-wide responsibilities while the others focus their attention on regional or national concerns. But the minimum condition for effectiveness is that the requirements of the alliance should not clash with the deepest aspirations of one or more of the partners.

These considerations are especially relevant to what has come to be called the "German problem." The reason the Berlin issue has been so sensitive is not primarily because the city is physically vulnerable, but because all Germany is psychologically vulnerable. To many in the West, the crisis over Berlin seems to turn primarily on an effort to find new modalities of access to that beleaguered city. To these Western observers, conditions in Germany as a whole seem more or less tolerable. Not everyone accepts the division of Germany, and some might prefer a unified Germany; but none of Germany's allies makes reunification a major goal. Underlying many attitudes toward Germany is distrust—particularly in Great Britain—based on the experience of two world wars. Thus, there are many voices in the West arguing that the logical solution is to negotiate new access procedures to Berlin in return for accepting the "fact" of a divided Germany. To concede the continuance of a status quo which is not intolerable seems a small price to pay for a promise of stability.

However, stability gained in this manner would upset the domestic equilibrium of the Federal Republic; indeed, this is what makes the Soviets so anxious to secure recognition of the status quo. If the West tacitly or explicitly abandoned the principle of national unity, the Germans would consider it a sacrifice of their basic interests. Whatever stability might result from the settlement would seem to have been purchased at their expense. No German political leader can accept as permanent the subjugation of 17,000,-

ooo Germans by Communist guns. His minimum goal must be to ameliorate conditions in East Germany—a goal which he will be under increasing pressure to pursue independently if the allies prove indifferent to it.

This difference in perspective has been at the heart of the disagreement between Bonn and Washington regarding the negotiations over Berlin. The United States has held the unexceptionable view that a showdown cannot be faced until the West has demonstrated that all honorable means of negotiation have been exhausted. It was widely assumed that the primary Soviet goal is to stabilize conditions in Central Europe. The United States was therefore inclined to seek some way to deal with the immediate irritant—the problem of access to Berlin—by making concessions which might enhance the status of the East German authorities without impairing the physical means of access. Progress on the national question would be achieved by increasing the contacts between the two parts of Germany. In these contacts, it was supposed, the superior strength of Western Germany could not fail to make itself felt.

All of these elements were contained in the United States plan leaked to the press in April 1962. It provided for an International Access Authority in which East Germany would enjoy the same status as the Federal Republic; a number of East-West German commissions to deal with German problems; a non-aggression treaty between NATO and the Warsaw Pact; and an agreement to prevent the spread of nuclear weapons to other countries.

Differing perspectives on Berlin created a diplomacy which combined the disadvantage of allied disunity with the inability to gain any real benefit from the negotiations. France refused to negotiate. The Federal Republic approved diplomatic contacts with the Soviets only with great misgivings. The "exploratory talks" were first conducted by Secretary Rusk and later by Ambassador Thompson with Foreign Minister Gromyko. Thus, the Federal Republic, on an issue affecting it most immediately, stood on the sidelines in a position to criticize the unfavorable features of specific proposals without having to weigh them against alternative courses. By assuming the role of chief negotiator we played into the hands of the French and disquieted the Germans, and all without being able to bring about a settlement. Since we could not commit the West as a whole, the Soviets were in a position to treat our offers as fishing expeditions or to engage in fishing expeditions of their own. If they considered allied discord a feint, this gave them an incentive to be rigid. If they took it seriously, they could in effect bank every concession and use it as the starting point for the next round of talks.

Moreover, our desire to "stabilize" conditions in Central Europe turned the conversations into an effort to find something in the Soviet catalogue of demands which could be conceded without destroying the freedom of Berlin. Instead of using the talks to define the West's conception of the future of Germany and of security in Central Europe, American spokesmen concentrated on what change in the status quo in and around Berlin might prove barely tolerable. They did not advance a program either for eventual German unification or for ameliorating conditions in East Germany. Such schemes were considered "non-negotiable," and therefore likely to undermine any chance of a settlement. The impression was thus created that only the issues which the Soviets chose to raise stood between us and lasting peace. This set up a pattern of negotiations in which, in return for Western concessions, the Soviets would withdraw the threat which they themselves had initiated.

The more negotiations were conducted in this manner, the more relations between Bonn and Washington suffered. The mere fact of bilateral negotiations raised the specter of a U.S.-Soviet accommodation at the expense of our allies. Our tactics thus encouraged the Franco-German entente. The French inclination to create a Third Force would probably have been pursued in any case; but it was given impetus and opportunity by German uneasiness about our course. In the resulting atmosphere of distrust, even our determination not to diffuse nuclear weapons to our allies could be represented as further proof that we were collaborating with the opponent against our friends.

By focusing the negotiations on access rights and modalities, we stressed an issue most likely to lead to misunderstanding. A city divided by a wall, surrounded on three other sides by barbed wire, and existing as an enclave in hostile territory is not ideally placed for the exercise of so-called "flexibility." This is illustrated by the original U.S. scheme for an International Access Authority which the Germans leaked to the press in April 1962, as a means of torpedoing it. It provided that the authority to regulate access to Berlin was to be composed of five Western and five Eastern nations and three neutrals, Sweden, Switzerland, and Austria. The Eastern nations included East Germany and East Berlin. The Western group included the Federal Republic and West Berlin. This implied the tacit recognition of East Germany, as well as a different political status for West Berlin, which lent color to the Soviet claim that it would be a free city. On the narrower question of access, the determining vote would have been in the hands of three neutrals, two of them living in the immediate shadow of Soviet power. The people of Berlin are not likely to believe that their security has been enhanced by substituting the judgment of Austria, Sweden, and Switzerland for the responsibility now exercised by Great Britain, the United States, and France. Of course, if an international authority actually manned the checkpoints on the access routes with its own personnel, the current situation would be greatly improved. If, however, the authority merely supervised the East German policy, three small nations would be in the position of having to defend current Western rights and in effect to decide questions of peace and war.

There are indications that we are rethinking our policy toward Germany—and in doing so it is important that we understand the proper priorities. Access to Berlin can be the subject of various face-saving formulas if the Soviets ever genuinely want a settlement. The issue, however, will not depend on our ingenuity in devising those formulas but on whether the Soviets decide to settle for real stability and to envisage a comprehensive settlement of the issues in Central Europe.

Since the issue of the future of Germany must be faced, it would be wisest to do so within an Atlantic framework.

The purpose should be to show reasonable elements in the Soviet leadership group and in the satellites that neither security nor economic advantage requires the maintenance of a Communist regime in a divided country. Failing that, it should demonstrate to the Federal Republic not simply that the Soviets reject the West's optimum program but that they reject any scheme consistent with even the loosest definition of self-determination. For example, it might be possible to accept the notion of a German confederation and thereby the existence of an East German state. But recognition should be made conditional on a degree of internationally supervised self-determination in East Germany. To make the proposal symmetrical, it might be proposed that any party operating in any part of Germany be permitted to function in every part. A confederation so constituted would permit special security arrangements to be made for East Germany—including its neutralization—and, if necessary, the maintenance of existing economic ties with the East for a specified term of, say, ten to fifteen years.

Beyond any specific program, it is crucial to keep in mind what is really at stake in Germany. One of Chancellor Adenauer's most notable achievements has been to bring about the optical illusion that conditions in the Federal Republic are as firm and stable as his policy. This is not the case. The problem of succession in Germany is therefore of vital significance—though not necessarily in the sense often mentioned. Whatever one may think of Chancellor Adenauer, he stands for a principle which it cannot be in our interest to undermine: Germany's Atlantic orientation.

Chancellor Adenauer knows that long-range policy, moderation, and political acumen have not been the outstanding characteristics of his compatriots in this century. Many of those in Germany who support particular American initiatives do not necessarily share our over-all views. Those who extol flexibility in the abstract, the political realists whose expertise consists in finding ways of adjusting to immediate pressures, are not always the most reliable allies in time of crisis. We must take care lest in the effort to achieve short-range objectives we encourage a political style which in the long run may prove demoralizing for the West. It would of course be desirable if Chancellor Adenauer's stanchness could be combined with greater diplomatic adaptability, but if a choice has to be made, the former is preferable. If we are equally consistent, the Atlantic partnership will still endure after the latest negotiating gimmicks have been forgotten.

NATO Nuclear Policy

Turning to the broader question of the defense of the West, the Atlantic Alliance is going through another of those critical re-examinations which over the past two years have been recurring at ever shorter intervals. Once again there is wide debate over the relative emphasis to be given to nuclear as against conventional arms, the nature of nuclear war, and the relationship of various national nuclear forces to each other. The United States has resurrected its proposal for a multilateral NATO force composed of mixed crews and is urging it as the touchstone of Atlantic solidarity.

This proposal has had a checkered history. It was first advanced for study by former Secretary of State Christian Herter in December 1960. It was then cold-shouldered in the first few months of the Kennedy administration. Then in May 1961, at Ottawa, President Kennedy announced a willingness to consider "a NATO seaborne missile force, which would be truly multilateral in ownership and control . . ." Our European allies were invited to make proposals to this end.

Given the fact that none of our allies possessed seaborne nuclear systems and that a command and control system even for a national force is not a simple matter, the probability that our allies would come up with a meaningful control system was not great. Indeed, many believed that the problem would be recognized as insoluble. Our allies were then expected to ask the President to act as executive agent of the Alliance with respect to nuclear weapons.

When this did not happen, the United States a year

later again offered to consider a NATO nuclear force, provided our allies first built up their conventional forces and came up with an acceptable control system. Since the control problem had not become any easier, and since most of our allies were dubious about the need for the kind of conventional build-up we were proposing, it was not clear whether our proposal was put forward in order to be accepted or to be rejected.

Three months later, in September 1962, McGeorge Bundy spoke in terms of a multilateral European force: "It . . . would be wrong to suppose that the reluctance which we feel with respect to individual, ineffective, and antiquated forces would be extended automatically to a European force, genuinely unified and multilateral, and effectively integrated with our own necessarily predominant strength in the whole nuclear defense of the Alliance." This speech said nothing about what we understood by "multilateral," "integrated," or "unified."

Two months later, Under Secretary of State George Ball returned to the theme of a NATO force. He argued that we thought "a European nuclear contribution" to NATO militarily unnecessary. However, "should other NATO nations so desire, we are ready to give serious consideration to the creation of a genuinely multilateral Medium-Range Ballistic Missile force fully co-ordinated with the other deterrent forces in the North Atlantic Treaty Organization."

At the regular NATO ministerial conference in December 1962, nothing was done about the creation of a NATO multilateral force. A week later, on December 21, President Kennedy and Prime Minister Macmillan signed the Nassau Agreement, which provided for two multilateral forces: one that would absorb the strategic forces of Great Britain and France together with a United States contribution of nationally owned submarines; another in which the nonnuclear countries of NATO would create a multilateral Polaris force, which was later explained to mean that it would be jointly financed, owned, planned, manned, and operated.

Nothing was said about how either multilateral force

was to be controlled, deployed, or targeted. On January 10, 1963, prior to President de Gaulle's press conference, Under Secretary Ball was back in Paris to explain to the NATO Council that the multilateral NATO force that he had declared militarily unnecessary in November was now a high-priority goal of the Kennedy administration. Indeed, he was reported to have suggested that the United States was ready to begin training submarine crews of mixed national composition immediately.

This sequence of events is important to keep in mind, because it well might have led political leaders even less suspicious of U.S. motives than President de Gaulle to doubt whether we really had a "grand design" or whether we were not simply offering palliatives to perpetuate our hegemony.

In any event, after President de Gaulle's press conference of January 14, 1963, the multilateral force composed of the presently non-nuclear powers was pushed energetically. "Informed sources" were quoted as having said that we would create a force so strong that the Federal Republic of Germany in particular would see that the advantages of our notion of multilateralism far exceeded any benefits to be gained by association with France.

In order to thwart French nuclear pretensions, we proposed to create a counterweight by bringing some of the non-nuclear European countries into the nuclear field. The already difficult issue of multilateral control had thus become further complicated because we have made membership in the "mixed" force a test of Atlantic solidarity. Livingston Merchant was appointed to carry out the negotiations to bring this force into being.

Since then, the U.S. position has continued to shift. We have indicated that surface ships are a better solution than submarines. Secretary McNamara and President Kennedy have spoken of both a European and a NATO multilateral force. But the practical requirements they impose make the distinction elusive. They agree that any NATO force must be "integrated" with our strategic forces; there must be a single chain of command and a single finger on the trigger. In the light of Secretary McNamara's strategic theories, this must mean that either a European or a NATO nuclear force has to be under ultimate U.S. command. "The American representatives also will make it clear," the New York *Times* reported on February 27, 1963, "that there will be only one finger on the trigger of any nuclear force established by NATO. It will be that of the President of the United States."

In giving multilateralism this definition, we are trying to defend Atlantic solidarity on an issue and with a solution certain to magnify allied disagreements in the long run. The valid and important concept of interdependence can only be discredited by association with schemes that deprive our allies of the physical possibility of independent action, while we reserve this right for ourselves. U.S. dominance in the nuclear field may be a desirable solution from our point of view—though it is apt to prove shortsighted. But we should not call such an arrangement a partnership, and we must recognize that it will generate rather than alleviate pressures for change.

It is difficult to see just what would be achieved by the proposed force. According to Secretary McNamara's testimony, it cannot be used independently of our much larger forces. In any event we presumably would keep control over the nuclear warheads of the NATO multilateral force —according to the McMahon Act, we would have no other choice. Even if the law were changed with respect to the physical control over warheads, the problem of the veto would remain.

If we retain the veto, one of two things would happen. If we decided to engage in nuclear war and our allies refused, we would use the Strategic Air Command and our entire Polaris force, including that part of it "assigned" to NATO. If the situation were reversed—that is, if our allies wished to use nuclear weapons and we disagreed—neither the NATO force nor SAC could operate.

Can we give up the veto? It is not easy to see how a country can abdicate so fateful a decision to a majority vote of allies, no matter how close. The constitutional issue would surely be formidable.

Moreover, what would giving up the veto commit us

to? Does it mean that we would not obstruct the utilization of the NATO force in which we participate? In terms of Secretary McNamara's testimony, this partial employment of nuclear power is what must in all circumstances be avoided. In any event, it is difficult to imagine making a commitment to go to nuclear war indirectly and with only the smallest part of our forces.

But if we agree to go to war with our entire nuclear arsenal, what is the point of creating a NATO force? Then it would be wiser to create a political control body for the Alliance as a whole and agree to go to war on the basis of whatever majority vote seems indicated. (Such a commitment would probably still not meet the need. Even under existing arrangements, we could refuse to aid our allies if we were reluctant to honor our NATO commitments, and that situation would not change under the new scheme.)

What of the argument that the proposed NATO force could in time be transformed into a European force if our allies request it? We have repeatedly hinted at our willingness to consider this prospect. However, there are two major obstacles. The first is our strategic doctrine. Our insistence on a unified command, a single target system, and the need for instant response is as inconsistent with a separate European force as with national forces.

Even if we were prepared to change our strategic doctrine, serious problems would remain. The only way a NATO force, as now conceived, could be transformed into a European one would be for our allies to ask us to withdraw from it. This would defeat the prime purpose of many of the smaller countries in joining the force: to demonstrate Atlantic solidarity. Such a step, even if it were politically feasible, is much more likely to accentuate allied divisions than beginning with an explicitly European program. Moreover, as long as France is not part of a NATO force and Britain's contribution is token only, any attempt to turn it into a European force will raise the specter of German domination and thus create powerful antagonisms in other European countries.

It can be argued, of course, that the fear of German domination will make Britain and France more eager to join the multilateral force. This is doubtful. But even if it were correct, such a process of arriving at a European force would be extremely worrisome. It would be better for the long-term stability and cohesiveness of Europe if West Germany joined a Franco-British program than for Britain and France to be obliged to seek membership in a grouping of which Germany is the senior European partner. History has been altered by smaller nuances.

This suggests the need to examine another of the assumptions behind our advocacy of the NATO force. The NATO force is often said to be a device to avoid the issue of nuclear weapons in German hands. The contrary is likely to be the case. The multilateral force as now conceived may wind up by frustrating every member. If West Germany is seriously interested in acquiring strategic weapons, the multilateral force is apt to prove only an interim step and may turn out to be the easiest way of getting Germany into the nuclear business. The danger in the multilateral force is that those who want effective control over their nuclear destiny will not long remain content with the projected arrangements, while those who go along for such motives as pleasing us, defying France, or keeping an eye on Germany will soon grow tired of the expense and will search for other options.

This becomes apparent when the financial implications of our proposals are examined. The number of missiles most frequently mentioned for the NATO nuclear force is three hundred. It is interesting that this represents four times the delivery vehicles of the French Mirage force and three times that of the projected British Polaris force. We are in the curious position of opposing the existing national nuclear forces, but in order to thwart them we are engaged in diffusing an even larger number of weapons to a group of countries not now in the nuclear business and with no immediate prospect of entering it.

The cost of a fleet of Polaris submarines is estimated at more than $1 billion a year, or an increase of 12 per cent in the defense spending of the participating countries. A fleet of merchant ships has been estimated to cost upwards of $500 million, or an increase of 7 per cent. And as the technical problems of placing Polaris missiles on merchant ships is studied and the requirements for assuring invulnerability are analyzed, the costs are liable to mount.

For this heavy expense, the participants would obtain no significant increase in control over nuclear weapons. Can anyone seriously believe that this can be a permanent state of affairs? Is it not infinitely more likely that after a few years we would face repetitions of our current problem with France in relation to some of the projected members of the NATO nuclear force?

Our present proposals grant the need for a separate force, but they do not grant the equality that would give that force meaning. In a few years, after they have gotten into the nuclear business with our assistance, some of the countries now projected as participants will indeed be much better able to raise the nuclear issue than France is today. They will not have to argue about the possession of nuclear technology—since this will have been conceded—but about the control of a force where their influence is patently out of proportion to their contribution. If we resist these pressures, we may bring about a violent swing toward de Gaulle's conceptions. Nothing is more likely to promote Third Force tendencies in Europe than for us to engage our prestige in pressing for a force which on our own showing makes no sense militarily, does not alter existing control arrangements significantly, yet requires a heavy European financial contribution.

The multilateral NATO force is thus likely to combine the disadvantages of every course of action. It will not prevent the diffusion of nuclear weapons; it may well accelerate it. It will neither stop the acquisition of nuclear arms by West Germany nor satisfy over any extended period whatever demands may exist there for a greater voice on nuclear matters. It will stop the building up of conventional forces, for none of the countries reported ready to join the NATO nuclear force is likely to increase its defense budget beyond the expenditures required for the multilateral force. Among the many inconsistencies of our present position is the simultaneous pressure for the NATO multilateral force and an increase in European conventional strength. The two policies are incompatible.

Finally, the NATO nuclear force will not represent any significant burden-sharing. Since some of the European countries will possess some kind of veto, our strategic planning could not count on the NATO force. The strategy envisaged by Mr. McNamara would then require us to maintain whatever strategic forces are thought necessary for a U.S. counterforce response—as if the NATO forces did not exist.

As for other political effects often advertised as the chief, if not the sole, purpose of the NATO nuclear force, allied cohesion is unlikely to be strengthened. On the contrary, Europe will be fragmented even further. France will be isolated, but at a heavy price. We will have shifted the relative weight in Europe toward countries which, while more pliable in the short run, may prove more unstable in the long run. If the influence of West Germany in the multilateral force becomes too great, neutralism may grow in Britain, Scandinavia, and the Low Countries. (The New York *Times* of March 9 reported that the Federal Republic would contribute about two thirds of the European share of the NATO force, or about 40 per cent of the total costs, and that influence in manning and operational control would be proportionate to the financial contribution.)

The effort to isolate France by developing in the nuclear field a structure in which West Germany would be the key European member may in fact overstrain the fabric of European cohesion and Atlantic solidarity and also undermine the domestic stability of West Germany. It is in nobody's interest—least of all West Germany's—to set in motion events that can only end with suspicion and concern in most of the countries of the West about Germany's nuclear role. This is bound to aid the Soviet thrust to divide the West through the fear of Germany. A divided country, which in the space of fifty years has lost two wars, experienced three revolutions, suffered two periods of extreme inflation and the trauma of the Nazi era, should not—in its own interest—be placed in a position where, in addition to its inevitable exposure to Soviet pressure, it becomes the balance wheel of our Atlantic policy. We are encouraging tendencies that we may later regret. There must be better ways for West Germany to demonstrate its devotion to the Atlantic Alliance than to become the largest European contributor to a multilateral nuclear force.

The danger of our present course thus goes far beyond disputes about strategic theory. An issue as complicated as the control of nuclear weapons within the Alliance cannot be expected to have a quick or a neat solution. Nevertheless, the frequent and rapid changes of our position undermine our reputation for reliability—whatever the merit of particular proposals.

How can the most well-disposed governments follow our lead when our proposals are in a constant state of flux, moving from indifference to eager advocacy of a NATO force and from submarines to merchant ships all within two months?

Even so stanch a friend as Great Britain must be bewildered. First we abruptly canceled Skybolt. Then Prime Minister Macmillan loyally supported the Nassau Agreement with the argument that the acquisition of Polaris submarines would align Great Britain with our strategic thinking and our NATO conceptions. A month later we proposed that the multilateral NATO force of mixed crews be composed of merchant ships, which left the British Prime Minister exposed to the criticism of having purchased an unnecessarily expensive system for Great Britain. It makes us vulnerable to the charge of foisting a second-best system on the Europeans. And the situation is made the more poignant by the fact that Britain has been asked to join both forces.

Our friends do not know what to support. Our opponents are encouraged to exert pressure or at least to procrastinate in order to elicit other offers. Open-mindedness is often a virtue. But we must remember that the leader of a great coalition simply cannot afford to do all of its thinking in public.

To be sure, we are still able to obtain support, partly because we remain the strongest ally and our good will continues vital; partly because many of the smaller European countries have developed a habit of dependence. Our influence is still sufficient to generate domestic pressures in many European countries. But all this is to no avail if the basic direction is mistaken. Then, the domestic forces we encourage may well produce long-term instabilities.

One of the major achievements of American postwar policy has been the growth of a moderate, self-confident Europe that is willing to assume a degree of responsibility for its destiny. We take this so much for granted that we tend to forget how difficult the process has been and how precarious the balance still is in many European countries. In our eagerness to advance our new strategic theories, we have failed to perceive that ultimately success or failure depends on the political forces associated with us.

In this respect, there is reason for serious concern. In too many countries, governments that painfully obtained a commitment to the existing defense programs and to the very concept of NATO find themselves charged with undermining U.S. relationships by those who opposed every step along that road. In several countries, our policies are supported by groups who see in the slogan of Atlantic solidarity a convenient tool to discredit the existing European structure. The Nenni Socialists in Italy have not become converts to our concept of nuclear defense; they half-heartedly support us because they want to retain an option for their favorite schemes of nuclear disengagement. Britain, if it abandons its nuclear program, will not introduce conscription. Conventional defense may be invoked to wreck the nuclear program; the result is much more likely to be a form of neutralism than a conventional build-up. Undermining the major program of an ally must produce upheavals that cannot be measured by purely technical standards.

Our present course may thus encourage simultaneously neutralism and rabid nationalism, a sense of impotence and frustration. In another five years we may be confronted by a Europe that can truly be described by many of the epithets presently applied to President de Gaulle. The fact that many of our actions are taken with the seeming agreement of much of our press and some of our allies is no consolation. The test of leadership is not tomorrow's editorial but what history will say of us five years from now.

Where Do We Go from Here?

It is always difficult to reverse course. The longer a given policy is maintained, the more vested interests—in dedication, in conception, and in bureaucratic persistence—it is bound to create. Yet sometimes the wisest policy is to resist the temptation to rely on momentum and to step back and take stock.

Perhaps the best way to begin a reappraisal would be to ask ourselves what our real interests in Europe are. We should examine what kind of structure we desire in the long run rather than seek for devices to head off immediate pressures.

The goal of a strong, unified, and self-sufficient Europe, which American policy has consistently pursued for a decade and a half, is as valid today as it was when first developed in 1947. We may not have fully understood then that an economically powerful Europe would be more self-assertive in the political and military field as well. We may have believed subconsciously that our policy would relieve us of economic burdens without requiring a redefinition of Atlantic relationships. But whether or not we fully realized the implications of what we were doing, the Europe of today stands as a testimony to our foresight and our ability to subordinate short-term advantage to long-term benefits.

However, in the past few years there has been a tendency to recoil before the inevitable implications of our policy. It was always in the cards—indeed, it was our stated purpose—that as Europe regained its economic health, it would also seek to develop its own specific policies. It never occurred to us originally that the relations of the European states to each other should not be closer than each of them was to the United States. On the contrary, the original conception was that cohesive Europe would be a more effective partner for the United States. Atlantic partnership was then thought of in terms of establishing a relationship with a Europe whose internal structure would be firmer than the Atlantic bonds.

This great conception can be reversed today only by undermining the structures that have been laboriously developed over the past fifteen years. Fifteen years ago it might have been possible to try to construct an Atlantic Community on the most-favored-nation principle: that is, that no nation have closer relations to any other than to the United States. Today this attempt jeopardizes all that has been achieved.

Yet, stripped to its essentials, this is the course we have been pursuing with Europe in the nuclear field. Our definition of interdependence has the practical consequence of discouraging the emergence of any European identity in nuclear matters. We are fostering a concept of multilateralism that will add new divisions to the existing rifts in Europe. A multilateral force in which France does not participate and to which Britain makes only a token contribution will lead to a structure in the nuclear field inconsistent with all our postwar policies. The result is likely to be either competing European groupings or the ultimate emergence of a European unity in which the leadership rules have been drastically altered with our assistance.

It is still possible—though it is getting late—to prevent these developments by fostering a European nuclear identity growing out of the British and French programs. It is often said that such a course would divide the Alliance. But surely we are not going to maintain that partnership is possible only with nations incapable of independent action. Moreover, if we cut through the phrases to the facts, a separate European entity need be no more divisive in the military than in the economic field. In both instances, it calls attention to the need for a political effort to devise common objectives.

It would be idle to claim that conceding European nuclear autonomy would by itself solve NATO's nuclear dilemma. The problem of relationships in the nuclear field is sufficiently complex to resist simple remedies. But, encouraging a separate European center of decision-making is a vital first step.

We have had two choices with respect to Europe's nuclear future. We could have accepted the British and French national efforts and encouraged first a common Franco-British and ultimately a European program. Or else we could have grouped the non-nuclear countries into a multilateral force more responsive to our notions of a single chain of command and an indivisible target system.

We have chosen the second course. The first is preferable by far. It is hard to conceive of a stable Europe that does not include France as well as Britain. Any genuine nuclear policy must grow out of existing programs that will continue whatever the fate of the multilateral force. A policy that cannot relate us to the existing nuclear powers—our traditional allies—is not likely to be more effective when the present non-nuclear powers have become members of the nuclear club with our help.

Thus, instead of being hostile to the French nuclear program and, at best, indifferent to the British effort, we should use our influence to place them in the service of a European conception. This would also be the most reliable road to Atlantic partnership. The emerging European force could then be related to ours through political co-ordination and joint strategic planning. Such a policy would require a change of attitude on our part: at the very least the technical pressures from the Defense Department would have to be subordinated to an overriding political direction.

It may be argued that once we help Britain and France, every European country will want its own national nuclear force. President Kennedy mentioned even a Belgian nuclear force as a possibility. We must distinguish, however, between the possession of some nuclear weapons and development of an indigenous nuclear program. The latter is beyond the present capability of any European country, for either political or economic reasons or for both.

West Germany is prohibited by the Paris treaties from manufacturing nuclear weapons. While treaties have been broken before, in this particular instance the international repercussions are apt to be so serious as to give any German government pause. At the moment and for at least the next legislative period—that is, until about 1969—there are in any event no signs of any domestic pressures in Germany for a national nuclear-weapons program. This may change, however, after the multilateral force has whetted appetites.

Italy has neither the resources nor the domestic support for a national nuclear program. As for Belgium and other smaller countries, it can hardly be argued that the French program exceeds France's resources but that we must gear our NATO nuclear policy to preventing the development of similar programs by much poorer countries.

To be sure, a joint Franco-British program would probably lead to efforts by West Germany and perhaps other European countries for a degree of participation in at least the control mechanism. But in this way the Franco-British effort could become a spur to European political integration. France and Britain would have a high incentive to foster European unity before the issue of nuclear weapons under German national control becomes acute.

Whatever is done in the military field, the current crisis underlines the urgent need for greater political cohesion in the Western Alliance. We are now in the curious position of pressing for military integration while practicing political bilateralism. On a variety of issues from Berlin to the test ban, we have claimed the right for independent approaches to the Soviets.

However, unity in the security field is bound to be ephemeral without a common diplomacy. We cannot have different conceptions of a possible *casus belli*—which is at least implication of different negotiating positions—and insist at the same time that the resulting strategy must be unified. If we want to spur integration, the political field would seem much more promising than the military. If the nations of the Atlantic Community follow common policies, the existence of different centers of military decision would present primarily a problem of technical co-ordination, not a challenge to allied unity.

The Atlantic Alliance requires urgently a political body to define common objectives and the means to achieve them. It might be useful to begin by developing a common position on such issues as Berlin, disarmament, or the test ban. If it should be argued that this is impossible, the emptiness of nuclear multilateralism is patent. Nations that cannot agree on common negotiating positions on such matters are not likely to be able to devise a common strategy for an apocalypse.

Withal, it is important to keep the difficulties of the Western Alliance in proper perspective. Deep as the divisions are, they are the result of the success of previous policies. They testify to the emergence of a strong and self-confident Europe—a consistent goal of U.S. policy in the last three administrations. Few of the recent fissures in the West have been produced by Soviet actions. This is another way of saying that the West is less imperiled by outside pressures than by a tendency to waste its own substance. It also means that the remedies are still within our own control.

SOVIET SATELLITES: CHALLENGE TO U.S. POLICY

by Milorad M. Drachkovitch

SOVIET SATELLITES:
CHALLENGE TO U.S. POLICY

by Milorad M. Drachkovitch

SOVIET SATELLITES: CHALLENGE TO U.S. POLICY

by Milorad M. Drachkovitch

tory remarks about the historical background of the region as such, as well as about a fundamental point in its fate at the end of the Second World War.

It is indeed relevant to emphasize at the outset that the so-called "satellite" states or officially "people's democracies" are, generally speaking, the old European nations with a rich, centuries-long past and multiform political experiences. Without going deeper into the history which has profoundly influenced their national consciousness and shaped their sense of individuality, one should recall that in many instances Western Europe has been protected and its free development made possible because the Asiatic invasions lost their strength and impetus in the struggle with the peoples of Eastern Europe, that "borderland of Western civilization" in the words of the great Polish historian Oscar Halecki.

The geopolitically privileged West has played a no less crucial role in the development and aspirations of the East. In particular the great revolutions of the West in the eighteenth and nineteenth centuries have had profound reverberations in East-Central Europe, igniting there the recollections of the past and introducing the great revolutionary ideas of national self-determination and the rights of man and citizen. There was hardly a political idea or movement in the West which, for better or worse, did not influence the East. To mention only one example, the entire constitutional engineering of the post-1918 period in East-Central Europe was an attempt to introduce forms and practices of Western democracies, combining the French, British, American, and Swiss systems. If many of these experiments failed it is above all because the ominous rise of modern totalitarian ideologies and states, as well as the weaknesses of Western European democracies and aloofness of the United States, prevented the possibility of living in peace and normalcy.

However, when in 1939 Great Britain and France declared war upon Germany to defend the state of Poland and the principle of self-determination, it seemed that all the hardships of war would not be in vain and that the destruction of Fascism and National Socialism would herald the dawn of democracy, as so eloquently proclaimed in the Atlantic Charter. The hope seemed even brighter when at the Yalta Conference the Soviets joined the British and American governments in signing, on February 11, 1945, the Declaration on Liberated Europe which contained the following solemn pledge:

> The establishment of order in Europe and the re-building of national economic life must be achieved by processes which will enable the liberated peoples to destroy the last vestiges of Nazism and Fascism and to create democratic institutions of their own choice. This is a Principle of the Atlantic Charter—the right of all people to choose the form of government under which they will live—the restoration of sovereign rights and self-government to those peoples who have been forcibly deprived of them by the aggressor nations.
>
> . . . .
>
> To foster the conditions in which the liberated peoples may exercise such rights, the three governments will jointly assist the people in any European liberated state or former Axis satellite state in Europe where in their judgment conditions require, (a) to establish conditions of internal peace; (b) to carry out emergency measures for the relief of distressed peoples; (c) to form interim governmental authorities broadly representative of all democratic elements in the population and pledge the earliest possible establishment through free elections of government responsive to the will of the people; and (d) to facilitate where necessary the holding of such elections.

The well-known and incontrovertible fact that the clear and precise postulates of this Declaration had been violated by the Soviet Union, becomes more meaningful if observed in the light of the following two considerations. First, the "Sovietization" of East-Central Europe was not imposed immediately after the war but only, some two years later, when it became obvious that the large major-

ity of people in all states were against Communist domination.[1] Second, the resistance to Communism was expressed
not by the prewar "bourgeois" parties, prevented from re-
appearing on the political stage after May 1945, but by
the left-of-center, agrarian, and in some countries social-
democratic parties. What unfortunately so many "liberals"
and socialists in the West were unable or unwilling to realize was that the actual building of "people's democracies"
coincided with the suppression of their own Eastern coun-
terparts. Thus, when throughout the year 1947 (in Yugoslavia even earlier), full-fledged Communist rule was
imposed through terror and fraudulent elections, two principles for which the Second World War was fought were
brutally trampled under foot: the right to self-determination for every nation and the basic human freedoms within
every state.

[1] This fact may be illustrated by several examples. In Hungary, the elections held on November 4, 1945, gave the following results: Smallholders (agrarians) 57%; Social-Democrats,
17.4%; Communists, 17%. In Austria, where elections were
organized a few days later, on November 25, the electoral returns were even more disappointing to the extreme left: Popular (Catholic) party received 1,598,474 votes and 85 parliamentary seats, followed by Social-Democrats with 1,428,441
votes and 76 seats. The Communists polled 174,347 votes and
obtained 4 seats. These defeats convinced the Communists in
the Soviet zone of occupied *Germany* of the necessity to impose
a fusion with the Social-Democrats, early in 1946. In Western
sectors of Berlin 82% of Social-Democrats voted against fusion,
while a similar referendum was forbidden in the Soviet sector.
But even after the enforced unification with the Social-Democrats, in April of 1946, the "United German Socialist Party"
(S.E.D.), dominated by the Communists, only narrowly de-
feated its opponents on the last elections in East Germany, in
October 1946, at which the other parties were still permitted to
compete. The S.E.D. received 47% of the votes; the Liberal
Party, 24.6%, the Christian Democrats, 24.5% and the "mass
organizations," controlled by S.E.D., 3.9%. After these experiences in Hungary, Austria, and East Germany the Soviet authorities and local Communists decided to change drastically the
electoral methods and to impose henceforth only "unique" electoral lists, without tolerating any sizable opposition. From 1947
on, this pattern was used with increasing intolerance toward any
non-conformist political force in the entire satellite realm.

To give but one example of the process of imposing "people's democratic" rule on Czechoslovakia, the most genuinely democratic prewar state in East-Central Europe, in February of 1948:

The insaturation of People's Democracy in Czechoslovakia . . . was made in a country liberated by the Red Army and in which the Communists have received, under official pressure of the USSR, control over the national army and police. When the Czechoslovakian reaction tried to escape the hold of the Czechoslovakian Party, the Soviet Government dispatched immediately an Ambassador Extraordinary to President Benes, Zorine, Deputy-Minister of Foreign Affairs of the USSR, to announce that the Soviet troops were moving along the borders and were ready to reoccupy the country. This was announced over the State Radio by the Minister of Information, member of the Party, while the armed patriotic militia, controlled by the Party, kept watch over the ministries, public buildings and patrolled the streets.[2]

Stalinist Rule and Post-Stalin Explosions

The ruthless efficiency of the Soviet "diplomat" and the Czechoslovakian local Communists, so aptly described above, reflects the truth contained in the statement of the late John Foster Dulles that "the Communist rulers have shown an immense capacity to extend their rule. But nowhere have they developed a capacity to make their rule genuinely and freely acceptable to the ruled." Still, it seemed that during the six years of full-fledged Stalinist domination over East-Central Europe (1947–53) the listless populations were resigned to their destiny. Monster

[2] This excerpt is taken from an anonymous mimeographed pamphlet, written in French, and entitled, *Long Live Leninism*, published in 1962 probably by the Albanian Embassy in Paris. The entire pamphlet is violently criticizing Khrushchev's "opportunism," and the excerpt quoted above is made not to blame Soviet behavior in Czechoslovakia in February 1948 but on the contrary to praise it as an example of justified revolutionary interference.

trials, executions, mass purges of the Communist parties, a truly colonial pattern of economic exploitation by the Soviet Union—all these elements of naked power used by the Soviet Union gave the impression that nothing could break the external and domestic framework of the Soviet bloc. The cult of Stalin's personality was promoted no less vigorously in Eastern Europe than in Russia itself. Workers appeared to be docile automatons, peasants passive objects of collectivization, intellectuals depersonalized servants of the imposed "new faith," youth the target of the most systematic "molding." National cultures and even languages were seriously jeopardized by enforced "Russification." The West was impassively watching the process of satellization of East-Central Europe, and many of its intellectuals were fascinated by the spectacle of the emergence of Stalin's "new world." At the same time, Western chancelleries never entertained the idea that the U.S. monopoly of the "absolute" atomic weapon prior to 1949 could be used for the purpose of diplomatic pressure on the Soviet Union to fulfill her international obligations toward East-Central Europe.[3]

Then Stalin died, and with extraordinary celerity his empire was cracking under the pressure of captive subjects. Inmates of the Siberian camp of Vorkuta gave a sort of symbolic sign by their strike against camp authorities; the proletarians in East Germany rose against their exploiters; and when in February of 1956 Nikita Khrushchev admitted to the Communist elite that Stalin's rule was that of a

[3] To dispel any misunderstanding, this is not a plea, even in retrospect, for a preventive war against the U.S.S.R. One should state, however, that today's knowledge about Stalin's initial caution and respect for Western military and technological might, would probably make him less inclined to build his satellite empire, if he were notified on time that the West was not willing to accept and had the means to prevent the new subjugation of the same region—East-Central Europe—for the freedom of which the war against Hitler was waged and the Yalta declaration proclaimed. The situation in the world today would be quite different if Churchill's famous Fulton address did not remain a piece of brilliant oratory instead of a guideline for action of principle-minded and self-confident democracy.

psychopathic murderer, the workers of Poznan and the entire people of Hungary rose in indignation, demanding the restoration of their violated national and human rights.

The most remarkable thing about these spontaneous popular outbursts was that they were largely initiated and carried through by precisely those on whom the Communist rule was supposed to rely: intellectuals and the school youth, workers of industrial centers, and even some segments of the Communist parties.

Khrushchev Moves to Save the Essentials

We know today that the Soviet leadership was taken unaware by these demonstrations of patriotic feelings in East-Central Europe. Khrushchev has recently revealed that after the uprising of June 17, 1953, some members of the Soviet Politburo advocated even relinquishing Communist rule in Eastern Germany. It is well known also that before reaching its decision to crush by military force the Hungarian revolt on November 4, 1956, the top Soviet leadership hesitated and argued for days about the kind of measures to take in dealing with Hungary.

All hesitations and repressions notwithstanding, Nikita Khrushchev realized that it was impossible to rule Stalinistically without Stalin, and that the very preservation of the Soviet Empire required some drastic changes in the "colonial" policies pursued heretofore in the satellite states. As a result of that awareness, the Council of Mutual Economic Aid (COMECON), founded by Stalin in 1949 as a counterpoise to the Marshall Plan, but functioning chiefly as sponsor of bilateral trade agreements concluded between its members, was resuscitated after Khrushchev's accession to power in 1955 and developed more systematically after 1956. Repudiating Stalinist practice, Khrushchev resorted to the old Leninist device of a "new economic policy" to be adopted this time in Soviet relations with East-Central Europe. Giving new substance to the rusty instrument of the COMECON, Khrushchev unfolded a perspective of a "Socialist commonwealth" to be attained by introducing a "socialist division of labor," i.e., increased specialization in various fields of production among the members of the COMECON. Thus, instead of the Stalinist economic absurdity that every satellite state, irrespective of its potentialities, should develop as a microcosmic replica of the Soviet Union, an autarchic unit controlled by Moscow, Khrushchev's grand design was to match the Western European process of supranational integration by superseding the existing national plans and replacing them progressively by a macro-economic plan, including the Soviet Union and all the satellites. In an article, "Vital Question of the Development of the Socialist World System," written in June 1962 after a meeting in Moscow of the first secretaries of the central committees of the Communist and workers' parties and heads of governments of the member countries of the COMECON, Nikita Khrushchev outlined the tasks and prospects of the COMECON as follows:

> At this level a special significance is acquired by coordinated national-economic plans, socialist international division of labor, and by coordination and specialization of production which will guarantee successful organic development of the socialist countries . . . The task now is to do everything to consolidate the national economy of each, broaden its relations and gradually advance towards that single worldwide organism embracing the system as a whole which Lenin's genius foresaw.[4]

At the same time, breaking with another of Stalin's habits, Khrushchev was willing to leave the individual Communist rulers a greater degree of freedom to manage their domestic affairs on condition that monopoly of political power of the Communist party is not relinquished and his line in foreign policy is followed without deviation.

"The Grand Tactician" . . .

To assess the real meaning of Khrushchev's intentions and his methods of achieving them, one might quote his

[4] *World Marxist Review,* vol. 5, No. 9, September 1962, p. 4.

own words from the same article: "For us, the Communists, the basic question in the struggle of the two systems is how, and in what way, to insure the steady growth of the influence of socialism throughout the world." Viewing his new course toward East-Central Europe in the light of this statement, three considerations appear as particularly relevant. The first is that by "de-Stalinizing" the Soviet imperial pattern, Khrushchev was actually opening some safety valves in order to forestall popular explosions and confuse the hard oppositional feelings. His reconciliation with Tito, intimacy with Gomulka, and the green light to Kadar to "liberalize" the regime in Hungary, are proofs that Khrushchev is determined to succeed where Stalin failed.

This leads to the second consideration, namely that the perennial Soviet goal of absorption of East-Central Europe might be fulfilled more easily by employing the co-operative devices of the COMECON type, rather than the brutal and primitive methods employed by Stalin. "Bloc-wide economic integration through extra-long-term supra-national planning"[5] may be a more efficient way to achieve the desired political integration, in particular when the "socialist division of labor" places "all the specializing countries in a relationship of dependence vis-à-vis their major supplier of raw materials and the only member not subject to effective specialization, the USSR."[6]

Last but certainly not least, internal liberalization and co-operative supranational planning serve also as an invaluable recommendation for a much more efficient Soviet influence and penetration of the Western and "uncommitted" worlds. As much as Stalin was involuntarily the "father" of NATO, Khrushchev aspires voluntarily to be its gravedigger. While Stalin's interest in Asia, Africa, and Latin America was of a perfunctory nature, and while he intended to keep his satellites confined behind the iron cur-

[5] Alfred Zauberman, "Economic Integration: Problems and Prospects," *Problems of Communism*, No. 4, vol. VIII, July–August 1959, p. 23.
[6] Zbigniew K. Brzezinski, *The Soviet Bloc: Unity and Conflict*. Harvard University Press, 1960, p. 285.

tain, Khrushchev tries to be the leading actor in such places as Laos, the Congo, and Cuba, assigning at the same time to "people's democracies" an increasingly active role in establishing all kinds of relations with the world's "neutrals."

Some of the results achieved thus far are impressive. At the September 1961 Belgrade conference of twenty-five "uncommitted" nations, militant anti-colonialism was directed exclusively against the West, and nobody raised a single question about the nature of governments in East-Central Europe. Moreover, Tito, who at the Sixth Congress of the Communist Party of Yugoslavia, in November 1952, branded the Soviet Union as an "imperialist power" and attacked her policy of "enslavement of Poland, Rumania, Hungary, Bulgaria, Czechoslovakia, and so on," was nine years later a most consistent advocate of Khrushchev foreign policies, including defense of Ulbricht's Stalinist regime in East Germany.

Likewise, the increasing closeness among the Polish, Yugoslav, and Italian Communists (the so-called Rome-Belgrade-Warsaw Axis) may be the target of Chinese and Albanian Communists' attacks, but in Western Europe it serves admirably well the purpose of softening the anti-Communism that Stalin's rule and even Tito's case in pre-Khrushchev time cemented. While it was difficult between 1948 and 1956 to find non-Communist intellectuals to defend Stalin's domestic and foreign policies, the wave of pro-Soviet sympathies in the Western intellectual circles today may be compared to the enthusiasm that Stalin's Constitution stirred up in the West in the 1930s.[7] Credited largely

[7] Particularly significant today, as in the 1930s, is the tendency to present the future of the Soviet Union in rosy colors. Such is, for example, the approach of Isaac Deutscher who in his recent book, *The Great Contest: Russia and the West* (1961), is rather lyrical in projecting the picture of a *necessarily* "vital and expanding" Soviet society, as if he had certified knowledge that things could not turn out differently. Likewise, in a disturbing analysis of pro-Communist inclinations of a large number of prominent Italian intellectuals, a shrewd observer noted their tendency to disregard both past and present and to talk about the way "things are going to be" in Russia. Joan M. Cook, "Tendency in Italy Veers to the Left," New York *Times*, May 25, 1963 (Western edition).

by the non-Communists with a sincere intention to find an accommodation with the West, Khrushchev is pumping blood with encouraging results into an old ghost of Western Europe, the "Popular Front"[8] which seemed to be buried between the coup of Prague in 1948 and the Hungarian rebellion in 1956.

Finally, and most significantly for the subject of this paper, while in 1956 access to Hungary was forbidden to the Secretary General of the United Nations, and a special UN committee was appointed to prepare its famous Report on the Hungarian uprising, today's UN Secretary General is busily engaged in putting off the Hungarian question from the UN agenda, all the solemn and unfulfilled UN resolutions notwithstanding.[9] It is indeed no minor achievement on the part of Nikita Khrushchev to convince so many people in the West that nothing happened between Yalta and the summer of 1963.

. . . And His Problems

It would be erroneous, however, to present only one, the successful though unfinished side of Khrushchev's endeavors to turn the liabilities of Stalin's reign into his own assets. To complete the picture one must take into account other elements which make Khrushchev's problems in deal-

[8] ". . . maybe he [Khrushchev] hopes for accommodation not with the West as such but with the Western left. A popular front in any important European state would undermine NATO." C. L. Sulzberger, "Pumping Blood into a Ghost," the New York *Times*, January 19, 1963 (Western edition). How much in France also the political atmosphere is changing for the worse may be seen from the following statement of a reputedly staunch anti-Communist Socialist leader, Guy Mollet: "Unity with the Communists will come about some day." The New York *Times*, May 25, 1963.

[9] We draw attention to a pamphlet prepared by The American Friends of the Captive Nations entitled *Hungary Under Soviet Rule*. Fifth Anniversary Issue, 1956–61. Its appendix contains a long list of the United Nations Resolutions on Hungary, pp. 60–73. The editorial committee of the pamphlet was composed of three prominent American public figures: A. A. Berle, Jr., Leo Cherne, and Clare Boothe Luce.

ing with East-Central Europe no less formidable than Stalin's. First of all, since he cannot apply Stalin's terroristic methods, Khrushchev must use arguments, seduction, and compromises in dealing with the satellites (keeping of course in ultimate reserve the element of naked power). He must in consequence be ready to make real concessions, and to expose himself to the danger which Alexis de Tocqueville formulated in 1856 in *The Old Regime and the French Revolution:* "A people which had supported the most crushing blows without complaints and apparently as if they were unfelt, throws them off with violence as soon as the burden begins to be diminished." This maxim which explains the 1956 events in East-Central Europe has not lost its potential meaning in spite of Khrushchev's success in reintroducing the reign of "order" in his European empire.

The experiment with the COMECON is also much more promising in theory than in practice. The concept of the "Socialist division of labor" sounds fine in propaganda pronouncements, but it acquires a much less appealing aspect to those national planners in the satellite states who are invited in the name of the future commonweal to change working habits and sacrifice many of the local interests. The phenomenon of protectionism tempts no less the Communist "new classes" than "bourgeois" governments, particularly nowadays, when there seem to be more people ready to write about the camp of "Ivan Denisovich" than there are inmates in the forced labor camps.[10]

Then, curiously enough, the old Marxist concept of "alienation," used solely to designate man's degradation in the capitalist environment, hounds the younger intellectuals today in all parts of the East Berlin—Moscow—Sofia triangle. The vilification of non-conformist intellectuals by

[10] The allusion made here concerns the already famous best-selling novel, both in the U.S.S.R. and in the U.S., *One Day in the Life of Ivan Denisovich,* written by the Russian author Alexander Solzhenitsyn about the subhuman conditions in Stalin's forced labor camps of which the author himself was an inmate for several years. There is reportedly a flood of non-published manuscripts in the Soviet Union as well as in the satellite states on the same subject.

Ulbricht, Khrushchev, Todor Zhivkov, as well as by Tito, points to two things: one, that the intellectuals are growing increasingly more daring than in Stalin's day by asking unpleasant questions and voicing their opinions; and two, that the official ideology has lost its subduing power, particularly for the oncoming generation.

Finally, the conflict with China exposes the fraud of the "scientific" nature of Marxism-Leninism, while disagreements about the most suitable methods of fighting the West and the Darwinian struggle for leadership of the international Communist movement introduce confusion into the Communist midst. Paradoxically enough, while the Sino-Soviet rift favors Khrushchev's policies vis-à-vis the Western world, it may, in the long run, be detrimental to world-wide Communist interests. The uncommitted nations may be less impressed and not inclined to follow the example of feuding Communist empires. Likewise, the East-Central European Communists might also be tempted to profit from Moscow's quarrel with Peiping in order to promote their own bargaining positions within the emerging polycentric world Communist movement.

Assets and Liabilities of "National" Communism

Ten years after the death of Stalin, some of the initial institutional and political features of his static and monolithic empire have changed beyond recognition. Khrushchev's "de-Stalinization" has been thus far a two-way street: the experiment fared rather catastrophically in the pre-Sputnik period (fall of 1957), but nearly six years later it appears to be paying dividends. Nobody can say, however, whether the fact, truly unthinkable a decade ago, of Soviet official endorsement of a previously heretical Titoist concept of "various roads" to Socialism represents a solid cure for the Stalinist disease or the decisive step toward imperial dissolution.

While only the future will bring the answer to this question, it might be appropriate to examine critically two antithetical but widespread opinions in the United States about the meaning of the present state of flux in East-Central

Europe. One is that differences among the Communists are irrelevant, and that they all should be treated *en bloc*, as unreconstructed enemies of all Western values and policies; the other is that the reputedly "liberal" Communists are potential friends of the West and as such should enjoy Western aid and support. Both of these views are in great need of clarification and confrontation with the historical record. On the first count, those who refuse to make any differentiation among the Communists should be reminded that the Hungarian 1956 uprising would probably not have materialized without the active role of the dissident Communists and their leader Imre Nagy. Likewise, the evolution and writings of a repented Stalinist, Milovan Djilas, indicate that the sternest indictment of the entire Communist enterprise may come even from the summit of the "new class."

On the other hand, it is a grave mistake not to draw a fundamental distinction between the genuinely disappointed Communists who, if they came to power, would be willing to take tangible steps in order to democratize (without quotation marks) the Communist systems (which incidentally would lead to the liquidation of Communism as practiced since the Bolshevik seizure of power in Russia) and the hard-boiled Communist Machiavellians who use some democratic forms in order to make their rule more acceptable to the people and therefore more secure. In this category, with some qualifications to follow, we would put Tito and Gomulka.

A full-dress discussion of "national" Communism in Yugoslavia and Poland, both controversial recipients of the U.S. multiform assistance,[11] is clearly beyond the scope of this paper, but a few observations on this issue are indispensable for the meaningful analysis of today's Communism in East-Central Europe. Even a cursory treatment is in order owing to the fact that Tito in the last fifteen years and Gomulka in the last seven have enjoyed a widespread

[11] For a detailed discussion of this problem see my recently published book, *United States Aid to Yugoslavia and Poland: Analysis of a Controversy.* Washington, D.C.: American Enterprise Institute, July 1963.

reputation in the West as "nationalists" and "liberals," often in striking contrast to their intentions and actual performance.

It is well to remember, first of all, that Tito was not initially a rebel against Moscow; he was kicked out of the Communist bloc as a result of one of the pathological crises of Stalin's suspiciousness. Tito was thereupon condemned by Stalin to become heretic and to turn to the West for help and protection. It is true that between 1950 and 1953 Yugoslav Communists experimented for the first time creatively in the realm of economic affairs and built up, with generous U.S. aid as an insurance guarantee, their model of a decentralized, collectivist, and still competitive economy. It is no less true, however, that soon after Stalin's death and the inauguration of the new course by his successors, Yugoslav Communists slowed down the pace of their reforms and abstained in particular from any experimentation with political democratization (which was the cause of the first Djilas deviation in 1953–54). Likewise, violent anti-Stalinists as they were between 1949 and 1953, when threatened by Soviet aggression of direct or "Korean" type, they changed their foreign political orientation fundamentally during the last decade. Branded by Stalin as a "Fascist criminal" and an "imperialist spy" Tito appeared in December 1962 before the Supreme Soviet of the U.S.S.R. and was greeted by Nikita Khrushchev as a worthy Communist comrade who was building a genuine Socialist society. Titoist rehabilitation coincided in fact with the comprehensive tightening of the screws in Yugoslavia during the last three years, and with a practically complete alignment of Yugoslavia behind the basic tenets of Soviet foreign policy.

The case of Gomulka in Poland is no less striking. He fell out of Stalin's favor in 1949 not because he was a "liberal" Communist but because, realistic Communist that he was, he thought it suicidal to impose upon Poland by violent means the Russian Communist model. Since his accession to power in October 1956 coincided with a tidal wave of popular revulsion against the existing state of affairs in Poland, Gomulka was rather universally celebrated as the champion of national independence and increasing civil freedoms. Viewed in retrospect, however, his rule has rather systematically disappointed the high hopes placed in him by Western wishful thinkers. He appears today as the closest adviser and friend of Nikita Khrushchev, who singled him out in the previously quoted article as artisan of COMECON's scheme of integration. The same record may be noted in Polish domestic affairs:

> The four great achievements of October [1956] were: the defeat of the Stalinists and their removal from positions of influence; the reaching of a modus vivendi between the regime and the Church; the abandonment of Soviet policies in agriculture; and a considerable degree of freedom to speak and write. The only one of these four that has been retained in full is the toleration of private farming.[12]

The question that legitimately arises is how to explain Tito's and Gomulka's moves to "decompress" and then "recompress" their regimes? To answer it we must take into account the complex and delicate interplay between the steady though diffuse popular pressure calling for "decompression" and the power interests of the Communist ruling class tending to limit and "recompress" popular demands. This phenomenon is described as follows by Milovan Djilas in what we believe is the key sentence in his book, *The New Class:*

[12] Jerzy Ptakovski, "Politics in Poland," *East Europe,* vol. 11, No. 12, December 1962, p. 20. Another appropriate quotation is worthy adding: ". . . Gomulka is a fanatical Communist by conviction and authoritarian by nature. He was swept back to power in October, 1956, on a wave of popular enthusiasm in which he was not even a participant, let along a protagonist, but almost a mere bystander. Far from being stimulated by the spontaneity which elevated him, he is profoundly distrustful of it, and during the last six years he has steadily chipped away at the flattering monument which the Polish people (and, even more so, Western observers) had erected to him. The so-called 'retrogression from October' has not been the result of Soviet pressure." James F. Brown, "Khrushchev's European Allies," *The New Republic,* March 30, 1963, p. 18–19.

Ideas, philosophical principles and moral considerations, the nation and the people, their history, in part even ownership—all can be changed and sacrificed. But not power. Because this would signify Communism's renunciation of itself, of its own essence. Individuals can do this. But the class, the party, the oligarchy cannot. This is the purpose and the meaning of its existence."[13]

A distinction should be made here between "Titoism," which has emerged as a variant of modern Communism with pretensions to wider applicability particularly in underdeveloped countries, and "Gomulkaism," which is destined for strictly local consumption.

The fact that "Titoism" was born as a reaction to Stalin's enmity and that "de-Stalinization" was pursued in Yugoslavia long before the same process was inaugurated in the Soviet Union, explains largely the Khrushchev-Tito rapprochement. By becoming partly "Titoist" himself, Khrushchev calculated to deflate the attractiveness of the Yugoslav example in the satellite countries, while using Tito's close relations with some of the world's most prominent "neutrals" to promote his own policies. As for Tito, the new friendship with Khrushchev serves as guarantee against any Soviet aggression and leaves him free to maneuver in both international and domestic fields. He can therefore play both cards: that of Khrushchev, ally in de-Stalinization and peaceful conquest of the world for Communism (the aim which Tito has never ceased to believe in and work for), and that of the Kennedy administration, which should be persuaded to continue U.S. economic assistance without any political concessions in return. To utilize the West in order to strengthen Communism in Yugoslavia is an old game for Tito.

Two conclusions emerge at the end of this brief examination of "national" Communism in its various manifestations. One is that it was a direct result of Stalinist rule in

[13] *The New Class: An Analysis of the Communist System.* New York: Frederick A. Praeger, 1957, p. 170.

Russia and the satellite countries and is changing nowadays, under Khrushchev, its former characteristics. In his attempt to replace Stalinist mold by a much more flexible pattern of integration, Khrushchev pursues the homeopathic course of injecting small doses of "national" Communism everywhere in order to cure in this way both the Stalinist disease of overcentralization and the opposite evil of centrifugal explosion. Tito himself, for a long time symbol of "national" Communism, is today assisting Khrushchev in his twofold venture: to stall the Chinese fractionalism within the Communist movement, and to subvert more efficiently the non-Communist world.

The second conclusion concerns the internal Communist problems, on both interbloc and intrastate levels. It is not easy to subdue the power of a genuine nationalism in East-Central Europe, even by employing the clever scheme of "national" Communism. It is not easy either to harmonize the views and interests of the Communist ruling classes in the various states they dominate. Likewise, all the experiments under way today in the satellite states (and also in the Soviet Union and Yugoslavia) are no less the result of the necessity to appease the people at home than of the intention to delude the enemy abroad. Indeed, *all* Communist regimes suffer today from an accumulation of internal contradictions, and no working devices have as yet been discovered to resolve them. It seems therefore accurate to designate today's situation in East-Central Europe as experimental and transitional, a situation which contains both the elements of salvation and ferments of dissolution with regard to the Communist rule.

What are then the implications for the U.S. policy of that paradoxical state of affairs when the Soviet Russian domination over the satellites appears to be at the same time more efficient and more vulnerable?

The Relevance of East-Central Europe for the United States

The problem of U.S. policy toward East-Central Europe under the present fluctuating conditions is subject of a controversy which should be briefly expounded.

There is in the United States an important school of thought on Communism that, with multiple variations, would argue in the following way:

Since the United States has never succeeded in influencing the Soviet attitude toward the satellites beyond merely verbal expressions of disapproval, it is even more difficult and might be dangerous to try to inaugurate now a policy designed to transform radically the existing Communist system. Since both the conventional and a fortiori atomic war must be excluded as means of policy, and since the U.S. does not have the right to incite the people in Eastern Europe to revolt and insurrection when it cannot help them militarily, the wisest attitude would be to recognize the status quo in East-Central Europe as a more or less permanent "fact of life." By normalizing and improving diplomatic relations with the satellite states, and helping them economically to achieve the highest possible degree of well-being, U.S. diplomacy would contribute to the unfolding of a liberalizing process within the Soviet bloc itself. The feeling of security from an outside intervention would encourage more moderate Communist elements and would help promote a more liberal and tolerable system, inclined to coexist peacefully with the West. In brief, to favor and hasten such an evolution, the United States should withdraw from any interference in Eastern European affairs.

Another school of thought, including also various shades of opinion, would argue a fundamentally different premise. Its basic argument is that the present Communist flux in East-Central Europe offers the United States a unique opportunity to develop an effective policy toward the satellites. At the outset, the "activists" (to be called so for the sake of identification) would agree that war and incitement to revolt must not be the means of U.S. policy toward East-Central Europe. Short of war and irresponsible revolutionary instigation, however, the United States should use all other means to encourage the captive nations in their resistance to Communist domination,[14] and to enable them

14 It is nonsensical and self-defeating in the eyes of the proponents of this school to grant the Communists the right to employ multiple means of unconventional warfare against the

ultimately to choose freely the governmental system of their liking.

Furthermore, according to the same reasoning, to follow the advice of the "passivists" and accept fatalistically the present status quo in the satellite realm would in fact, to paraphrase Talleyrand, be worse than a crime; it would be a mistake. For in the global, world-wide U.S. policy, East-Central Europe plays, potentially, an extremely important role.

First of all, by a series of electoral or revolutionary manifestations in the last eighteen years millions of East-Central Europeans have given every tangible proof that they have never freely chosen the form of government under which they still must live. For the United States and the West in general to be reconciled to this permanent denial of the right to self-determination solemnly promised in the Atlantic Charter and the Yalta Declaration on Liberated Europe means to disregard the moral foundations upon which during the last two centuries the entire fabric of Western civilization and the entire process of political life have been built.

Second, in the paradoxical situation of the world today, when sympathy for the United States seems to increase with geographical distance, East-Central Europe, despite or perhaps because of the systematic Communist "hate-America" campaign, is probably one of the shrinking areas on this planet where the concept of "America" still enjoys its pristine attractiveness. Richard Nixon, who narrowly escaped violent death in Caracas and whose motorcades through the Latin American towns a few years ago aroused usually limited enthusiasm, was greeted with such a display of fervor in Warsaw in August 1959 that in his own words his short visit to the capital of Poland remained "the most moving experience of all my trips abroad. I know this welcome was not for me personally. It was an expression, a

---

West, while refusing in principle and in advance to turn the same methods against them, particularly when a well-planned and executed counteraction, on the ground chosen by the West, could put them on the defensive, and consequently either defeat them or thwart their aggressive attempts elsewhere.

spontaneous outpouring of warm feeling, toward the country I represented."[15] To be reconciled, in the long run, to the loss of such an invaluable and unfortunately not so universal human and political source of popular good will toward the United States, would represent a major failure of U.S. statesmanship, as well as a fatal setback for democracy in the world.

Third, in the deadly military game of our time, the East-Central Europeans' resistance to the Communist rule constitutes a popular deterrent to the temptation of Soviet leaders to use their numerical superiority and launch a conventional military attack, no less important than the nuclear deterrent itself, against the West. An East-Central Europe resigned to the fate of irreversible absorption by the Soviet Union (whatever the method of integration employed) stimulates Soviet westward expansion today or in the future. An East-Central Europe with the hope that freedom is the perspective of the future and not a remembrance of the past, is a guarantee that a new world conflagration will not recur where it happened twice, in 1914 and 1939.

Fourth, the issue of Stalin's "colonialism" and Khrushchev's "neo-colonialism" in East-Central Europe should particularly interest the new, emerging nations of the world, with their so loudly proclaimed and understandable sensitiveness about "imperialism." The task of U.S. diplomacy should be to remind them constantly that the problem of

15 Richard M. Nixon, *Six Crises*. New York: Doubleday, 1962, p. 285. It is worth quoting more extensively from Mr. Nixon's description of the behavior of the Poles who greeted him in Warsaw: ". . . I had a chance to look closely into the faces around me. Some were shouting, others were singing, and many were crying—with tears running down their cheeks . . . Two-hundred-and-fifty thousand people lined the streets of downtown Warsaw, according to the official and unofficial estimates. It was unprecedented and unexpected. So many flowers and bouquets were thrown at us that our driver had to stop the car several times to clear the windshield. Dr. Lange [Polish Vice Premier] could not believe what he saw. I could not believe it. The press corps could not believe it. But there it was before us—a crowd almost twice as large as that which had greeted Khrushchev only three weeks before."

self-determination and independence, largely solved in the former imperial parts of the Western world, still awaits its solution in the region they usually tend to overlook—East-Central Europe.[16]

The enumerated reasons why East-Central Europe is such an important factor in U.S. foreign policy explain also Nikita Khrushchev's aversion to any mentioning of the satellites' problem and his emphatic insistence on their "sovereignty" as well as his denial of the right of anyone (except, of course, himself) to interfere in their internal affairs. It corresponds exactly to his attitude when dealing with the West about controversial subjects: "What's mine is mine, what's yours is negotiable." Western policy should be not to acquiesce in Khrushchev's cunning but to counter his own inroads outside the Soviet bloc by opening the problem of legitimacy of all Communist regimes in East-Central Europe. Likewise, to influence effectively the course of events in that part of the world, the United States

---

[16] The importance of enlisting the support of the "non-aligned" nations in the cause of freedom in Eastern Europe, is suggested by a Hungarian scholar, author of probably the most comprehensive and objective study of the Hungarian 1956 revolt: "Perhaps the best opportunity of reactivating the satellite problem is offered by the contest for the sympathies and support of the uncommitted nations of Asia and Africa. A clear Asian and African recognition of Soviet duplicity—its contradictory treatment of East-European and non-European problems—might have a sobering effect on Moscow's rigidity, both political and ideological. A necessary Soviet choice between the sympathy of these Asian and African nations and the maintenance of a colonial empire in the center of Europe might possibly influence its attitude concerning that problem. The belated acknowledgment of the truth in the Hungarian crisis by the Indian leader can no longer be helpful; but a conception of the satellite problem by the uncommitted nations and a readiness to exercise diplomatic pressure on the Soviet Union for the sake of its satisfactory solution might have an unpredictable value. This encircling diplomatic pressure might even grow into the greater evil beside which a dignified withdrawal from East-Central Europe might not seem so repugnant as before. The enlightenment of Asian and African leaders on their real kinship with the peoples of East-Central Europe should be a principal task of Western diplomacy." Ferenc A. Vali, *Rift and Revolt in Hungary*, Harvard University Press, 1961, p. 513.

must deny to the Kremlin the opportunity to offset its own
imperial weakness by foreign political successes—the case
in point is Cuba.[17]

The case of U.S. "activism" in East-Central Europe,
which the present writer shares, requires a few concluding
remarks. One is that totalitarian regimes do not perish because of internal contradictions alone. For such regimes to
be fatally weakened, short of international war, two specific conditions must be fulfilled. One is the existence of a
deep internal rift within the ruling political class, which in
time of crisis would paralyze the functioning of the entire
system and offer the hitherto powerless popular masses the
unique opportunity to have their say (the classical case of
that situation is Hungary on October 23, 1956 and a few
days after). The second condition requires that the insur-
gents receive multiple foreign assistance against their imperial rulers. (Exactly what the Hungarian freedom fight-
ers lacked on November 4. The recognition by the West of
the Imre Nagy government would have at least complicated the Soviet dilemma, and could have made them more
amenable to deal with Nagy instead of crushing him.) The
lesson of 1956, and the possibility of new disturbances in
the satellite countries (or in Yugoslavia if Tito's successor
fails to maintain order in the case of a struggle for power)
point to the necessity for U.S. policy makers not to be surprised by events and to try to react swiftly to aid the people regain their liberty.

On the other hand, just because of the present experimental and transitional situation in East-Central Europe,
as described above, the possibility must not be dismissed
that centrifugal forces will continue to grow without leading to the explosion. In such an eventuality it would be es-

---

[17] Although U.S. policy of "containment," formulated in
1947, was strictly defensive in nature and presented therefore
only an inadequate answer to Stalin's enslavement of East-
Central Europe, it had a valuable point, namely that internal
contradictions within the Soviet bloc could have disruptive consequences only if not compensated by the external successes of
the empire-builder.

sential to distinguish clearly between the Communist regimes which make some concessions to the people in order to strengthen their own power and the growth of genuinely democratic oppositional forces including the disillusioned Communists. To help the former with unconditional economic assistance or, to give a specific example, to recognize the Kadar regime and acquiesce to the dropping of the Hungarian question from the agenda of the United Nations would not favor the cause of freedom among the satellites, as the huge amount of aid to Tito (and partly to Gomulka) without any strings attached did not bring their regimes closer to the West. At the same time a constant pressure on the Soviet Union should be exercised, reminding Khrushchev—and the world as well—that the best contribution to the lessening of international tension and the real de-Stalinization of Soviet foreign policy would be to go back to the imprescriptible principles of the Declaration on Liberated Europe.

TOWARD A COMMUNIST ASIA

by David Nelson Rowe

David Nelson Rowe, Professor of Political Science at Yale, was born in China and educated there and at Princeton, the University of Southern California, the University of Chicago, and Harvard. He has been a specialist in Chinese and Far Eastern affairs for thirty years and is the author of thirty-five books and articles in that field.

The main trends of United States policy toward East Asia since 1960 are quite easy to see, and it is in the light of these trends that future problems may easily be predicted in advance.

Generally speaking, the main trends of our East Asian policy have all led in the direction of disaster. In Laos, for example, we have abandoned the previous policy of aggressive containment in favor of a so-called policy of "neutralization" for that country. In East Asia this is universally interpreted at the minimum as a serious defeat for U.S. policy, and usually it is taken as a mere preliminary step to a Communist takeover of Laos and the opening thus of all Southeast Asia to Communist conquest.

Again, our China policy, from being one of firm containment has deteriorated into one of accommodation within the framework of the so-called "two Chinas" policy. This is generally accepted to be the basic framework for our whole policy toward both the Chinese Communists and the Republic of China on Taiwan. It is no denial of this to cite our clear-cut opposition to the admission of Red China to the United Nations, for it has just as clearly been indicated in official statements there and elsewhere that if only the

Chinese Communists will accept the so-called "two Chinas" solution, this formula will apply in the UN as well as elsewhere, and both the Chinese Communists and the government on Taiwan would be expected to secure and hold representation in the UN. That no such result is likely to ensue, because of the steadfast opposition by both Peiping and Taipei to any such solution, does nothing to diminish our government's commitment to the policy and the clear understanding of this commitment everywhere in Asia.

In South Vietnam we are attempting what may well prove to be an impossible task, namely, to destroy invading Communist forces there without formally committing our own forces to the conflict. This is bound to impress all observers, in Asia or elsewhere, as a genuine retreat from the position we took previously in the case of Communist aggression in South Korea and to indicate accurately the degree of weakening and softening in our posture of armed defense against Communist aggression that has taken place since 1950. And we undertake this only partial commitment, stopping short of using our own divisions, in an area and under circumstances even more difficult than those we met squarely in Korea previously.

In still another area the clear indication of our softness has been offered openly to the observing public both in Asia and elsewhere, namely, in West New Guinea. Here we have brought all our pressure to bear on a stout anti-Communist ally, The Netherlands, to give up territory under its control and to which its title could hardly be challenged and to hand it over to the tender mercies of Indonesia. Justification? Well, only the usual argument of "inevitability," and the supposed need to sacrifice an anti-Communist ally to prevent a pro-Communist country from becoming even more hostile to the free world than its already clear-cut pro-Communist orientation makes it. Relying as we do on the promises of Indonesia to grant self-determination to the native population of West New Guinea, we have seemingly forgotten that every promise the new Indonesian regime made to the Dutch in connection with the independence of the former Dutch colonies of Indonesia was flagrantly disregarded by the Indonesians and broken at will. Can the UN do better by the Papuans than it did previously with the Indonesians of the outer areas, whose pledged freedom to have local government of their own under a federal system, was callously destroyed by the Indonesian authorities of Java after independence?

These are but samples of the trends of our East Asian policy during the past three years. We cannot hope that these cases have escaped the detailed and careful observation of all Asians. What has been the result?

In Japan, the most important economic and political stake of the cold war in East Asia, our recent Asian policies have done much to strengthen the forces of neutralism and pacifism, not to mention those forces directly allied to the world Communist revolution. The strength of these forces is generally underestimated in this country. When we remember that thousands of card-carrying Communists hold positions in the Japanese governmental business and economic enterprises, we have only begun to tell the story of Communist penetration in Japan. The chief danger here lies in the creeping growth of Communist influence among the youth, the intellectuals, in the press and other media of communications, and in the most influential sectors of religion and of the great labor organizations.

In Japan today, neutralism and pacifism are largely a mere cover for a trend toward ultimate one-sided commitment to the Communist bloc. At just such time as the conviction really takes hold in Japan that the United States and its friends represent the ultimately losing side in the cold war, both neutralism and pacifism will disappear, swamped in a new wave of Japanese activism and positivism with the ultimate aim of restoring Japan to a genuine position of power and influence in the world as a whole. The question is: who is going to win? Since that question is increasingly answered in Japan in favor of the U.S.S.R. and the Communist world revolution, the current trends in Japan are perfectly understandable, and their increase in the future is predictable as long as we convince the Japanese by our actions that we are weakening in our stand and the other side is strengthening its position.

Hence the recent revival of interest in Japan in trade with the Chinese Communists. There is no observable conviction in Japan that this trade will become important in the near future in terms of volume or monetary value. But it is the long future they are interested in. The Laos "settlement," generally accepted as opening the door to Communist takeover in Southeast Asia, has convinced the Japanese that they must get on the Communist Chinese bandwagon, for surely the Chinese Communists, and not the Russians, will be the immediate economic beneficiaries of a Communist takeover of Southeast Asia. Such a takeover would mean that this important trading area, now valuable to Japan, could thereafter be available to them only in an indirect way, through Communist China. They are convinced that, after such takeover, and in view of the inability of the Soviet Union to contribute materially to the long-term economic development of Communist China, Japanese money and technology would have to be called in, in Southeast Asia at least, if not in nearer areas such as Manchuria and North Korea. The Japanese policy of aiding and abetting the repatriation of Korean residents in Japan to North Korea seems clearly designed to augment the possibilities, at least in the northern part of Korea, for Japanese economic penetration some time in the future.

With the United States Government seemingly committed to the so-called "two Chinas" policy, why should we not expect the Japanese to engineer their own rapprochement with the Chinese Communists, and to try to beat us to the punch with it also? The slightest clues to our policy in this respect will be avidly picked up by the Japanese, to whom East Asia is by no means merely a playground of somewhat academic policy makers but an area always considered vital to the welfare of Japan.

In respect to Taiwan, the result of this trend of Japanese policy has already been to strain relations between Japan and the Republic of China. The Japanese are trying to buy their way out of this by extending some long-term credits of a comparatively minor nature to the government in Taiwan. But any evidence that Japanese advances to the Chinese Communists are succeeding will cause tensions with

Taiwan that may well result in rupture of relations. This is why the Japanese have sedulously avoided any hint of their rapprochement being developed in the "political" sphere, including recognition and diplomatic relations either formal or informal. They hope to eat their economic cake with the Chinese Communists and have their political cake with Taiwan at the same time.

An interesting and not at all unimportant aspect of this whole situation is the increasing Japanese pressure on the U.S. position in Okinawa and our gradual retreat in the face of this pressure. The accentuation of American civil authority in Okinawa and the diminution of the power of the military there is an important breakthrough in the Japanese campaign, pushed steadily and with sophistication for a thoroughgoing establishment of Japanese civil authority over this island fortress in the Pacific. Any such takeover by the Japanese would clearly jeopardize our defense posture there, for it would be followed by the same type of "anti-militarism" in fear of the U.S.S.R. that is now so prevalent in Japan itself, with all its results in the sphere of U.S. defense provisions. Here is where, if we surrender to Japanese demands in the hope of "keeping Japan on our side," we would really be surrendering to forces quite hostile to us and favorable to our enemy, Communism.

What of Korea in all this? The fall of the Syngman Rhee regime was openly approved by our diplomatic establishment, but the weak and impotent government which followed it, suffused as it was with the spirit of accommodation with the regime in North Korea, created far more problems than it ever solved. We were really rescued from this situation only by the intervention of the Korean military whose coup clashed with our own civil-oriented democratic traditions. But the military junta now ruling Korea, while incapable of working miracles, has achieved substantial results, only to be faced with the inevitable demand, strengthened from our side, for the "restoration" of civil rule in 1963. The military have promised such a shift for 1963, but it is questionable whether any such thing can or should take place. Our problem is more likely to be one of adjusting ourselves to the maintenance of military control by generals in civilian dress.

This is the only logical answer, certainly for the time being, to the pervasive factionalism and inherent instability of Korean political life. We must face it: Korean desire for full independence and self-government under democracy is only exceeded by Korean political inexperience and quarrelsomeness, added to which is a built-in tendency toward instability of their higher social echelons. It is a question hard to answer, as to which of all these features of the Korean environment is the more repulsive to us. As of now, we stick with the military rule which is the natural concomitant of the other features of Korea that have been listed here. But we ourselves are far from given to stability of adherence to chosen alternatives. If military rule is prolonged, under whatever disguise, we are almost sure to react against it ultimately, with possible disastrous results. Military rule is the only thing that has really worked in Korea since the establishment of independent government in the Republic of Korea. We must realistically determine to put up with military government, not only in Korea, but in numerous other areas in which we are inclined to help work for something else in the ultimate long run.

The ever present problem of Korean-Japanese relations plagues us now as it has ever since the war ended. After the departure of Syngman Rhee it was widely anticipated that an improvement would set in. But subsequent events have demonstrated the bilateral character of Korean-Japanese discord and disorientation. Both countries are involved in it, and equally. There is not much use trying to apportion blame: Koreans by and large hate the Japanese, and Japanese by and large despise Koreans. The United States should base its policy toward both countries on the certainty that this psychological complex will not soon pass away. It severely handicaps our efforts in the western Pacific not only in the area of defense and security but in economic and political fields.

Directly involved in this situation is Taiwan, seat of the government of the Republic of China. Like both Japan

and the Republic of Korea, it is tied to us by a treaty of
mutual defense, which still remains the cornerstone of the
policies of the United States and the Republic of China toward each other. With our aid, the Chinese on Taiwan
have built a veritable showcase of social and economic
progress and development, in addition to steadily maintaining a very large standing armed force, trained and
equipped with U.S. aid. Now, however, we have begun to
make deep cuts in our military support of the Chinese
Government, seemingly based on the idea that its military
posture should be exclusively "defensive," and that for
their ultimate strategic defense the Chinese on Taiwan
should depend on the might of the United States.

Perhaps contrary to the expectations of our own policy
makers, this tends to force the government on Taiwan into
a posture of *offense*. The dilemma presented to President
Chiang Kai-shek and his government is this: Shall we attack the mainland soon, or wait for our present armed
power to wither under the steady deprivation imposed on
it from the American side? Thus our own policy of down-
grading and de-emphasizing the military side of U.S. aid
to Taiwan has had the effect, not of placing it in a position
purely defensive, but of forcing it to take the offensive.
That the dilemma confronting the Nationalists is that of a
choice between military weakening and what our policy
makers consider a suicidal military offensive against the
mainland, does not mean necessarily that the choice will
be refused. The only thing certain is that if such a choice
is presented, the government on Taiwan will choose attack
against the mainland, with all that this means in terms of
possible U.S. involvement. We have done everything possible, in the view of our policy makers, to make such a
choice impossible, including denying to the forces on Taiwan everything classified as offensive weapons of war. But
the criteria here are not very clear, and in times of stress
the distinction between offensive and defensive weapons
is apt to disappear entirely.

Further impelling the Taiwan Government toward attack
is the trend, cited above, of U.S. policy in the direction of
the "two Chinas" solution of what we have come to term

"the China problem." The government on Taiwan felt the impact of this U.S. policy orientation most recently in connection with the Laos settlement, under the terms of which the Chinese Communists came into Laos and brought with them a full-scale diplomatic establishment of several hundred members. This, of course, confronted the Republic of China with the problem of its own pre-existing and established diplomatic representation, much smaller than that of the Chinese Communists. The United States brought pressure on the Republic of China to remain in Vientiane and retain its representation in Laos. But the Republic of China refused, withdrew recognition from Laos, and terminated its diplomatic relations with that country. As explained by the Foreign Minister in Taipei, Free China could not condone any solution of this problem which would countenance the "two Chinas" approach.

The question of course is: how far can the Republic of China go in tolerating the "two Chinas" approach before it succeeds in destroying its very *raison d'être*, namely, the destruction of the Chinese Communist regime on the mainland? Thus, again, by our policy, instead of mitigating the tensions between Communist China and Free China we are actually and inevitably contributing to their heightening and intensification. That the Chinese Communists react in just this way is seen in their recent almost unprecedented concentration of armed forces in the areas of the South China coast fronting on Taiwan. They know, and probably hope, that our policy toward our ally on Taiwan can easily force him into armed action, and they must prepare to exploit such a situation to their own advantage if possible. They would gain the ultimate advantage from it if, in case of an attack from Taiwan against the mainland, the United States definitely refused to back up its ally. This would, once and for all, convince every country wholly or partially dependent upon the United States for security, that such dependency was nothing but a rotten stick that would collapse at the first hint of danger.

Our total policy in respect to the Republic of China today also has its share of responsibility for the heightening of tensions inside Taiwan itself. The decreasing defense support to Taiwan by the United States has caused the imposition of new surtaxes there for military purposes. These surcharge taxes, heavily aimed at consumption, hit hardest at the salaried and business classes. They are somewhat costly, since their result is to decrease private expenditures in certain areas and thus to diminish sales, restrict business, and contract the tax base. On the other hand, they do not materially affect the vast bulk of the farming population but cause strong dissatisfaction among the city population most directly connected with the operation of government itself. In Taiwan today, it is probably impossible to substitute for them a general income tax with any prospect of success.

Thus, even with economic development in Taiwan constantly reaching to new heights, marked dangers exist. There is a veritable powder keg in the Taiwan Strait, and recently, the more we have tried to dampen it down, the more explosive we have rendered it. Thus we are inextricably involved, still today, in the Chinese civil war, that "fratricidal strife" to which President Truman in 1945 said he would not permit the United States to be a party. Eighteen years later we cannot deny its existence, nor, seemingly, can we plan or plot it out of existence. We can only take sides in it. Unless we do, we magnify the chances of war. Only if we do take sides in it can we magnify the chances that the Chinese Communists will destroy themselves by their own fatuous and fatal domestic errors, compounded by our own policy of denying them external outlets for their huge internal problems.

Going directly south from Taiwan we come to the Philippines. Here, after a successful military, economic, and social campaign against Communist revolution, the Philippines has seemed internally secure. But the strategy of the Philippine Communist Party has shifted. Their target now is not the peasantry but precisely the more privileged elements of Philippine society, namely, the intellectuals and students. As in Japan, these elements are quite able to see from their vantage point among the well-informed the real impact of U.S. policy elsewhere in Asia. In the spring of 1961 the Philippine Government responded to the obvious attitude of impotence and vacillation of SEATO by a spontaneous and voluntary offer of Filipino forces to fight Communist infiltration in Laos. Of course this offer and others like it from other nations in the area were turned down and smothered in a thunderous silence of the so-called Great Powers. In the Philippines, such a response by the United States to the immediate problems of the area tends to bring together in a common opposition to the United States both the neutralist, pacifist, and left-wing or pro-Communist elements on the one hand, and the most violently anti-Communist elements who are otherwise supporters of the United States on the other hand. It is quite true that even with such an alignment the forces that can be brought to support Communist aims in the Philippines are still small and weak. But it is also true that in the light of our policy these forces are bound to grow larger and stronger.

These threatening elements will not plunge to commit themselves to any course of direct action so easily countered by overt measures as was the earlier armed Communist revolution in the Philippines. Their program is aimed, on the other hand, at long-term results, namely the progressive disaffection of the youth and the intellectuals from the United States and in the direction of accommodation with the Chinese Communists and the Communist bloc in general. Here again it is the overwhelming motivation of the weak to be on the strong and winning side in the eventual showdown. No amount of counterorganization or counterpropaganda can win the struggle unless, as a minimum, the course of policy on our part is shifted toward a more aggressive containment. Positive and aggressive containment of the Chinese Communists is what is required here as elsewhere, to hold our allies with us.

South Vietnam is the first place in which to do this. Here, where we have a real war on our hands, we try to fight it without committing our own troops. But in neighboring Thailand, where there is as yet no open war, we have stationed divisions. What is the rationale of such a seeming contradiction?

The explanation can only be sought in the realm of politics. In South Vietnam we have a war on our hands at least partially, if not wholly, because in that country we had in President Diem a genuine focus of anti-Communist sentiment and a genuine source of direct anti-Communist action. In Thailand, on the other hand, while general sentiment is overwhelmingly anti-Communist, there is no strong figure around whom to focus this opinion and from whom may come direct action against the Communist threat to the country. In South Vietnam, neutralists are apt to be in jail. In Thailand, the amount of open neutralism has to be seen to be believed, and it is of long duration.

In fact, the whole tradition of Thailand, seen during the past century, has been to avoid entire takeover by accommodation with the would-be aggressors. In an age of colonial rivalries between Britain and France in this area, such a policy could pay off. The balance of power, the system of so-called "buffer states," these things were compatible even with the much-maligned colonial system. But more latterly, Thailand was rescued from complete Japanese domination only by the victory of the Allied Powers in World War II. And today, any idea in Thailand of confronting the aggressor with a smile, however appealing it may be, can end only in disaster.

The threat to Thailand today, nevertheless, is from internal subversion, something that divisions of U.S. troops there cannot prevent any more than our bases in Japan have arrested the political deterioration inside Japan. What is needed in both cases (and without it we can do nothing) is a clear-cut aggressiveness of our own, such as we demonstrated in Korea under the leadership of President Truman. That particularly strong response is what held Japan on our side for as long as she has remained there. More of the same is required today. The recent conclusion of a trade treaty between Thailand and the U.S.S.R. is a very large straw in the wind, indicating which way things are going in Southeast Asia today. Only a few years ago such a thing would have been unheard of, since, in view of the genuine lack of substantial economic relations between the two countries, the only real import of such a treaty is as a symbol of political readjustment.

On the other side of all this it is customary to cite the supposedly disturbed state of relations between the U.S.S.R. and the Chinese Communists as something in which we can take a material amount of comfort from other woes. In my opinion, the state of relations between the two Communist powers is, rather, no comfort at all. This is not to deny the existence of unhappiness between them. Not at all. The Chinese Communists are severely unhappy with the disastrous state of their own internal economy, and they are even more unhappy because they have awakened to the truth that the U.S.S.R. can really not do too much to help them directly in these matters. The U.S.S.R., on the other hand, has awakened to the truth that Communist China is a great and heavy weight about the neck of the Communist world revolution to the success of which both countries are so completely dedicated.

The inevitable strains between these partners are thus highly exacerbated. But what are they doing about it? Are they *merely* indulging themselves in vicious displays of disagreement about such matters as high theory and practical policy in respect to such areas tangential to both as, say, Albania? Not at all.

The current successes of the Sino-Soviet bloc are indeed measured in all the failures and shortcomings of our own policy which have been listed and briefly described above. Communist progress in Japan is supported financially and materially by both the Chinese Communists and the Russians. The seemingly fathomless swamp we are caught in in Korea is the joint making of the Chinese Communists and the Russians since 1945. The current tensions between ourselves and the Republic of China on Taiwan are surely a product of the alliance between the Chinese Communists and the U.S.S.R., without which the Chinese Communists could constitute no danger to anyone, least of all to the United States.

But perhaps it is in the Laos case that we see the clearest evidence of the way in which the Communist-bloc members, in this case the Soviets and the Chinese Communists, are working to extricate themselves from the difficulties and dangers into which their own errors have plunged them. If there is to be any mitigation now of Chinese Communist internal economic and social dangers and pressures, surely it can come from a takeover of Southeast Asia. The Laos case shows how the two partners are co-operating to bring this about. While the Russians advertised their presence in the area and in the Laos case by supplying Laotians on their side with war materials from Russian supply planes flying from Chinese territory, the Chinese Communists massed 250,000 troops near the Laos border in Chinese territory. *This time* there was no futile and disastrous discussion and argument as there was before in the Korean case, as to whether the Chinese Communists *would* come in. We believed it before it happened, and because we believed it could happen, it did not have to happen. Instead of fighting in Laos, we skipped the war and sat down at the conference table in Geneva to negotiate Laos into a highly questionable state of "neutrality," implemented in Laos by the establishment there of what Syngman Rhee would never tolerate in Korea, namely, a coalition government. This was forced by joint and collaborative Russo-Chinese Communist blackmail and intimidation. And if their strategy works in the takeover in Laos, as it gives every sign of doing, this will be a joint Russo-Chinese Communist victory which would probably lead to the takeover of all Southeast Asia.

Even if the joint strategy of the Chinese Communists and Russians in this matter does not succeed, surely there can be no doubt that the strategy is joint.

The obvious aim of this strategy is to relieve the intolerable pressures inside Communist China through a takeover of the economic resources of Southeast Asia, and in the process to win, so as to win more in other areas. Success of the Communist strategy in Southeast Asia, it can confidently be predicted, will do much to pull Japan over to the Communist side, in reality if not in name. And such successes as these are rightly calculated to ease in turn the existing tensions between Russia and the Chinese

Communists, to the general welfare of the Communist world revolution everywhere.

As is usually the case, a policy of retreat anywhere necessitates a policy of aggressive defense elsewhere. Otherwise we are trapped into general retreat all along the line, which cannot be covered up, no matter how hard we try by, for example, spending $20 billion to send an expedition to the moon.

As of now, the right place to initiate an aggressive defense is in South Vietnam. It will probably be forced on us later on, at any rate. For if and when the enemy there becomes convinced of what we are trying hard now to convince ourselves, namely, that we are *winning* in South Vietnam, he must prevent it. He must put in what it takes to do this. With Laos secured, he can easily do it. If we wait until then to put in divisions of our own, we will find necessary a commitment far greater than we previously made in Korea.

If we do not have the divisions, and what goes with them in the shape of air, land, and sea implementation, we must create them as soon as possible. Unless we do, and use them in Southeast Asia against the enemy, we will lose all of East Asia to Communism. If and when that happens, we will face a future of isolation and defeat, for all the rats will scurry to abandon the sinking ship, and to find some other craft in which to live, no matter how waterlogged or disarrayed it may be, so long as it is still afloat.

These are the issues in East Asia. How are we going to handle them?

FOREIGN AID DOCTRINES

by Edward C. Banfield

Dr. Edward C. Banfield is a member of the Joint Center for Urban Studies of MIT and Harvard. He is the author of many books, among them *The Moral Basis of a Backward Society* (1958).

Technical assistance and capital grants and loans to under-developed countries for non-military purposes ("foreign aid" or "aid") have in the last decade become a conspicuous feature of our foreign policy. In comparison with the total of defense spending the amount of aid has not been large (roughly 3 per cent for the decade), and in comparison with Gross National Product it has been very small (less than 1 per cent). But aid is nevertheless coming to be regarded as a principal instrument of our foreign policy. The use of it to supplement, and in some degree to substitute for, the traditional means of diplomacy is to be explained in part by the impracticability of using force or threats of force under the conditions that now prevail. Many people, however, believe it is in general a better way of achieving our objectives. In their widely read and influential book, *A Proposal*, Max F. Millikan and W. W. Rostow, for example, say that "we have put relatively too much emphasis in recent years on pacts, treaties, negotiations and international diplomacy and too little on measures to promote the evolution of stable, effective and democratic societies abroad," and they emphasize this by subtitling their book "Key to an Effective Foreign Policy."

Most of those who write about aid justify it mainly or ultimately, but usually not solely, on the ground that it will contribute to national security. This position is based on one or the other of two largely incompatible doctrines. One, which will be called the doctrine of indirect influence, asserts that national security will be promoted by using aid to transform fundamentally the cultures and institutions of the recipient countries. The other, which will be called the doctrine of direct influence, takes the cultures and institutions of the recipient countries as given and seeks to achieve the purpose (promotion of national security) by bringing influence to bear directly either upon the governments of the countries concerned or upon their public opinions.

A widely accepted doctrine asserts that foreign aid may serve the vital interests of the United States by setting off or bringing about fundamental changes in the outlook and institutions of the recipient societies and that these changes will lead to others—especially the spread of freedom and democracy—that will promote peace and thus indirectly serve our ultimate purpose, which is to increase our national security.

One school of thought emphasizes economic effects. A marked rise in average income will change profoundly the outlook of the masses of the people in underdeveloped countries. People who have enough to eat and something to look forward to will be much less receptive to Communist and other extremist appeals. Prosperity and opportunity will engender a taste for democracy and peace as, presumably, they have in our own society. The one great need, therefore, is to bring about rapid economic development. All the other effects that are desired will follow automatically.

On this theory, aid should be distributed among countries solely on the basis of their ability to use it to increase incomes. In principle, Russia and China might be given the highest priorities.

Another school of thought, represented principally by Millikan and Rostow, says that increases in income will not of themselves produce the desired effects (freedom, stability, democracy, and peace). To be sure, "some" economic improvement is a necessary condition for achieving these effects. But Millikan and Rostow are severely critical

of the "crude materialist" thesis that economic development will of itself either reduce revolutionary pressures or
lead to orderly political development. They regard it as a
serious misconception to think that the spirit of revolt
spreads easily among people who are chronically destitute
or that the mere creation of wealth can satisfy a people's
expectations. In their view, aid is important principally because it will set off social, political, and psychological
changes that will energize the society.

Since they insist that the desired effects can only be
secured through certain social, political, and psychological
changes, Millikan and Rostow might be expected to make
suggestions for using aid to bring about these changes.
They do not. All of their recommendations would be con-
genial to a "crude materialist."

They refer to the purpose of aid as "economic development" and make recommendations that are all directed
toward purely economic goals and that have little or no
relation to (indeed, are probably somewhat in conflict
with) the goal of setting off social, political, and psychological changes. For example, the key recommendation is
that the distribution of aid "be determined by absorptive
capacity rather than by considerations of equity or politics."

Millikan and Rostow, then, not only say nothing about
how the changes they regard as crucial are to be brought
about, but, by laying out a program which looks entirely
to economic objectives, they implicitly contradict the main
point of their analysis.

All who hold the doctrine of indirect influence agree that
a significant (Millikan and Rostow say "some") improvement in levels of living is necessary to secure the effects that
are ultimately desired. "Crude materialists" believe that
the greater the improvement the more marked these secondary effects will be. To the extent that there is reason
to believe improvements will not take place, confidence in
these doctrines must be weakened.

The improvement that is necessary is in the income of
the ordinary man, not in aggregate income. A large increase in aggregate income could leave most people in the
society worse off than before if, for example, population

grew faster than income or if the growth in income was accompanied by an increased concentration of income in the hands of a small elite or was siphoned off for military or other governmental purposes that did not raise standards of life. In order to bring about the necessary improvement in levels of living, therefore, a proper equilibrium must be achieved among three variables: the productivity of the economy, the size of the population, and the evenness with which income is distributed. Conceivably a satisfactory relationship among these variables might be secured by changing only one of them; in the usual case, however, it will be essential to change them all.

In most of the underdeveloped areas aggregate income has been increasing in recent decades. These gains, however, are being nearly offset, and in some cases more than offset, by growth of population. The rate of population growth is in most places enough to absorb the increase in aggregate income that will result from normal saving. Although their incomes are rising, the underdeveloped countries, with some exceptions, are not increasing their per capita food supply.

Estimates by Professor P. N. Rosenstein-Rodan on very optimistic assumptions (e.g., that the underdeveloped countries will get all the aid they can absorb and that they will make reasonably good use of it) indicate that from 1961 to 1976 gross national product in the underdeveloped parts of the world may rise from an average of $140 to $192 per capita. Whether an increase of this magnitude would suffice to change the political outlook of the underdeveloped countries decidedly is, of course, anyone's guess.

If the aid doctrine requires not merely *some* improvement in levels of living but the "modernization" of the economy, the outlook is even more discouraging. That aggregate and in some cases per capita incomes in these countries have been growing in recent years does not mean that they will continue to do so. The growth that has occurred so far may be in the nature of "taking up slack"; additional growth may be impossible without basic changes within the societies—changes that will not occur.

Some societies may never develop. The American Indian is a case in point. The cruelty, indifference, and stupidity of whites can explain only in part why many Indian cultures have not entered modern society after several hundred years of contact with it. In the last thirty years a vast amount of effort has been put forth on behalf of the Indians. The United States Government, for example, has spent several thousand dollars per Navaho to help them adapt, and has spent it with much intelligence and good will—as much, at any rate, as is likely to be found in any underdeveloped country. Yet the problem of the Navaho remains almost as it was a generation ago.

Even those underdeveloped countries which are not primitive may lack certain cultural or other prerequisites of development. One such prerequisite is the presence in the society of at least a small class of persons having talents and incentives that lead them to organize, innovate, and take risks. Other prerequisites are traits which must probably be fairly widespread in order for such a class to arise, or to function effectively if it does arise. These include the desire for material improvement, the belief that economic activity is worthy of respect, willingness to concert activity for common purposes or at least to allow others to concert it without interference, and ability to maintain at least that minimum of political stability that is essential in order for the government to carry out certain critical tasks.

These and other prerequisites are not all present in any of the underdeveloped areas.[1]

Such factors are in general more important obstacles to development than are lack of technical knowledge or of

[1] After listing four prerequisites of development "each as critical as capital" (viz., a substantial degree of literacy and that small number of people with knowledge and skills for managerial and technical tasks, a substantial measure of social justice, a reliable apparatus of government and public administration, and a clear and purposeful view of what development involves), J. K. Galbraith declares, "In practice, one or more of these four factors is missing in most of the poor countries." "A Positive Approach to Foreign Aid," *Foreign Affairs*, Vol. 39:3, 1961, p. 444–57.

foreign capital. If cultural and other conditions favor development, it will occur without aid. (Japan and Russia, to cite recent cases, did in fact develop without it.) If cultural conditions do not favor development, no amount of aid will bring it about. (Haiti, for example, has received large amounts of both technical assistance and foreign capital without development taking place.) *Probably no country is so poor that it cannot accumulate capital, Simon Kuznets has written, and the Western world could not if it tried prevent the wholesale borrowing of its technical knowledge by underdeveloped countries able to make use of it.*

American aid doctrine certainly exaggerates greatly the importance of both technical assistance and foreign capital in the development process. Only in the most backward countries can either kind of aid make a crucial difference, or perhaps even an important one. In the nature of the case, the greater the need of a country for aid, the less evidence there is that it has a capability to develop. The most prosperous and promising of the underdeveloped countries—Mexico, for example—may not require any aid in order to grow at a satisfactory rate. There is, to be sure, an important middle group of countries—India is a conspicuous example—which can absorb large amounts of aid and which offer some promise of developing. In time, too, some of the most backward countries may be brought by aid to the condition of this middle group. Nevertheless, despite these qualifications, there is a built-in perversity in the situation which makes it impossible to use large amounts of aid with effectiveness in most places.

Although aid is seldom, or perhaps never, an indispensable prerequisite to economic development and although even under the most favorable circumstances it is not likely to be the "key" to development, it may, as such dissimilar analysts as Milton Friedman and J. K. Galbraith have emphasized, do much to retard development if improperly used. There is much that should be done by government in underdeveloped areas (e.g., provision of roads, elementary education, a monetary system, law and order), Friedman says, but there are crucial advantages in letting private business do as much as possible. *One such advantage is that private individuals, since they risk their own funds, have a much stronger incentive to invest wisely. Another is that private individuals are more likely than state bureaucracies to abandon unsuccessful ventures.* The availability of resources at little or no cost to a country inevitably stimulates "monument-building," i.e., investment in projects adding little or nothing to the productivity of the economy. Under these circumstances, he concludes, countries would develop faster without aid than with it.

But even if economic growth does occur it will not necessarily lead to the spread of freedom and democracy. In the literature on aid these terms are usually left undefined. One cannot tell which is meant: wide distribution of power, rule of law, regard for civil liberties, free elections, consumers' choice, national independence, a distribution system favoring the poor, or something else. Obviously these need not all go together (e.g., national independence is compatible with dictatorship).

If by democracy and freedom are meant "respect for the individual" and its corollary "government by discussion" (however these principles are expressed institutionally), there is certainly little basis for optimism. Respect for the individual is unique to the Judaeo-Christian tradition. In those parts of the world which do not participate in this tradition, the idea is unintelligible or nearly so. That this particular conception—of the sacredness of the individual— might enter into and transform alien cultures in those parts of the world where the worthlessness of the individual human life is a conspicuous fact of everyday experience (a circumstance which indeed constitutes the very problem that aid seeks to solve) is so improbable as to be incredible.

The prospects are better if democracy is defined to mean merely government through institutions that are in some sense representative (i.e., which take account of the wants and interests of the major elements of the population and which by a peaceful process like an election can be made to respond to public opinion). But democracy even in this restricted sense will have a slow and fitful growth in most of the underdeveloped world. The political institutions of the West cannot be copied, as its technology can, by people whose ways of thinking and valuing are fundamentally different.

The expansion of state activity which aid engenders tends in some ways to discourage the growth of democracy. In a prosperous and politically experienced society, democracy and extensive governmental participation in economic affairs may coexist. But the situation of the underdeveloped countries precludes this. The best choice open to many of them is between governments that are not incompetent and ones that are not tyrannical. Aid, by encouraging governments to undertake tasks beyond their capabilities, is likely to lead to waste through the incompetence of the recipients, to the extension and hardening of governmental power—or, perhaps most likely, to both at once.

Where propaganda is to be the basis of governmental power, the West is at a great and probably hopeless disadvantage. It is identified (unfairly, of course, in the case of the United States) with the hated system of colonialism, the horrors of which increase with every retelling and the virtues of which have already been forgotten. The great principles for which the West stands, such as the worth of the individual, are unintelligible to the masses in the underdeveloped areas; the meaning of democracy, it need hardly be said, cannot be shouted over the radio to a street mob. The Communists, on the other hand, are under no such handicaps. The Marxist ideology provides people who are undergoing transition from a pre-industrial to an industrial society with a doctrine that makes sense of what must otherwise appear to them a senseless world. The Soviet Union, moreover, is an underdeveloped country that has "made good," whereas the United States, the richest country by far, is the conspicuous symbol of all that is hateful and threatening.

Reasons for hating the West, the capitalist, the white, and the foreigner exist to some degree in most of the underdeveloped countries. They account in part for the hostility often manifested toward the United States by the

leaders of countries which have no "objective" grounds
for hostility. In such countries, it may be much more important to the ruling clique, and perhaps also to the whole
nation, to have us for enemies than for friends.

Successful application of the doctrine of indirect influence (supposing this to be possible) will require concentration of aid efforts on the most promising and amenable
countries, and this, of course, will almost certainly create
disaffection among those that are not favored. It is quite
likely that the promising and amenable—and hence favored
—countries will be ones of little strategic importance to the
United States and that the disfavored—and hence dis-
affected—ones will be of great strategic importance.

Millikan and Rostow assert that as underdeveloped
countries gain confidence they will become easier to deal
with.

> Once they see that they are wholly capable of
> standing on their own feet, they can afford to be less
> quixotic and nervous in their foreign policies. A con-
> fident nation, making progress at home is likely to con-
> duct its foreign policy with poise and good sense.

This also overlooks the fact of power. The Soviet Union
is a confident nation, but it is nevertheless infinitely dangerous to us. Twenty-five years ago, when its confidence
was much less, it was no danger at all. The difference is
that its power has increased. What counts is not the confidence of nations but their power.

Along with the probability of achieving the effect that is
ultimately desired must be considered another: that of
achieving it *in time*. The peril to America exists now and in
the immediate future; it makes little difference to us how
peaceful the presently underdeveloped countries will be
a hundred years from now, or even thirty years from now,
if by then we will have been destroyed. One unit of present
advantage is worth much more to us than many units of
advantage thirty years hence, and more, perhaps, than any
possible number a hundred years hence. It is certainly
wildly optimistic to believe that the underdeveloped areas
may become "mature" and "healthy" democracies within

a generation, but even if they did, success might come too late.

Whatever the benefits that may be judged probable on this basis, account must also be taken of the costs. One cost which may not be obvious is the possibility of making matters worse. We may, for example, set off armaments races and wars between the underdeveloped countries. Indeed, there is reason to suppose that we have already done so. Israel's attack on Egypt was probably made possible by American aid, for although the aid was non-military, it freed foreign exchange for the purchase of armaments. In time, perhaps, our non-military aid to Egypt will enable that country to attack Israel. The arms competition between India and Pakistan is largely financed by us. By giving India non-military aid we make it possible for her to buy arms (Indian expenditures for arms have for several years equaled the value of the aid received from us), which causes Pakistan to demand ever larger amounts of military assistance. We are therefore financing both sides of an arms race.

This is not the only danger. We ourselves may eventually be menaced by countries that are now weak and friendly but will by our aid be made strong and hostile.

Another doctrine asserts that aid may serve the vital interests of the United States by directly influencing the recipient governments and peoples to act as the interests of the United States require or, more often, to refrain from acting in ways injurious to the United States. In contrast to the doctrine of indirect influence, this doctrine does not expect aid to work by changing the character of the recipient society economically or otherwise, though it acknowledges that economic and other effects may be by-products.

Several versions of this doctrine may usefully be distinguished:

1. *Quid Pro Quo.* The aid is part of a bargain between two governments in which there are clearly specified advantages to both sides. For example, we might agree to build a system of highways in return for assurances that

the Soviet Union would not be allowed to penetrate the country.

2. *Business Friendship.* The aid is given to create or maintain a relationship that is expected to have mutual advantages over time. The aid is, so to speak, a payment on an open account, it being tacitly understood that political advantages will be given in return.

3. *Maintenance of Friendly Governments.* The aid is intended to strengthen and to keep in power a government which is friendly, or at least not unfriendly. This may be done by undertakings, including of course economic development, which will increase the prestige of the recipient government or the confidence its public have in it.

4. *Prestige.* The aid is intended to exhibit dramatically the power of the giver and thereby to increase it. As Hobbes said in *Leviathan,* "Reputation of power is power, because it draweth with it the adherence of those that need protection."

5. *Good Will.* The aid is intended to make the recipient feel well disposed toward the giver and to put him under an implied obligation to return kindness for kindness. Few people expect governments to be moved by such sentiments as gratitude, but it is fairly widely believed that public opinion may be so moved and that it may have some effect on the policy of governments.

6. *Moral Force.* The aid is expected to affect public opinion by exerting moral force. The giver expects that the nobility of his action will inspire the recipient to act nobly too.

In most discussions of the doctrine of direct influence, these differences of approach are not clearly recognized. The term "impact" is sometimes used to describe any approach that is expected to make its effect by influencing opinion. It is evident, however, that different approaches require different means. For example, measures to promote "business friendship" would not generate "moral force."

It is not obvious why Americans so generally condemn the *"quid pro quo"* and "business friendship" versions of the direct influence doctrine. To bribe a foreign government to keep its country free may not be evil at all. But if it is, it is a kind of evil that respectable statesmen have always deemed it their duty to do when the security and welfare of their countries demanded. Where bribery is not involved, the justification of "reason of state" is not necessary. If a government is willing to give political favors in exchange for material resources, it is hard to see why either it or a government which accepts its offer should be criticized. As Aristotle remarked, the expression "friendly governments" means governments that exchange favors, not ones that love each other.

Instead of regretting the occasional necessity of putting aid on a business basis, we should wish that we could do it more often. Unfortunately, our opportunities will be few. The underdeveloped countries are in most cases pathologically sensitive about national "honor," and the suggestion that we should get something for what we give is always bitterly resented.

For the United States to seek to increase its prestige by the use of aid makes little sense. The power of this country is not underrated. (The Soviets are in a different position; their power is new and has to be seen to be believed.) Military prestige, moreover, is of little value so long as it is understood on all sides that Soviet power, world opinion, and our own scruples will prevent us from using force in any event. Our experience with Cuba is a case in point. The case for using aid to increase our reputation for non-military power is even poorer. No underdeveloped country doubts our ability to give or withhold enormous advantages.

"Good will" and "moral force" can make their effect only by working upon public opinion rather than upon governments. The public opinion in an underdeveloped country does not include the opinion of the peasants, who in most places are the vast majority. If our grain prevents the peasant from starving, he may be grateful, but his gratitude has no effect upon the policy of his country because politically he does not exist. Those who *do* make a difference are the people of the cities, especially the primate cities, and, above all, the small group which rules.

To suppose that the masses in the cities will feel grateful

toward us because we have improved the peasant's lot or
saved him from starvation is probably unrealistic. It is
hardly less so, perhaps, to suppose that the ruling groups
will be moved to gratitude or respect by our generosity.
They will assume that our actions are really selfishly moti-
vated and that our claims to the contrary are hypocrisy.
Although they are largely Western-educated, these elites
do not entirely share our moral standards. In some places,
the very idea of public-spiritedness is incomprehensible;
actions we think noble appear as merely foolish.

These considerations suggest that if aid is to have political effect it must work upon the educated class. Undertakings which stir national pride or afford direct material
benefits to that class are likely to succeed best. Building
an ostentatious capital city or supporting schools, theaters,
and supermarkets in primate cities may do more to create
politically significant sentiment in favor of the United
States than much more costly projects in the hinterland.

Even at its most effective, "impact" aid is not likely to
change matters fundamentally. To make countries that are
already friendly somewhat more so will avail us little. To
bring friendly countries into a condition of "total dependency" (assuming this to be desirable) would require vast
amounts of aid. To change basically the policy of uncommitted countries by this means is probably out of the
question. There is a danger too, as President Kennedy
pointed out to Congress, that "if we encourage recipient
countries to dramatize a series of short-term crises as a
basis for our aid . . . we will dissipate our funds, our good
will and our leadership."

It is often asserted that if we do not give them aid the
underdeveloped countries will eventually fall under the
control of the Soviet Union and be used by it to bring
about our destruction. There is, however, reason to think
that this is not a realistic view of the alternative. For one
thing, assistance for non-military purposes (the only kind
of aid under discussion here) is not our sole means of preventing countries from falling under Soviet domination. Except where aid is the practical equivalent of military assistance (the recipient using it, as India does, to release for

military expenditure funds that would otherwise have to be used for non-military expenditure), it is not decisive in keeping a country out of the hands of the Soviets. *What is decisive is military assistance or the threat of it.*

However, even if we gave neither aid nor military assistance, it is not likely that all of the underdeveloped countries would fall completely under Soviet control. Nationalism would be a barrier to Communist imperialism, as it has been to Western, and even if all of the countries in question did become in some sense Communist, the Kremlin probably could not impose a tight discipline upon all of them in all things. Tensions like those that now exist between the Russians and the Chinese and between both the Russians and the Chinese and the Yugoslavs would certainly arise. But even if they did not—even if all of the underdeveloped countries entered fully into a monolithic bloc hostile to the United States—we would not necessarily be cut off and isolated.

Let us, however, assume the worst: viz., that all of the underdeveloped countries fall completely under the control of the Soviet Union and that it uses its control to try to isolate and destroy us. Even in this event, we could probably survive and we might even prosper.

The economic consequences of such isolation would be endurable. Trade with the underdeveloped countries is relatively unimportant to us. They are comparatively cheap sources of certain raw materials, but at some additional cost we could either produce these raw materials ourselves or find substitutes for them from within our borders. The cost might be no greater than that of extending aid at the levels that would be necessary in order to achieve much by it (say $6 billion a year).

That we could probably survive if all of the underdeveloped countries fell to the Communists is not, of course, a reason for letting them fall to them if we can help it— any more than the fact that one can survive with a broken leg is a reason for letting one's leg be broken. The dangers and disadvantages of such a thing to us, even though not likely to be fatal, obviously justify very strenuous efforts— more strenuous, perhaps, than we are now making—to prevent it from happening. Even if aid is only moderately effective in keeping the underdeveloped countries out of the hands of the Communists, it is a small price to pay for a large benefit.

This, however, is very different from saying that our very existence as a nation depends upon our giving aid.

There are those who believe that a humanitarian desire to improve the welfare of the people of the underdeveloped areas amply justifies extensive aid and would justify it even if no security advantages could be expected from it—even if, indeed, there were some loss of security to be expected from it.

Statesmen have usually assumed that the object of policy is to increase the relative power of one's own nation— something that may be done by decreasing the power of others—and accordingly they have thought themselves virtuous when they have merely refrained from inflicting injuries.

As applied to aid, the doctrine of altruism presents two especially grave difficulties. One is that "doing good" may be impossible either because we do not know what is "good" or because, if we do know, we cannot bring it about and may, despite our best intentions, bring about "bad" instead. The other is that it may not be a proper function for our government to do good for people who are not its citizens.

1. It is hard to say what constitutes welfare, especially the welfare of people whose culture is radically different from our own. Our common humanity offers some guidance: food obviously serves the welfare of the starving. But even the matter of food is not so simple. By preventing starvation, we may, if we cannot at the same time reduce the rate of population growth, lower the average income and perhaps prevent the occurrence of those fundamental changes that would lead to sustained economic growth.

We do not have to analyze the matter very far to see that "welfare" cannot be defined in purely physical terms, i.e., as amounts of food, clothing, and shelter. "Doing good" cannot then, be equated with raising incomes, or with bringing about self-sustaining economic growth. The choices that we have to make when we extend aid must in the last analysis express a conception of the good life and of the good society. But if we are liberals, we believe we have no way of deciding for another culture what its ends of life should be.

2. Doing good for those who are not its citizens may not be a proper function of our government. Foreign aid, like most government activities, involves taking property from some by threat of force in order to give it to others.

It may be thought that if a large number of Americans —say a majority—want very much to have aid given through the instrumentality of the government, the giving of it will *ipso facto* serve the common good: the common good, that is, may be defined as "whatever will serve the convenience of a large bloc of voters." But this is not consistent with the philosophy on which our government was founded. According to this philosophy, government is justified in coercing some of its citizens (e.g., by taxing them to support aid) not in order to serve the convenience of others (even though these others may be an overwhelming majority), but only to maintain the society and to make it a good society.

Although academic political theorists do not seem to be much concerned about these questions, a kind of common law political theory appears to be coming into existence with regard to them. It maintains, as does the traditional theory, that government should restrict itself to serving the common good, but it defines the common good in terms that transcend the nation. A government, people seem to think, should serve the common good *of the world as a whole*. Those who take this view think that the ultimate purpose of aid ought to be the promotion of a world community.

Attractive as it may be, this position is full of difficulties. World community, even if desirable, may not be a possibility. It is obvious that the world is very far from agreeing as to what constitutes its common good and that it is entirely unwilling to let the United States decide for it.

Those who think that America has a responsibility to raise the level of living of mankind ought, if they are to be consistent, to think that it also has a responsibility to save the world from Communist tyranny, for that is an even worse thing. But the responsibility, if it exists, cannot stop there. Communist tyranny is not the only kind of tyranny and may not be the worst; our responsibility must therefore extend to preventing, or eradicating, all tyranny, including, of course, that which results from a people's own folly or immorality.

Those who expound the doctrine of our world responsibility ought to be prepared to acknowledge that to whatever extent we have a responsibility we must also have a right to exercise authority. The claim that one has responsibility for another implies the inequality of the two and, consequently, the right of the superior to give, and the duty of the inferior to accept, tutelage. The doctrine of American responsibility is therefore really an incomplete and confused version of the now unfashionable notion of the "white man's burden." The difference between the two doctrines—a very important one—is that whereas the old one frankly recognized the necessity of joining authority to responsibility, the new one passes over the subject of authority in embarrassed silence.

The writing on aid not only lacks the systematic relating of means and ends that is the defining characteristic of rational planning, but much of it conceals the hard problems of choice behind a fog of moralizing. By "moralizing" is meant advocacy, as a basis for action, of moral principles that do not take account of elements of the situation which render them inapplicable or inappropriate. The moralizer averts his gaze from those features of the real situation that constitute the crux of the problem and then, unhampered, tells us how to act in a world different from the one in which we must act. For example, he warns severely against extending aid to corrupt tyrannies or reactionary ruling oligarchies. This would be good advice if the choice were really between a corrupt tyranny and an honest democracy. Alas, this is seldom the choice, and when it is, the advice is usually not needed. The real problem exists when we must choose between a corrupt tyranny and a Communist one—and here the advice of the moralizer is at best confusing and at worst wrong. He refuses, however, to acknowledge the real problem.

Sometimes moralizing is half hidden behind an affectation of political realism. For example, Eugene R. Black, president of the World Bank, tells us that by sacrificing our present political advantage to promote long-term economic development we will serve our *real* political interests. And Reinhold Niebuhr, who is known as a political realist, explains that the art of statecraft is to find "the point of concurrence" between the national and the international common good; apparently he is confident that there is such a point, for he goes on to say that "this policy means that we must try to persuade the nation that what is good for the alliance of the free nations is good for our own Nation *in the long run.*" Such statements conjure the crucial problems of choice out of existence by making it appear that conflicts of interest only *seem* to exist—that "in the long run" there are no conflicts and "the proper and the practical courses coincide," presumably at the "point of concurrence."

This mentality, evident in most of the writing on aid, ignores the very facts that constitute the problem: that vast areas of the world show little prospect of achieving self-sustaining economic growth or of governing themselves reasonably well within the foreseeable future; that development, when it does take place, is as likely to be inspired by blood and hate as by peace and rational management; that the development of the underdeveloped countries may not on balance be in the interest of the United States or, indeed, of civilization; and that the measures most effective in relieving misery and promoting economic growth are in general least effective in serving the urgent necessities of the West. Instead of facing up to these tragic facts and endeavoring to frame a course of action that is workable and represents the least among evils for us and for mankind, writers on aid generally proffer a few sententious principles of everyday morality and issue stern warnings against using aid for political purposes.

When policy based upon such misconceptions fails, the moralizer knows whom to blame. Not, surely, anyone in

the underdeveloped countries—not even if the obvious
cause of the trouble is there. Still less those like himself
upon whose naïve and sentimental notions the policy was
based. The fault, he says, is with the United States; it was
not generous enough, or not tactful enough, or not firm
enough, or it did not organize and plan effectively. That
the failure may have been unavoidable, the natures of
givers and receivers being what they are, is a possibility
that escapes him altogether.

THE UNDERDEVELOPED NATIONS

by Karl Brandt

Dr. Karl Brandt is Director of the Food Research Institute at Stanford University and Professor of Economic Policy. A frequent consultant on agricultural economics to the United States Government and former member of the President's Council of Economic Advisors, he is the author of *Reconstruction of World Agriculture* (1945) and *The Management of Agriculture and Food in the German-Occupied and Other Areas of Fortress Europe* (1953).

Aside from the tug of war in military strategy and tactics and simultaneous ideological warfare, the power contest between the West and the Communist powers will proceed primarily by expansion in the economic realm. What counts in the long run is growth of the potential of an economy, or the development of its human, man-made, and natural resources in their aggregate capacity to produce goods and services, not merely expansion of output. The gross national product of nations can be expanded for many years with serious depletion of the productive assets and resources, including particularly the human resources.

Since the economic contest affects all human action of a nation, strategy in the free world, with its non-coercive economy, requires first of all that the faith of the people in the basic fairness and equity of their economic system must be maintained and strengthened, and that the public must be aware of and alert to the crucial issues of over-all economic strategy.

Economic growth in the Atlantic Community and Japan will outdistance the results of forced industrialization within the Communist world still further if Western private enterprises are encouraged, even more than they are now, to invest freely across the national boundaries. Such initiative of American firms in different parts of Europe and in Japan, of some European firms in the United States, Canada, and Japan, and similarly of Japanese firms in Europe and in the United States, can expand productivity by blending advanced techniques, procedures, and innovations, and by promoting the mobility of capital as well as research and skilled personnel within the industrial heartland.

The greatest prospect for growth lies, however, in joint ventures of enterprises from two or more industrial countries in underdeveloped countries. They are that part of the free world which is subject to large scale and intensive Soviet offensive. These countries comprise all the geography outside the Communist realm and outside the West's industrial heartland. In them the conflict poses much more difficult problems.

There are enormous differences among these countries in every respect. They include old and long independent ones, even much older ones which have become independent only since World War II, and some where primitive tribal societies are still under colonial administration. Among these less developed countries are some with a much improved per capita income and prosperity, while others suffer from utter poverty and stagnation. There are some with developed oil resources and big foreign-exchange earnings and some which are making great strides in industrialization. And finally there are quite a few with overwhelmingly agrarian rural economies. To cover all these diverse conditions with world-wide statistical averages of dubious conceptual adequacy does not necessarily contribute to understanding the nature of specific problems in individual countries.

Yet there are certain common traits. The underdeveloped countries are all exporters of primary products and importers of industrial products, including particularly producers' capital goods. In a substantial number of these countries, particularly in the tropical and subtropical climates, the major part of the population lives on small farms and expects and demands economic development.

These vast areas, most with high rates of population growth, are particularly exposed to indigenous political and social unrest and to Communist infiltration. All of these areas need an increase in the productivity of farm labor, which in turn requires a substantial increase in the output of food, feed, and fibers per man year of the labor force employed in agriculture.

In most of these areas certain commercial crops are produced with hired labor on plantations which are highly capitalized and competently managed large-scale enterprises, while some of the plantation crops as well as a multitude of others are also produced by small family farms.

In considering the agrarian policy issues of underdeveloped countries, it is important to realize that in semi-arid climates the main remunerative agricultural land utilization other than irrigated crop farming is extensive grain production or even more extensive grazing of cattle and sheep, or a combination of grain farming and grazing. If the vast expanse of such lands with several times the acreage of all arable land is not to go entirely to waste, there must be very large units of ranches or *estancias* with very large capital in land and livestock, and with a very few hired ranch hands employed. To bring the size of such units into comparison with intensive crop farming in humid areas or with irrigation farming serves only to confuse the issues of land reform. However, intensive animal husbandry fits very well into small farming with intensive crop production or arable land in humid climates or on irrigated land.

It is widely asserted that the underdeveloped part of the free world (excluding, of course, such agriculturally advanced economies as Australia, New Zealand, and Canada) cannot begin to attain economic growth unless there is a thorough agrarian reform with distribution of the land among landless farm workers and small holders. It is also widely taken for granted that in the interest of greater equality for the small farmer the large scale enterprises must be liquidated.

The whole area of problems connected with rural development and agrarian reform is an ideological and economic battleground where the West, through confusion about basic principles and by too ready an acceptance of seemingly plausible yet vastly oversimplified and ill-advised solutions, has a very good chance to lose the battle for freedom and human dignity just as it was lost in mainland China by supporting the supposedly benevolent "agrarian reformers."

A few basic observations may indicate some points of orientation for constructive policies for the underdeveloped countries.

Land as such neither produces income nor is it wealth per se. It offers an opportunity to apply management, labor, and capital. To carve up productive, large-scale plantation enterprises which are well managed, capitalized, have a high productivity, and provide steady employment at competitive wages, and to distribute their land in small parcels is the opposite of what economic development demands. The destruction of the large and efficiently operating private farm enterprises and their parceling is precisely the recipe prescribed by Stalin and his book *Lessons in Leninism,* namely, the first necessary stage of the Communist revolution, which, according to party doctrine, must precede the second stage of collectivization. Political hostility to plantations has ruined the world's former leading natural rubber and cane-sugar industries in Java, and it impedes a potentially prosperous agricultural development of tea, cocoa, oil palm, and banana culture in many tropical zone countries.

Sound economic strategy of the West requires the finding of a more rational solution. Since the plantations are in many underdeveloped countries the only enterprises which have the full command of up-to-date production techniques and of scientific research, these enterprises should be enabled and induced to share the benefits of their modern farming methods, processing plants, and marketing facilities with small farmers, and to act as their extension service agency. Such *symbiosis* between a plantation and a large number of small farmers could be organized either on a contractual basis or in the form of a corporation in which the plantation and a small farmers' co-operative association would be equal partners. Such an arrangement would be particularly attractive in all cases where the specialized production of a farm commodity requires a processing factory, or packing houses and elaborate shipping installations, as is the case for sugar cane and sugar beets, oil palms and coconuts, bananas, pineapples, and many tree fruits, nuts, and vegetables.

To provide by legislation for such *symbiosis* between small farmers and modern large-scale farm enterprises or agricultural corporations seems just as important as legislation passed throughout the world in the latter part of the last century on behalf of the farmers' co-operative associations as a form of corporative private enterprise.

In large areas of the underdeveloped countries it is apparent that even under the most favorable circumstances of industrialization and expansion of nonagricultural employment a major part of the population will continue to earn its livelihood on small family farms. To assist these people in their effort to improve their living conditions and real income ought to be a primary concern of economical social strategy. Unfortunately, reasonable action is impeded by too many popular but erroneous assumptions.

It is taken for granted that

(a) The income of small farms consists for all practical comparison exclusively of products sold in the market.

(b) Small farms are bare of capital.

(c) Small farmers are unable to form capital.

(d) The most important aid to small farms is the enlargement of their acreage.

(e) Farm tenancy is a destructive form of land tenure, which cannot be improved and must be replaced by ownership.

These assumptions are demonstrably not in accord with facts. It is far worse that they obscure the opportunities for genuine improvement. Small family farms yield in terms of real income, aside from cash sales of products, home-consumed food, housing, fuel, and potentially some clothing as well as transportation. How good or how poor the aggregate real income is depends on skills, work discipline, the art of good husbandry, the existing capital in real estate, and improvements, the dead and live inventory, the stores of food, feed, and seed, as well as on the opportunity to earn enough cash to purchase or rent means of production such as tools, implements, or fertilizer. The concept of a farm, no matter how small and poor, as being totally void of capital, is just as much sheer fiction as is the notion that small family farmers are unable to form capital. Blindness to the opportunities for forming capital on even very primitive farms excludes from development policy one of the great sources of wealth in countries stricken by rural poverty. Raising of draft animals or breeding stock of food-producing animals is the formation of capital. So is the clearance of woodland, the digging of drainage ditches and wells, improving walks and roads. In fact, these improvements of productive real estate are considered vital capital investments in most advanced economies. A large part of the wealth of the United States was formed by farmers when this country was still underdeveloped.

It is the new situation in the Western world that—as a result of unforeseen overabundance of oil and natural gas, the enormous expansion of the petrochemical industries, and the decline in transportation costs—plant nutrients and irrigation water are becoming available to farmers in all parts of the free world at declining costs in terms of marginal product. The progress in plant breeding, in chemical weed and pest control, combined with lower prices of fertilizer and of small combustion engines for pumping irrigation water, offers the opportunity for intensifying the production of crops, animal feed, and animal products. Since on the small farm interest and depreciation on the real estate, the work stock, and the labor must be considered as overhead or fixed costs, the adding of purchased inputs such as seed, fertilizer, pesticides, and energy for irrigation lowers the unit costs.

From the absurd claim that the rural farm population cannot form capital, many development strategists jump to the *non sequitur* that, therefore, the government must form the capital for industrial development by taxing the farmers through foreign-exchange controls and multiple-exchange rates, or through government purchase of farm commodities at stable prices. Such stable prices then serve the purpose of confiscating a substantial part of the farm income. This kind of development strategy is the unchanged Soviet doctrine. It is the abrogation of the entire philosophy of the West and undermines most effectively the economic philosophy of the humane society and prepares underdeveloped countries for a materialistic state capitalism. Besides this immeasurable harm, the squeezing of income from the farm population has the logical result of preventing or crippling the increase in productivity of farm labor which is essential to economic growth. It is claimed that small farmers will use improved cash income only for senseless consumption or for working less. The evidence in most parts of the world is different. Small farmers acquire bicycles, sewing machines, better work clothes, better breeding stock, radios, and a multitude of goods which all tend to improve their work capacity. This in turn gives a healthy boost to the rise of private industries.

Therefore the greatest aid to family farms is the improvement of their supply with the "small means" for increasing their productivity by making production credit available and by improvement of their access to urban markets for their increased output.

Since an underdeveloped economy suffers typically from underemployment or seasonal unemployment of farm people, improvement of their income must begin with making constructive use of the idle time of this large part of the labor force. This can be done on the farm as well as in part time work off the farm. If even in advanced industrial countries the weight of food in the consumer cost-of-living index (including beverages and tobacco) has a range between 29 and 38, while in some fairly progressing underdeveloped countries it exceeds 50 for the nonfarm population, then it seems worthy of maximum effort to increase this part of farm family income to its optimum by diversification of food and feed crops and animal products, and by improving home economic skills. Beyond that, family farmers should be assisted in improving their housing, their furniture, and clothing by developing their vocational woodworking and metalworking skills, and by making better tools available to them through effective merchandizing of such imports. Vocational training at the apprentice level in the villages promises almost immediately effective development aid for the greatest number of the rural population.

Since gaining time is essential, it is faulty strategy for underdeveloped countries to rely primarily on education and research at the highest level in the development of human resources at the expense of building up from the grassroots. The underdeveloped countries have the opportunity of utilizing, free of charge, the results of enormously costly agricultural and technical research undertaken in the advanced countries. The same applies to the importation of farm equipment. However, it would be a wise policy decision if, instead of trying to jump from the oxcart and draft-animal level of farm transportation to the immediate abolition of draft animals and to the motorization of farms with trucks, underdeveloped countries would take the step of increasing the effective draft power by adopting used truck chassis with roller-bearing axles and pneumatic tires. This stage, which has preceded the full mechanization of farm transport in all European countries, requires far less capital, while it increases the farm efficiency very substantially by making the animal draft power 30 to 40 per cent more effective. The most important decision for underdeveloped countries concerns the necessity of establishing an economic climate that attracts the investment of indigenous as well as foreign capital. Private foreign investment capital has the enormous advantage, compared with government-to-government loans or grants, of bringing with it the managerial experience and the technical skills so essential to economic development. Since such capital investors take the risk of losing if their new enterprises are unable to compete and to yield amortization and depreciation, the host country has the best assurance that it will continue to develop and will not end up with white elephants.

The national interest can well be satisfied by offering

shares in such foreign investment to citizens of the host country and eventual sale of the remaining stock.

The creation of such confidence and stability is closely connected with the way in which any agrarian reform is handled. That efficient plantations should not be destroyed has already been stressed. If colonization of unsettled land is undertaken, it is advisable to open up first of all fertile land in the public domain, if need be by making it accessible through construction of roads or by granting concessions for construction of water dams for power and irrigation use.

If land for settlement of farmers must be acquired from large landed estates, the best method is acquisition by a colonization bank or a settlement agency in the farm real estate market. The next alternative is expropriation by condemnation procedures. In that case protection of the confidence of all parties in the security of property requires prompt, fair, and adequate compensation of the former owner in such terms and with such means of payment that the acquisition does not amount to partial or total confiscation. Confiscatory policies do not deserve the name of agrarian reforms. They are plainly acts of revolution and violence.

Fair and adequate compensation has the advantage that the indemnified former owners will have a keen incentive to invest such funds in remunerative enterprises. In that case the funds will tend to accelerate the process of private industrialization, which is less prone to lead to failures by decentralization than under centralized expansion of public enterprises.

The strategy of wise and successful agrarian reform requires the cautious amendment of the institutional framework of the underdeveloped economies. This applies first of all to the institution of private property in land, which comprises the right to encumber, to divide, to lease, to grant easements, to sell, and the obligation to pay land taxes. Reform requires corrective amendments with due respect for the secondary effects. Instead of condemning farm tenancy, wise reforms of legislation have in many countries not only corrected the defects in the performance of both parties, landlords and tenants but have made farm leases one of the socially and economically most progressive arrangements for efficient land utilization. The same applies to the supposed innate evils of farm-labor contracts on large scale enterprises. In a number of underdeveloped countries in several continents, wise reforms have given the hired farm workers and their families more social security and more equitable wage schedules than industrial workers have in the cities.

What is needed for wise reform is the hard work of resourceful lawyers, economists, and sociologists who have a full knowledge of the many alternatives which the rich historical experience of the advanced countries of the West has yielded.

ECONOMIC PRIORITIES: Needs v. Expediency

by Roger A. Freeman

Roger A. Freeman is a Senior Staff Member at the Hoover Institution on War, Revolution, and Peace at Stanford University. He served on the White House staff during the Eisenhower administration and as Assistant to Governor Arthur B. Langlie of Washington. He is a member of the executive committee of the National Tax Association, acted in 1956–57 as fiscal adviser to the Bolivian Government, and has been chairman of the state and local government advisory committee to the U. S. Bureau of the Census, and is a member of the Advisory Council of the Tax Institute of America.

If we assembled a representative group of economists and of political, business, and labor leaders and asked them to draw up a list of major economic goals, they could without too much difficulty agree on such objectives as rapid and steady growth in national product and income, full employment, stable prices, wide diffusion of well-being, balanced foreign payments, etc. But if they then proceeded to draft policies necessary to attain those goals, they would soon be in each others' hair and wind up with two or more reports with widely differing and often contradictory recommendations.

Why, we may ask, should there be such discord on the means of economic policy when there appears to be a reasonable accord on its ends?

For one, economics has not yet become as exact a science as, for example, physics or chemistry, in which cause-and-effect relationships are more apparent and, as a rule, can be verified by test series. We cannot test economic theories by laboratory experiments; our much beloved models are fascinating intellectual exercises but can seldom be regarded as empirical evidence.

For another, it seems that politics tends to override economic considerations.

THE PRIMACY OF POLITICS

Harvard economist Seymour Harris has suggested the existence of a widening "gap in understanding between professional economists and professional politicians."[1] It may sometimes so appear because a majority of economics professors are to the left of the general public and, to a lesser degree, of its elected representatives. But the real conflict is not between occupations—between the professor and the politician—but between opposing political ideologies. Most persons accord political goals a higher priority in their hierarchy of values than purely economic goals. A set of economic facts may not convert a man to whom the policy which the evidence at hand suggests is repugnant. If he is a "true believer" he will reinterpret the facts and devise an economic rationale that supports his views—which he calls mature judgment, while his opponents are more likely to label them preconceived notions or prejudice.

The perpetual argument over federal v. state financial capacity offers a good example: not so many years ago the advocates of governmental centralization asserted that the revenue sources of state and local governments were inflexible and could not be as rapidly expanded as those of the national government. ("The whole is greater than the sum of its parts.") So they asserted that the national government would have to assume a greater share of the financial responsibility for education, welfare, and other public services. When state and local revenues kept growing at a much faster rate than federal receipts in the period since World War II—as they had always done except during shooting wars—the argument shifted: state and local gov-

[1] Seymour E. Harris, "The Gap between Economist and Politician," the New York *Times Magazine,* April 14, 1963.

ernments, they said, had exerted such an effort by quad-
rupling their income while federal receipts only doubled
that they had exhausted their fiscal capacity and from now
on would have to depend more heavily on the national
treasury. Of course, if state and local revenues had *not*
climbed so steeply, the centralists would have advanced
this as proof that the states lacked the power to do it. No
matter what they did, the states could not win. Such a
"heads I win, tails you lose" line of reasoning is frequently
found expedient to sustain a preferred policy and achieve
political ends in the face of adverse economic facts.

We can, as the result of much observation, study, and
analysis in this and other countries, advance a reasonable
and documented case why the unburdening and strengthening of private enterprise is more likely to lead to *sustained* industrial expansion than forced draft by central
planning and direction of economic activities. But we cannot, in the true sense of the word, *prove* it, particularly not
to the satisfaction of those who believe in the greater intelligence and efficacy of governmental action.

We may adduce dozens of examples over the past thousand years, in Asia, Europe, and the Americas, of the eventual and apparently inevitable results of a policy which depends on the banknote printing press for the solution of
fiscal, economic, and political problems. But they won't
convert those to whom the alternative course of fiscal discipline—which may mean austerity and self-denial—is vis-
cerally repugnant or politically inopportune.

WAGES, PROFITS, AND UNEMPLOYMENT

An economist usually recognizes that the price of a commodity has a powerful impact on the size of its market and
its sales potential and may even admit that this rule also
applies to the price of labor. But some will find many reasons why this conclusion must not be translated into wage
policy. As wages were pushed up faster than productivity
in the postwar period, prices climbed, and the international and domestic competitive standing of many of our
industries began to slide. In an effort to hold their ground,
companies started absorbing a growing share of the higher

costs and thus stabilized prices but in the process squeezed their profits, which in turn slowed down industrial expansion and tightened the job market.

It will come as a surprise to many to learn that John Maynard Keynes recognized the relationship between profits and unemployment. He wrote: "Unemployment, I must repeat, exists because employers have been deprived of profit. The loss of profit may be due to all sorts of causes. But, short of going over to Communism there is no possible means of curing unemployment except by restoring to employers a proper margin of profit."[2] But our present-day neo-Keynesians prefer soothing the pain to curing the ailment. They seek correction in politically expedient inflationary policies and liberalized welfare and unemployment benefits rather than in putting the needed brake on wage rises and letting greater productivity restore adequate profits and gradually lower prices.

REDISTRIBUTING INCOME

Some pursue a similar line in tax and expenditure policy. A man who holds that success and failure in our society are largely fortuitous and devoid of personal merit or demerit is hard put to accept the proposition that greater reliance on market decisions in regard to income distribution might in the long run lead to faster and sounder economic growth. Facts to the contrary will not make him waver in his belief that human welfare can best be promoted by more extensive governmental action to "improve" income distribution than we have yet seen. To give his preference an economic rationale, he will wax enthusiastic over schemes of income equalization as a means to augment and stabilize consumer purchasing power.

Such ever greater redistribution of income, whatever its economic virtues may be, is unacceptable to those who believe that the widest personal freedom—defined as the power of choice between known alternatives—and individual responsibility for one's fate are supreme values. They

2 John Maynard Keynes, *Essays in Persuasion*. New York: Harcourt, Brace & Co., 1932, p. 275.

may favor some mitigation at the lower end of the income scale for reasons of charity and justice, but maintain that the rewards and punishments of a free market system are the fuel that drives the engines of economic expansion and that with less fuel we shall drive fewer miles. They hold that there is no substitute for strong incentives.

It goes without saying that an individual's economic situation and interests powerfully affect his position on economic policy, though they do not necessarily control it. Pocketbook considerations are persuasive, and with the exception of those who are ideologically committed to a particular cause, men are rarely eager to support a program which does not seem to benefit them immediately or directly.

Such personal interests may, on the whole, be expected to balance each other in the normal process of free government. But political arithmetic only counts and seldom weighs. An officeholder or candidate, for example, may be well aware of the paralyzing effect of overly steep graduated income tax rates. But before taking a public position he tunes in on a wave length on which he learns that—based on 1960 income tax returns—taxpayers with an adjusted gross income under $4500 account for a majority (52 per cent) of all individual returns, those with $25,000 and over for less than 1 per cent of all taxpayers (and voters). Then he wrestles with his conscience—and *he* wins. So, although political leaders knew of the pernicious effect of excessive income tax rates, they found it expedient to impose them upon the American people in successive steps between 1932 and 1944 and did not, except in a token manner, reduce them in the eighteen years following World War II. We have, for the past thirty years, been paying a high price for this classic example of demagoguery.

LIBERALS AND CONSERVATIVES

On the whole, economic policies in recent decades have often dealt with symptoms more than with causes and were guided by political expediency more than by sound and proven principles. Arguments and positions have by and large divided along the line of the political dichotomy between Liberals and Conservatives. These labels, as has often been pointed out, are not very appropriately chosen. Those who call themselves Liberals tend to favor policies which would increasingly restrict individual liberty, while the Conservatives, far from wishing to conserve and continue policy trends of recent decades, propose to alter the direction in which we are traveling. But the terms Liberal and Conservative have become so widely accepted and generally used in the United States that to avoid further confusion we may as well keep using them—provided that we spell them with a capital L and capital C. After all, proper names are not necessarily descriptive labels. The difference between Democrats and Republicans is not that the former are against republican forms of government or that the latter oppose democratic principles of government.

Political goals which divide Liberals and Conservatives and tend to enjoy priority over purely economic considerations in the setting of economic policies may be identified by three major antitheses:

1. More government—or less?

Liberals favor extending the scope and magnitude of governmental activity; Conservatives prefer to enlarge the range of individual decision-making power. A crude measure of the trend is the share of national product or income channeled through government.

2. More centralization of government—or less?

Liberals favor greater national uniformity of public services through the centralization of policy making; Conservatives prefer local autonomy in the setting of domestic programs. A crude measure is the division of public revenues and the flow of funds between levels of government.

3. More redistribution of income—or less?

Liberals aim to overrule, through the political process, the rewards and punishments of the free market more decisively than we have so far done; Conservatives believe that government should disturb relative economic positions only to the extent to which compassion and justice demand it. Crude measures are the relative tax burdens and public benefits in high and low income brackets.

ECONOMIC POLICY AND ECONOMIC GROWTH

With political goals tending to override purely economic goals, it is small wonder that the results of economic study have had only a modest impact on policy formulation. Yet the volume of economic study and the institutional setting for such studies have vastly expanded over the past twenty to thirty years. This growing search for more facts and new truths probably expresses a widespread and nagging uncertainty over the soundness of our current economic policies, a call for an "agonizing reappraisal," which typifies recent decades far more than earlier periods.

Looking back over the sweep of American history we can hardly question that on the whole our economic policies must have been sound: the proof of the pudding is the fact that no country in all recorded history has ever expanded its national product and income as rapidly for as long a time as has the United States for well over a hundred years or achieved such widely diffused well-being and vertical socio-economic mobility. It is no mere accident that violent class struggle, which has plagued so many other countries, has been absent. Much of the credit must go to the institutional setting and the rules of the game under which the American economy operated.

SLOWER GROWTH?

The United States still is by far the richest country on earth and controls between one half and one third of the world's major economic goods with only 6 per cent of its population and land area. But our rate of economic growth seems to have been gradually slowing down. Raymond W. Goldsmith, in a study for the Joint Economic Committee of Congress, computed average annual growth rates of Gross National Product (GNP) for three forty-year periods since 1839 as follows:

1839 to 1879	4.31 per cent per year
1879 to 1919	3.72 per cent per year
1919 to 1959	2.97 per cent per year[3]

[3] Employment, Growth, and Price Levels, Hearings before the Joint Economic Committee, 86th Congress, 1st S., Part 2, 1960,

Dissatisfaction with our economic growth rate has been spreading and deepening in recent years. Concern has focused not so much on the secular trend apparent in the figures above but on the post-World War II period which, it is said, showed rapid growth in its earlier part, followed by a slowdown in the later 1950s. Typical of such comments is one by Senator Paul Douglas, a former economics professor, that GNP grew an average of 4.6 per cent per annum between 1947 and 1953 but only 2.3 per cent per annum between 1953 and 1959. That computation averages the years of the Korean and Cold War build-up of 1950 and 1951 with peace periods. In 1950 and 1951 GNP grew 8.2 per cent each. Both in the preceding and in subsequent years the growth rate was much lower. Only the early part of World War II showed similar growth rates. But the spurt in war production in World War II or in 1950 and 1951 can hardly be counted as normal economic growth.

The record shows that GNP did not expand at all in the four to five years prior to 1950 and grew at an annual average of 2.9 per cent between 1952 and 1962—with identical rates in the first and the second half of that period.

In other words, GNP grew about as fast in the past ten years as it averaged over the forty-year period 1919 to 1959. This does not at all mean that a rate of 3 per cent per annum is satisfactory and should be accepted as "normal." After all, the span from 1919 to 1959 includes the decade of the Great Depression, during which unemployment averaged 19 per cent of the labor force and exceeded 14 per cent in each year between 1931 and 1940.

Unhappiness with our present growth rate is justified for several reasons:

1. Unemployment, which has averaged 6 per cent of

---

p. 271. It is not generally agreed that GNP is necessarily the best or a reliable measure of true economic growth. But it is so widely used that for reasons of comparability and availability I am using it too.

the civilian labor force for the past five years and shows no signs of improving, must be at least partially attributed to slow economic growth;

2. Demands are strong, in this country as everywhere else, for a steady improvement in living standards. They can be more easily met, and internal tensions kept to moderate proportions, if the size of the pie to be sliced is sufficiently bigger each succeeding year than if one group's gain must be another group's loss;

3. The outcome of the struggle for men's minds all over the world depends to some extent on the relative economic advance achieved by free societies and by totalitarian systems. If our expansion lags, people in less developed countries may turn their hopes in other directions. This would threaten our position as leader of the free world and diminish our ability to act as its bulwark against aggression.

Last but not least: most observers are convinced that the United States possesses the human and material resources to sustain a much faster expansion of production and income but that the natural dynamism of its economy is obstructed by ill-conceived governmental policies. So the search is on for wiser economic policies.

Economic policy covers a wide range of subject fields, ranging from banking, credit and currency to foreign trade and tariffs, utility regulation, anti-trust action, and many others. In this paper, I shall deal with three problem areas which in my opinion rate priority because in terms of impact they presently appear to be the most important: taxes, public expenditures, and wage levels.

TAX REDUCTION OR TAX REFORM?

That taxes are too high and exert a depressing influence upon the economy has long been charged by Conservatives and denied by Liberals. Roy Blough, former Treasury official and member of the Council of Economic Advisers, retorted to high tax complaints in his book, *The Federal Taxing Process* (Prentice Hall, 1952): "The pessimists who have continued to forecast the destruction of industry by high taxation have been faced instead by an expanding economy." Kenneth Galbraith proposed a breakthrough to a higher level of taxation in his controversial book, *The Affluent Society* (Boston, Houghton Mifflin, 1958). Another Harvard economist, Arthur Smithies, in 1957 expressed to the Joint Economic Committee the view then held by the great majority of academic economists: "The problem in the tax area is tax reform rather than tax reduction."

The AFL-CIO wrote as late as 1960 in its handbook, *Federal Taxes,* that "the period of high taxation that has prevailed for the last twenty years has also been a period of very high income, savings, and investment, indicating that there has been little if any loss of incentive."

TAXES ARE TOO HIGH

But in the early 1960s something approaching a national consensus developed that taxes are too high for the country's good and need to be cut. There appeared to be general agreement when President Kennedy said in his television address of August 13, 1962 that the tax structure "is a drag on economic recovery and economic growth, biting heavily into the purchasing power of every taxpayer and every consumer." The rates "are so high as to weaken the very essence of the progress of a free society—the incentive for additional return for additional effort. . . ." Four months later, speaking to the Economic Club of New York, the President stressed that "the accumulated evidence of the last five years that our present tax system, developed as it was during World War II to restrain growth, exerts too heavy a drag on growth in peace time —that it siphons out of the private economy too large a share of personal and business purchasing power—that it reduces the financial incentives for personal effort, investment, and risk-taking."

Taxes had indeed soared, not only in amount, but also relative to the size of the economy. All governmental revenues in the United States (federal, state, and local combined) equaled less than 10 per cent of Gross National

Product prior to World War I, moved to about 15 per cent in the 1920s and 1930s, and reached a record of 32 per cent during World War II. They dropped back to 25 per cent by 1950 but soon started climbing again and came close to matching their highest war level in 1962, when they equaled 31.2 per cent of Gross National Product or 38 per cent of the national income.

In this case, as so often, it is impossible to prove empirically that the level of taxation is primarily responsible for our economic lag. Some of the European countries which have been growing more rapidly than the United States bear a tax load which is at least as high as ours and possibly higher. Tax cuts in the United States were followed by economic upswings in 1919, 1921, 1945, and 1954 but by downturns in 1929 and 1948 and by no conclusive trends on other occasions. It may well be that the tax structure, the type of taxes, bears more strongly on economic growth than the magnitude of the burden.

WHAT'S WRONG WITH THE TAX STRUCTURE?

The American tax structure, which until a few years ago was the joy and pride of many of our economics professors and tax specialists, has recently fallen into disrepute. "Nobody spoke up in defense of today's tax structure" at the panel of tax experts whom *Life* Magazine assembled late in 1962. The summary conclusion was: ". . . [our tax system] is one of the worst in the world." (*Life,* January 11, 1963)

Much of the criticism of our tax system over the past six to seven years focused on the so-called "erosion of the tax base." Ever widening loopholes, it was asserted, enable many wealthy people to avoid paying their fair share and let more than half of all personal income escape.

It is true that in recent years only 43 per cent of all personal income was subjected to federal personal income taxes. That, incidentally, is up from 34 per cent at the end of World War II.

But, contrary to a widely held belief, most of the $230 billion difference between personal income and taxable income (in 1960) consists of exclusions, exemptions, deductions, and credits, which Congress granted in order to ease the load of low-income persons and families, or to achieve other desirable objectives: $100 billion, or almost half the total, is attributable to the exemption of $600 per person. Another $38 billion consists of tax-free social-welfare payments; standard deductions account for $11 billion, while $34 billion of personal income are merely "imputed" and not actually received, such as imputed income on owner-occupied homes, employer contributions to social insurance, etc. It comes as a surprise to many that the percentage of personal income subjected to federal taxation increases sharply with the size of the income, as Table I demonstrates:

TABLE I

TAXABLE INCOME AS A PERCENTAGE OF ADJUSTED GROSS
INCOME IN 1960

Income Class	Per cent Taxable:
All	54%
under $3,000	26%
$3,000 to $5,000	42%
$5,000 to $7,000	49%
$7,000 to $10,000	58%
$10,000 to $15,000	67%
$15,000 to $25,000	74%
$25,000 and over	80%

SOURCE: U. S. Treasury Department, *Statistics of Income . . . 1960, Individual Income Tax Returns.*

Itemized deductions for charitable, educational, religious, and similar contributions, state and local taxes, interest, medical expenses, casualty losses, etc., total $33 billion. Here also, the lower income brackets benefit relatively more than high brackets: itemized deductions equal 24 per cent of adjusted gross income for taxpayers with an income under $3000, 17 per cent for those between $10,000 and $15,000 and 15 per cent for those between $25,000 and $100,000. Persons with incomes from $100,-

000 up, however, list deductions which average 20 per cent of their income, because, typically, they make large charitable contributions.

It is small wonder that the drive to restrict deductions and close "loopholes" has made little progress and appears doomed. Its success would unfavorably affect too many taxpayers and might lessen rather than improve the equity of the tax system. The Administration declared early in 1961 tax reform by closing loopholes to be a main objective of its tax program. But as the year 1962 progressed, official spokesmen for tax reform were talking less and enjoying it more when they shifted to the subject of tax reduction. The argument focused more on *how* than *whether* to cut taxes. The "how" is controversial, because views differ widely on what is wrong with our tax system.

It is well known that the American tax system is like no other in the world. The governments of other industrial nations obtain the bulk of their revenues from consumption, sales, or turnover taxes, and a smaller share from income taxes. The United States relies more heavily on steeply graduated, high-rate income taxes than any other country, but shies from sales taxes, which so far have remained a comparatively underdeveloped area of taxation in America.

The ideological conflict is between Liberals who favor sharper income redistribution from the rich to the poor through more steeply progressive income taxes, and Conservatives who stress reliance on the market and favor proportionate taxes that leave relative income positions more undisturbed; so they support consumption taxes or *less* steeply graduated (or proportional) income taxes.

CONSUMPTION V. INVESTMENT

Liberals justify their position economically by suggesting that economic growth is retarded by inadequate purchasing power and consumer demand which ought to be augmented by concentrating tax relief in the lower income brackets. Conservatives hold that the economic sluggishness of recent years can be traced to a weakening of profit incentives by punitive taxation and a deficiency in investment funds, which should be corrected by focusing remedial action on the medium and upper brackets and on the corporation income tax.

The historical record suggests that capital formation rather than consumption is the primary determinant of economic growth. Simon Kuznets so demonstrated in a major analytical study (*Capital in the American Economy*, National Bureau of Economic Research, Princeton University Press, 1961) in which he found that investment has been in a steady, long-range relative decline due to the effects of taxation, inadequate savings, and a general preference for consumption.

What has lagged in recent years is not personal consumption nor government spending but profits and investment. Between 1956, the year before the rise in unemployment began that still plagues us, and mid-1963, the annual rate of personal consumption has grown $100 billion, of residential construction over $7 billion, of governmental purchases $45 billion, and of all governmental spending $72 billion. A federal *cash* surplus of $5.5 billion in the fiscal year 1956 was converted into a deficit of $4.1 billion in fiscal 1963. The annual rate of labor income grew $90 billion between 1956 and mid-1963, of all disposable personal income $107 million; but the rate of business and professional income increased only $5.5 billion, of net corporate profits less than $3 billion, and of expenditures for new plant and equipment $2.4 billion—and when expressed in constant dollars, actually declined. Simultaneously, unemployment jumped from 2.8 million to 4.1 million. The contrast may be even clearer when expressed in relative terms (see Table II).

Table II shows that labor income, personal consumption, and government expenditures expanded while corporate profits and business investment stagnated. The President's Economic Report, January 1963, discussing the disappointing trends in 1962, recognized that "it was therefore the failure of expenditures other than consumption to rise as far as had been expected that held down the rise in incomes and in turn consumers' expenditures" and that "the

TABLE II

ECONOMIC TRENDS BETWEEN 1956 AND 1963
(FIRST HALF, SEASONALLY ADJUSTED)

	Increase or decrease in per cent	
Number of unemployed	+49%	
Unemployment rate	+38%	
	In actual $	In constant $
Gross National Product	+37%	+22%
Personal consumption	+37%	+21%
Labor income and transfer payments	+40%	+25%
Business and professional income	+16%	+ 3%
Corporate profits	+11%	— 1%
Expenditures for new plant and equipment	+ 7%	— 5%
Government purchases, defense	+40%	+24%
Government purchases, civilian	+74%	+55%

SOURCE: *Economic Indicators,* October 1963, and 1962 *Supplement.*

error, then was in the area of business investment, which fell about $8 billion short of the level that had been expected for the year 1962" (p. 15). But, changing from a recognition of needs to political expediency, it managed, with a remarkable display of dialectic sophistication, to avoid some of the obvious policy conclusions. That net corporate profits between 1950 and 1962 shrank from 16 per cent of the corporations' gross income to 9 per cent (while the employees' share jumped from 73.6 per cent to 81.3 per cent) may have been economically harmful. But it is hard to deny its political appeal. Whose heart would bleed for the big corporations?

A comparison between the United States and the countries of the European Economic Community (EEC) is illuminating. Between 1950 and 1961 GNP grew 40 per cent in the United States, 82 per cent in the EEC countries (in constant prices). Other significant changes were:

SHIFT IN SHARES OF GNP IN THE U.S.A. AND EEC COUNTRIES,
1950 TO 1961

GAIN OR LOSS IN PERCENTAGE POINTS

	U.S.A.	E.E.C.
Private consumption	– 3.8%	– 6.7%
Public consumption	+ 6.9%	+ 1.4%
Capital formation and stock changes	– 3.5%	+ 3.0%
Net exports	+ .4%	+ 2.3%

SOURCE: OECD, *Statistical Bulletin, General Statistics,* November 1962.

The most significant changes were: a sharp relative decline of private consumption in Europe, a rise of equal proportion in the share of public consumption (government) in the United States, a growth of capital formation in Europe, a decline of it in the United States. As a result, the industrial plant of Western European countries is now of more recent origin and presumably more modern than the U.S. plant.

The data from EEC countries certainly suggest that their rapid economic growth was related to a high rate of capital formation and not adversely affected by a relative decline in consumption. Conversely, sharp expansion of government in the United States could not make up for the shrinkage in capital formation.

MORE PROGRESSIVITY—OR LESS?

Income improvement in the United States has been truly dramatic, particularly at the lower end of the scale, and still continues. For the first time in history in any country, income is not distributed in the shape of a pyramid, with a large mass of poor people at the base, but in the shape of a diamond, with a majority of the population bunched in the middle. The have nots have decidedly become a minority.

The income of the average American family equaled $6706 in 1956, $7660 in 1960, and exceeded $8000 in 1962. This is no reason for us to rest on our laurels. The question is how further progress can best be achieved. It is likely that a country, like an individual, cannot increase its wealth by consuming more but only by saving and productively investing a larger share of its income and output. If it were possible to assure and accelerate national growth by the simple expedient of increasing purchasing power through fiscal and monetary means, there would soon be no underdeveloped countries or poor areas left in the world.

An income tax which is as steeply graduated as our present scale is widely regarded to be punitive and acts as a penalty upon the most enterprising and productive element in society, namely, those who aim to expand business activities and succeed. The most damaging consequence of our redistribution policy may well be its impact on morale. A society which is characterized on one hand by its idolization of the average—of "the common man" —by its suspicion of the talented, its envy and resentment of the venturesome and ambitious, and on the other by its ever ready alibi for the failure as "disadvantaged," "underprivileged," as the spotless victim of the community's imperfections should not be surprised when it winds up in mediocrity; it dozes and eventually quenches the fires of progress. We don't drive our outstanding men into exile by ostracism, as the Athenians did, we just "cut them down to size" by making leisure more attractive to them than effort.

The effect of this policy resembles that of speeding fines which grow with the number of miles by which the driver exceeds the speed limit. A graduated scale has, however, a political appeal for those who regard high incomes to be unearned and low incomes undeserved. Calvin Coolidge once remarked: "You can always get a lot of votes by telling people that their troubles are not their own fault."

Economic expansion is promoted by widening the range of industrial ventures. But a corporate tax which results in $2.08 earnings being required for every $1.00 of needed *net* return eliminates many new projects from consideration. So does a restrictive depreciation policy.

The tax program which the Administration proposed

early in 1963 by advancing payment dates would grant corporations no effective reduction for several years and give the relatively greatest cuts in the personal income tax to the low brackets. A table attached to tax message shows the proposed reduction of liability in the various income brackets:

TABLE III

REDUCTION IN PERSONAL INCOME TAX LIABILITY ACCORDING TO THE PRESIDENT'S RECOMMENDATIONS IN 1963

Income Class	Reduction
to $3,000	39%
$3,000–$5,000	28%
$5,000–$10,000	21%
$10,000–$20,000	15%
$20,000–$50,000	12%
$50,000 and over	9%

Those changes would have made our tax system *more* progressive and would not have been effective in promoting long-range, sound economic growth.

TAX REFORM MEANS TAX REDUCTION

Conservatives believe that the "double-pronged" approach of tax reduction and tax reform and the argument that has developed which of the two should receive priority, is a false dichotomy. They hold that the most urgently needed tax reform, which merits priority, is a substantial cutback in the corporate income tax rate and of the excessively high rates in the higher and medium brackets of the personal income tax. The aim of such a program is not to help stockholders and wealthy persons amass greater fortunes, as its opponents claim, but to augment savings, increase incentives for the most productive individuals in our society, and to widen the employment opportunities for many of those who are now involuntarily idle, and to improve the rate of growth in the national economy. Conservatives do not believe that the poor can be effectively helped by the expediency of soaking the rich but rather by untrammeling the expansive forces and by freeing the natural dynamism of our economy which has been repressed for too long.

MORE GOVERNMENT SPENDING—OR LESS?

Many Conservatives who are convinced that oppressive taxes are a major obstacle to industrial expansion nevertheless insist that to cut taxes while boosting expenditures at a time of huge budgetary deficits is self-defeating and a sure road to inflation and economic chaos. Liberals, on the other hand, maintain that to reduce public expenditures below their prevailing inadequate levels would multiply unemployment and precipitate a depression besides crippling essential public services. They hold that every additional dollar of governmental spending adds two or three or more dollars to the GNP, due to the so-called "multiplier," and primes the economy.

DO DEFICITS PROMOTE GROWTH?

That raising governmental expenditures is an effective method of spurring the rate of economic growth is believed by many but hard to prove. If the public dollar comes from taxes, then it merely replaces a private dollar which otherwise would have been spent or invested. If it is deficit-financed and thus newly created purchasing power, then it does add to the demand for goods. But whether this promotes economic growth and full employment or inflation is highly controversial.

The experience with planned federal deficits in the 1930s is not very convincing as to the efficacy of this policy. Federal outlays in the fiscal years 1933–34 through 1938–39 were twice as large as in the preceding six years, with virtually all of the additional funds coming from deficits. But unemployment declined only from an average of 12.4 million in 1932–33 to 9.9 million in 1938–39, at which time one of every five workers was still unemployed. The federal deficits of the mid-1930s were, in relation to the size of the economy, the equivalent of a present annual cash deficit of $20 to $25 billion. If a red balance of that size year after year does not bring back full employment and prosperity, how big an annual deficit would our present-day Keynesians deem necessary—$40 billion or $50 billion, or more?

Federal cash transactions in the dozen years 1946 through 1957 yielded an aggregate *surplus* of $11 billion, and the unemployment rate averaged 4.2 per cent. In the succeeding five years, from 1958 to 1962, the federal government ran a net cash *deficit* of $24 billion, and the unemployment averaged 6.0 per cent. An aggregate $18.6 billion cash deficit was proposed for the fiscal years 1963 and 1964 and in the 1964 budget. But few expect that this will reduce the unemployment rate to anywhere near the level which prevailed until 1957.

The national debt stood at $270 billion at the end of 1946 and at $273 billion in 1956—almost unchanged. By 1962 it had grown to $299 billion and was scheduled to reach $316 billion by 1964. This sharp rise in governmental debt—not counting the simultaneous jump in state and local debt—was accompanied by growing unemployment.

I showed earlier that during the 1950s governmental spending increased as a percentage of GNP in the United States but declined in the EEC countries. Meanwhile national product grew in the EEC countries twice as fast as in the United States. Nor do developments in the United States over the past six years bear testimony to the prosperity-creating power of governmental spending: government expanded much faster than any other major sector of the economy, but unemployment grew worse and GNP merely inched upward.

I could easily multiply the number of examples if space permitted. Many countries have learned that deliberate deficit management is a political expediency which more often leads to inflation than to economic growth. But some circles in the United States find it difficult to assimilate that lesson and only recently seem to grow more aware of the threat posed by a continued foreign-payments deficit and a loss of confidence of foreign nations in the economic policies and in the financial strength and stability of the United States.

Those who contend that sharply enlarged deficit spending leads to economic bloom usually favor greater governmental activity for its own sake. If our GNP were growing rapidly, they would assert that the nation surely could afford to allocate a bigger share of its larger product and income to the expansion of public services. To the true believer in Leviathan a fast-growing economy is as good a reason for boosting governmental spending as an impending recession. The prescription is the same regardless of the ailment. Some doctors, it seems, are more interested in selling their patent medicines than in helping the patient.

The record shows (Table IV) that over the past two decades total governmental spending in the United States quadrupled, as did GNP. This seems to cast some doubt on the "multiplier" effect of the governmental dollar: it may have retarding as well as stimulating effects and in the end, like the private dollar, total no more than one hundred cents.

TABLE IV

GOVERNMENTAL EXPENDITURES (FEDERAL, STATE, LOCAL)
IN THE UNITED STATES AND GNP 1902 TO 1962

Fiscal year ending in	Total government expenditures	GNP	Government expenditures as a percentage of GNP
	billions		per cent
1902	$ 1.7	$ 20.7	8.2
1922	9.3	72.6	12.8
1932	12.4	67.4	18.5
1942	45.6	140.5	32.4
1952	99.8	338.8	29.5
1962	175.8	539.0	32.6

SOURCE: U. S. Bureau of the Census, *Historical Summary of Governmental Finances,* 1957. U. S. Bureau of the Census, *Governmental Finances in 1962,* 1963.

GROWTH IN PUBLIC SPENDING

The growth in governmental expenditures since 1940 is widely attributed to the demands of national security. High government officials have asserted that allocations to the domestic functions of government have grown very little when related to expanding population, rising prices, and increasing national product and income. John Kenneth Galbraith charged in *The Affluent Society* that government was being scandalously starved while private consumers lavished in luxurious abundance. The charge was taken up by Walter Lippman, Adlai Stevenson, and others who clamored for a breakthrough to higher levels of spending for domestic public services. But the historical record disproves this charge: governmental spending *for domestic purposes* has been growing much faster than GNP or personal consumption, particularly over the past ten years.

TABLE V

GOVERNMENTAL EXPENDITURES FOR DOMESTIC PURPOSES*
IN THE UNITED STATES,
1902 TO 1962

Fiscal year ending in	*Billions*	*Per cent of GNP*
1902	$ 1.3	6.3
1922	6.8	9.4
1932	10.1	15.0
1942	17.4	12.4
1952	41.5	12.3
1962	109.2	20.1

* = all expenditures except: national defense, international relations, veterans services and benefits, interest on the national debt.

SOURCE: U. S. Bureau of the Census, as in Table IV.

Since most of the debate over public spending has focused on the *national* government, it may be well to take a closer look at the rise in federal spending over the past ten years. Table VI shows that between the fiscal years 1954 and 1964, based on the President's 1964 budget, federal expenditures for war-connected purposes increased 31 per cent, for domestic functions, 245 per cent. On a per capita basis, and adjusted for a 17 per cent loss in the value of the dollar, federal spending for domestic services multiplied two and a half times, while personal consumption improved only 13 per cent.

TABLE VI

FEDERAL EXPENDITURES IN 1954 AND 1964
(PROPOSED) AND RELATED DATA

(Consolidated Cash Statement)

Fiscal year ending in:	1954	1964	*Increase Per cent*
	billions		
Total	$ 71.9	$ 122.5	+ 70%
War-connected purposes	58.6	76.7	+ 31%
Domestic functions	13.3	45.8	+245%
Gross National Product (calendar year 1953 and latest official estimate calendar year 1963)	365.4	583.0	+ 60%
Personal consumption (for same periods as GNP)	232.6	375.0	+ 61%
Population (millions)	161.7	191.0	+ 18%
Prices (GNP, est. 1962 = 100)	84.0	101.5	+ 21%
PER CAPITA IN 1962$: Federal expenditures for domestic functions	$ 98	$ 236	+141%
Personal consumption	1,712	1,934	+ 13%

SOURCE: U. S. Budget, 1964, Economic Report of the President, 1963, *Economic Indicators*.

Most of the $32 billion rise in federal spending for domestic purposes was for welfare, education, health, highways, agriculture, etc. In the light of the relative rates of growth in civilian government and in private consumption, it is hard to understand how it is possible for some participants in this debate to claim that public services are being squeezed while the consumer luxuriates. The statements by some of our highest officials that federal nondefense spending has been rising at a slower rate than population and prices or GNP are contradicted by the U.S. budget.

It required 160 years—from 1789 to 1948 for federal spending for civilian purposes to reach $7 billion. It took only another sixteen years—from 1948 to 1964—to boost it to $46 billion. If this rate of progression were to continue for another twenty years, virtually all income and product in the United States would be channeled through and distributed by the government. This would just about create the conditions which George Orwell so vividly described to exist in that year—1984.

BIG GOVERNMENT AND FREEDOM

It is natural that those who, like the Founding Fathers, "aim to secure the blessings of liberty to ourselves and our posterity," are deeply troubled at this trend, particularly when they hear statements such as made by the President at a news conference on April 3, 1963, referring to federal civilian outlays: "I am concerned that we are not putting in enough rather than too much because the population is growing 3 million people a year." The population is in fact growing 1.5 per cent a year, but government civilian spending, in *constant* dollars, grows four to five times faster.

The Liberal forces which promote the steady expansion of government are, on the whole, well-intentioned but fail to think the consequences of continuing the trend through to the eventual outcome. They ought to take to heart the counsel of one of their own, Mr. Justice Brandeis:

> Experience should teach us to be most on our guard to protect liberty when the government's purposes are beneficent. Men born to freedom are naturally alert to repel invasion of their liberty by evil-minded rulers. The greatest dangers to liberty lurk in insidious encroachment by men of zeal, well-meaning, but without understanding. (Olmstead *v.* U. S. 277 U. S. 478 (1927).

That the size of government and the extent of liberty are inversely related has long been known. Thomas Jefferson remarked that "the natural progress of things is for liberty to yield and for government to gain ground," and Woodrow Wilson warned that "liberty has never come from government. . . . The history of liberty is the history of limitations of governmental powers, not the increase of it."

PRIORITY FOR CIVILIAN SPENDING OR FOR NATIONAL DEFENSE?

It is apparent from Table VI that war-connected outlays have been rising only slightly faster than prices; in fact, the budget classification "national defense," a somewhat narrower concept, climbed only 19 per cent and has not even kept up with prices over the past ten years.

International affairs, meanwhile, expanded 62 per cent. Foreign aid has accomplished excellent results in *some* countries but in more recent years has been increasingly used to make up for the unwillingness of governments, particularly in certain newly independent countries, to accelerate economic development by the same methods by which the industrial countries achieved their advanced stage: by consuming less than they produce, by promoting domestic savings, and by making investment attractive to foreign capital. Some of those governments find it politically more expedient to pin the "rising expectations" of their people not on their own efforts but on the American taxpayer and enjoy having "decadent capitalists" involuntarily finance socialistic experiments.

Concern has been rising over the decline in the priority accorded to national defense. From 66 per cent of all federal expenditures in 1954, national defense gradually shrank to 46 per cent in the program for 1964. Earlier, the Bureau of the Budget had projected defense outlays to shrink during the 1960s, while civilian costs were to increase 71 per cent. May we assume from all this that the international situation has so improved and the strength of our potential enemies so weakened that we can afford to relax our defense effort? There is little evidence to support such hopes.

Many people comfort themselves with the thought that the leaders of our government allocate to defense whatever is required. Budget Director David E. Bell expressed this in a speech on May 18, 1962: "We give top priority to defense and then argue about what comes second." (Congressional Record, July 3, 1962, p. A 5085)

Analytical studies of the postwar record by Samuel P.

Huntington, Warner R. Schilling, Paul Y. Hammond, and Glenn H. Snyder, at Columbia University's Institute of War and Peace Studies suggest that civilian functions enjoyed priority over defense.[4] Huntington reported:

> . . . the tendency was: (1) to estimate the revenues of the government or total expenditures possible within the existing debt limit; (2) to deduct from this figure the estimated cost of domestic programs and foreign aid; and (3) to allocate the remainder to the military (Huntington, *loc. cit.*, p. 221).

There is much evidence that repeatedly weapons systems and other major military programs recommended by the military experts and the chiefs of the armed services were scaled back, terminated, or rejected for budgetary reasons. Among the best-known recent examples are the scrapping of such development projects as the Skybolt air-to-ground missile, the nuclear aircraft carrier and the decision to build a general purpose TFX warplane rather than the specialized types recommended by the navy and air force chiefs. Simultaneously, dozens of schemes to expand domestic services were pushed ahead, many of which were carried out—as Table VI clearly proves.

Frequently the President tried to force welfare programs through a reluctant Congress while Congress attempted (usually without success) to have the President give priority to some of the defense projects he opposed for monetary reasons. There is ample evidence in Gallup and Roper polls and from other sources that on the whole the American public is ahead even of Congress in its willingness to spend for defense purposes but less than enthusiastic about the multitude of welfare schemes. The best evidence that our government leaders are aware of the public's attitude are their repeated attempts to justify the soaring size of the budget by claiming that much or most of the rise in spending is allocated to defense.

[4] Samuel P. Huntington, *The Common Defense*. New York: Columbia University Press, 1961.
Warner R. Schilling, Paul Y. Hammond, Glenn H. Snyder, *Strategy, Politics, and Defense Budgets*. New York: Columbia University Press, 1962.

HOW TO ASSURE PRIORITY FOR NATIONAL SECURITY

The question is: can the American people reverse the trend and assure priority for defense needs over expedient welfare programs? The greatest obstacle to a shift of priority to defense requirements is well-organized interest groups which promote various special benefit schemes. A member of Congress, or the President, can often only at his peril refuse to lend such groups a ready ear and a willing hand. The transfer of jurisdiction over numerous domestic functions of government to the national level subjects our top officials in the executive and legislative branches to greater pressures than many of them are able to resist and politically survive. Their inability under present arrangements to control the magnitude of spending more effectively, even if they try, has repeatedly been demonstrated by keen observers, sometimes in quite entertaining fashion (e.g., George Cline Smith, "Economy is for Others," *Nation's Business,* November 1952; Robert D. Novak, "The Uncuttable Budget," *The Reporter,* April 25, 1963).

This is not at all a new experience. Aristotle proposed more than two thousand years ago: "Where there are revenues, the demagogues should not be allowed after their manner to distribute the surplus; the poor are always receiving and always wanting more, for such help is like water poured into a leaky cask." (*The Works of Aristotle,* translated under the editorship of W. D. Ross; Oxford, Clarendon Press, 1921. Vol. X, *Politica,* by Benjamin Jowett, Book VI [VII] 5, p. 1320)

History suggests that in the later years of the great city-states Greek politicians devoted more thought and funds on how to be popular than how best to serve the nation. The tragic consequences we all know. If our governmental leaders are to place needs above expediency in making decisions on national security, some way must be found to protect them from extraneous political pressures.

DIVISION OF LABOR IN GOVERNMENT

By intent of the Founding Fathers and in actual practice for close to a century and a half most of the domestic public services were left in the realm of state and local government while the federal government concentrated on national security and similar inevitably national tasks. In recent decades however the federal government has increasingly entered numerous local civilian programs and assumed policy control, particularly in such fields as public welfare or health. This left the President and Congress with inadequate time for due consideration of international relations, weapons systems, or space activities. Attempts to remedy the situation by adding staff or reshuffling the congressional committee system miss the point and are futile. There is only one way to correct it: the federal government must quit trying to bite off more than it can chew.

CENTRAL POWER V. HOME RULE

The major purpose of having a federal system of government rather than a unitary system with a direct chain of command is, of course, local autonomy through deconcentration of power. But Liberals, as a rule, prefer unified national control. They believe that under the domination and within the financial limits of state and local governments essential public services would suffer. They reject suggestions to help the states financially, to the extent necessary, by methods that would maintain their autonomy, in other words, through programs other than earmarked and closely controlled grants-in-aid. They find no appeal in plans of tax reallocation, or of unconditional, purely monetary grants. Proposals to allow individuals income tax credits for educational expenses and school taxes instead of allotting federal funds to states and institutions are anathema to them. Such measures would preserve and enhance the decision-making power of individuals, communities, and states, while the purpose and effect of programmatic grants is to extend the reach of the national government and to strengthen the powers of the federal bureaucracy.

EXPENDITURE PRIORITIES

What then are the Conservatives' priorities in regard to public expenditures? Outlays for defense should be granted first and overriding priority and not be controlled by goals other than the assurance of national security. Therefore, decisions on military expenditures should be made strictly on their merits and be divorced from considerations of economic growth and expansion of domestic services.

Economic growth should, however, be a prime consideration in deciding the magnitude of spending for public functions other than national defense. Conservatives do not accept the Liberals' belief that the more government spends, the faster the economy grows. They seek to achieve a sound balance between governmental and private spending by subjecting public outlays for domestic purposes to the same acid test as private outlays: the test of willingness to pay for them.

Such a test is seldom feasible at the federal level, where there is little connection between the advocacy and approval of spending proposals and political responsibility for raising the equivalent funds. Federal money too often appears to come for free or to have been paid for by somebody else.

A true weighing of costs versus benefits is possible only at state and local levels where the pleasure of spending public funds is diminished by the pain of raising them. From the struggle of opposing forces in states and communities, public budgets are likely to emerge which express a broad consensus of what needs to be done.

Economists have long debated how best to shape fiscal policies that counteract undesirable economic trends. Which steps should be taken to add to the force of the "automatic stabilizers"? What counts in terms of economic effect is not so much the magnitude of public expenditures as the net result of taxes and spending: surplus or deficit. Experience with contracyclical or compensatory fiscal policy suggests that a cutback in taxes is likely to be a more effective means of spurring a sluggish economy than increased spending.

That expenditures should, *over the course of the business cycle*, be kept within revenues may appear puritanical, old-fashioned, and unenlightened to Liberals. Conservatives believe that any other course will not help but harm the economy and, if pursued long and vigorously enough, must lead to disaster.

HIGHER WAGE RATES—OR MORE JOBS?

Heavy unemployment, which has plagued the country for over five years and shows no sign of dwindling, is our most serious economic problem. It exacts an unconscionable toll in terms of human misery, erodes morale here and confidence abroad, threatens the job security of many millions, tends to aggravate social tensions, and throws a dark cloud over the job prospects of our boys and girls now nearing graduation. There can be little doubt that unemployment is related to the slow rate of economic growth. Faster industrial expansion would widen job opportunities and reduce unemployment materially. It is thus understandable that the major attention is focused on means to accelerate the rate of growth and, of late, particularly on tax cuts as the most obvious tool in the hands of government. But a growing number of economists and others are gradually coming to the conclusion that tax relief, essential as it is, may not be an adequate answer to our present unemployment problem. President Kennedy remarked at his news conference of October 11, 1962, that "we could have a great boom and still have the kind of unemployment they describe."

IS AUTOMATION RESPONSIBLE?

Some blame automation, charging that machines are wiping out jobs. But automation is merely a new name for technological changes which have been taking place since man emerged from the caves and which accelerated with the industrial revolution. Dramatic examples of people losing their jobs to machines notwithstanding, technological progress has, in the long run, increased and not narrowed job opportunities. European countries have been modernizing their industrial plant faster than the United States since World War II but are not suffering from unemployment. We would seriously harm our economy if we attempted to stop automation—and it is doubtful that we could stop it if we tried.

The fact is that there are many unfilled jobs, as a reading of the advertising pages of any metropolitan newspaper proves. While between 5 per cent and 6 per cent of the civilian labor force is unemployed, from 6 per cent to 7 per cent of the production work is now done on overtime, and close to 5 per cent of all workers engage in moonlighting, i.e., hold more than one job. It should give us reason to think why many employers prefer paying a 50 per cent premium over regular wages to hiring some of the available unemployed. Also, what the effect would be of reducing the regular workweek to 35 hours as has been suggested as a means of spreading the work: would it not result in more overtime and more moonlighting?

UNEMPLOYED YOUNGSTERS

Unemployment is heaviest among the young people, both those who dropped out and those who graduated, who cannot find anybody to hire them. In Great Britain, which also suffers from some unemployment, young people encounter little difficulty in locating. They start in apprentice jobs which pay them very little for several years until they have acquired sufficient skills to justify a regular wage. In the United States, the apprenticeship system is little used and favored neither by the youngsters nor the labor unions. Minors are protected by minimum wage laws and union contracts which call for the payment of regular wages that are higher than the value of their output is likely to be for some years. Thus employers are reluctant to hire any but the most highly qualified at rates that would mean a net loss to them.

THE "HARD CORE" UNEMPLOYED

Many of the other unemployed are in a similar predicament. About 500,000 men and women have been idle for over half a year and another 500,000 for 15 to 26 weeks. They constitute the "hard core" and most serious aspect of the unemployment problem. Most of them are unskilled or semi-skilled. The common explanation for heavy and lasting unemployment among the unskilled is technological advance, which has upgraded requirements and wiped out hundreds of thousands of common laboring jobs. This sounds plausible enough, but some stubborn facts seem to contradict it.

In any free market the price of scarce goods will rise faster than the price of goods that are in surplus. But studies of wage trends have shown that occupational differentials have been narrowing and that the pay of skilled workers has been climbing more slowly than of unskilled workers (e.g., Paul G. Keat "Long-Run Changes in Occupational Wage Structure 1900–1956," *The Journal of Political Economy,* December 1960).

The *Economic Almanac* for 1962 shows (p. 60) the following earnings of skilled occupations as a percentage of the earnings of unskilled occupations:

1907	205
1931–32	180
1937–40	165
1945–47	155
1955–56	138

The 1960 *Census* showed inverse trends since 1940 in the number and pay of workers by level of skill:

TABLE VII

INCREASE IN THE NUMBER OF PERSONS AND
EARNINGS IN CERTAIN OCCUPATIONS,
1940 AND 1960 CENSUS

	Increase in per cent, 1940 to 1960	
	Number of persons	*Earnings of year-round, full-time workers, in constant dollars*
Men		
Professional and technical workers	+115%	+ 53%
Craftsmen and foremen	+ 68%	+ 76%
Operatives	+ 43%	+ 84%
Laborers	− 1%	+ 83%

Computed from: 1960 Census of Population, Supplementary Reports, PC(S1) − 17

If a shortage of professional workers paralleled a surplus of laborers, assuming a free market, the pay of the first group should have climbed at a faster rate than the pay of the second. That the reverse actually took place suggests several possible explanations. The two most obvious are:

1. The shortage of professional workers has not been as great as it is often pictured, and the supply met the demand amply, if not in quality, then at least in numbers.

2. The wages of the less skilled and unskilled workers were not set in a free market but, at least partially, by political factors which boosted their contractual or legal (minimum) wages to a level that exceeded the productivity of many of them. This suggests that a vast number of unskilled jobs were not wiped out by automation nor by slow economic growth but by wage rates which left an employer only the choice between hiring certain workers at a loss or not hiring them. As a result, the lowest-skilled occupations have the highest unemployment rates:

TABLE VIII

UNEMPLOYMENT RATES IN CERTAIN OCCUPATIONS,
OCTOBER 1963

	Unemployment rate	
	Total	Jobless for more than 26 weeks
Professional and technical workers	1.5%	.1%
Craftsmen and foremen	3.6%	.5%
Operatives	6.0%	1.1%
Laborers	9.0%	1.7%

SOURCE: *Monthly Report on the Labor Force,* October 1963.

Measures which were declared to be for the protection of workers at the lowest skill and wage level resulted in their being deprived of employment opportunities and made dependent on unemployment pay and public assistance. With the steady rise in contractual and legal wage rates, and the continuous liberalization of unemployment and welfare benefits, we are bound to have an ever-expanding group of men and women who will at best find casual employment and be idle most of the time.

RETRAINING

Retraining of workers who have lost their jobs and whose job skills are obsolete is one essential answer to this problem. Such programs have proven successful with skilled workers who found it necessary to shift from one trade or industry to another. Results have been less encouraging with the upgrading of unskilled workers who needed not *re*training but simply training. Only a limited number participated in the courses and acquired sufficient skills to land and hold jobs.

The unpleasant fact which often is conveniently overlooked or deliberately bypassed is that there are men and women with low occupational trainability. Between 4 per cent and 6 1/2 per cent of the population possess an I.Q. from 70 to 79, and about 2 per cent between 60 and 69. Many of these will never be able to produce the equivalent of a current union wage or even a minimum wage rate.

Education will help some but not all. A study of welfare recipients in the Woodlawn area of Chicago in February 1962 found that 93 per cent had attended school up to at least the sixth grade, but almost half could not read at the fifth-grade level and were classified functionally illiterate. Persons of low intelligence and skill can find jobs in European countries—at wages they are worth. But under the American system of compensation there is and will continue to be a large—and increasing—number of persons who cannot by their own effort earn a current American wage. Retraining offers a solution for only some of them. The others are the victims of a wage policy to which they cannot adjust. If the policy is not modified, they will have to be maintained in more or less perpetual idleness or on simple work relief projects.

EDUCATION AND VOCATIONAL TRAINING

The number of unemployed and the lack of skills among young people suggest that our schools are not doing an adequate job of preparing some of their pupils for the task of earning a living. It has been suggested that the schools have "concentrated heavily on the 20 per cent of American children who will graduate from college and have neglected the vast majority who must find jobs while they are still in their teens."

Others have asserted, particularly in the past six or seven years, that the schools have lowered their standards, that they cultivate mediocrity, fail to provide excellence, and do not challenge nor pay adequate attention to the gifted children.

Unfortunately there is some truth in both charges. It is unlikely that a school system which focuses on averages rather than differentiation, and which moves children through its twelve grades in chronological order regardless of educational progress can do justice by them. The talented children who are not adequately prepared for college and those of low intelligence who are not being trained in marketable skills are paying a high price for this "noble experiment" which is a wonderment and a mystery to the rest of the world.

If an attempt is to be made to prepare all children for the life that awaits them and for which nature endowed them, then we must give priority to finding a way toward an education which challenges the academically talented, educates the great mass "in the middle" for their civic and occupational tasks, and trains those of low intelligence in the type of work they have the capacity to perform.

SOME WORKERS ENJOY HIGH WAGES—OTHERS ARE JOBLESS

It may be a mere coincidence that in America where workers are paid by far the highest wages in the world, a greater percentage of the labor force is unemployed than in the other industrial countries. The Council of Economic Advisers wrote in the *Economic Report of the President, January 1962,* that "The post-Korean years were marked by the *coincidence* of relatively large wage increases with declines in industry employment." (Emphasis supplied.)

Further analysis could produce more such "coincidences." Some of the industries in which strong unions succeeded in making their members "aristocrats" of labor in terms of wage rates, such as printing, particularly newspapers, movie making, soft-coal mining, railroads or merchant marine, can tell lively stories of shrinking employment opportunities, or flight to foreign suppliers or locations. It also suggests that there is a causal relationship between wages that rise faster than productivity and an economy which is unable to employ all workers who are available at those rates.

Almost thirty years ago, when he still was a university professor of economics, Senator Paul Douglas explained (in line with the classical theories of Boehm-Bawerk, Menger, et al.):

> As has been stated, the curve of the diminishing increments attributable to labor seems to be so elastic that if wages are pushed up above marginal productivity there is a tendency for the employed workers to be laid off at approximately three times the rate at which wages are increased. Labor under the capitalistic system, there, tends in the long run to lose appreciably more through diminished employment when it raises its wages above marginal productivity than it gains from the higher rate per hour enjoyed by those who are employed. The converse of this is that when wages are thus above the margin, a reduction in the wage rate will help labor as a whole and increase the total amount paid out in wages by causing appreciably larger increases in the numbers employed and hence a decrease in the volume of unemployment.[5]

That American wages have long been rising faster than productivity was shown by Albert Rees and other economists.[6]

The *Economic Report of the President, January 1962*, reported the average annual increase in output per manhour in private non-agricultural industries during the post

---

[5] *Controlling Depressions*, Chicago, Norton, 1935, p. 221.
[6] Albert Rees in *Wages, Prices and Productivity*, The American Assembly, 1959, p. 11.

war period (1947 to 1961) at 2.9 per cent, the corresponding boosts in hourly compensation at 5.1 per cent. Much of the sharper increases in wage rates was, of course, expressed in and consumed by the resulting price rises. But part of it benefited some of the workers—those who were able to hold onto their jobs; another part was at the expense of profits. Corporate profits declined sharply in relation to national income: They averaged:

1948 to 1952	7.7% of national income
1953 to 1957	6.3% of national income
1958 to 1962	5.4% of national income
1963 (first half)	5.5% of national income

The unemployment rate meanwhile jumped from 3.8 per cent to 5.6 per cent. Some of the wage boosts apparently were at the expense of those who lost their jobs and were unable to find others.

If wage rates had been set by unhampered market forces through free bargaining between management and labor, they might not have gotten so much out of line. The natural adjustment to which the then Professor Douglas referred could well have provided the needed corrective. But for more than a quarter century government has powerfully interfered in the process. It has conferred privileges and immunities upon labor unions, has been less than impartial in strikes, and has, through administrative methods and political pressure, put its weight behind the upward push in wages. With cards stacked against it, management yielded, often against its better judgment. The employment record after some of the "successful" strikes speaks a clear language.

Increase in private job opening has been sorely inadequate. Between 1956 and September, 1963 (seasonally adjusted) the civilian labor force grew by 5.6 million persons. Slightly over one third—37 per cent—found jobs in private employment. Forty-one per cent were added to government payrolls, and the remaining 27 per cent swelled the army of the involuntarily idle. So, over the past six years, government jobs accounted for more than half of the employment growth. During those years the civilian labor force expanded by about 800,000 persons per year. What will happen during the balance of the 1960s, when annual labor force increases will average close to 1.4 million? Will government continue to provide the majority of additional job openings? Or will steps be taken to enable private industry to expand at a satisfactory rate?

PUBLIC WORKS ACCELERATION?

Some believe that sharply enlarged public works could accommodate many of the idle workers, and on first glance such a program might appear well suited to cope with the situation. But on closer analysis such a "direct" approach might be like putting a half-frozen man next to a red-hot stove or one racked with high fever in the snow.

The construction industry offers a good example how self-defeating direct governmental action can be. For half a century—which is as far as our statistics go back—construction prices have been climbing about twice as fast as other prices. Since 1915 construction costs have risen 439 per cent, retail prices 202 per cent, wholesale prices 163 per cent. A consumer now pays between $6500 and $7500 for merchandise which he could get for $2500 in 1915. But the type of house that would then have cost $2500 now sets him back $13,500 (quality being even). That is beyond the capacity of "marginal" workers. Soaring construction costs have pushed millions of potential home buyers and renters out of the housing market and have restricted employment. When government expands its works programs and offers billions of additional contracts—with Davis-Bacon wage rates set by the Secretary of Labor—it helps to push up construction wages. That drives prices beyond the capacity of additional potential buyers and exerts a depressing influence on private building. Thus, construction, which has been raising wages faster than other industries, also has for some years experienced the highest unemployment rate, at more than twice the average for all industries. Craft unions, such as the electricians', carpenters', painters', plumbers', bricklayers', became, unintentionally, the biggest boosters of do-it-yourself and just-don't-have-it-done movements.

INTERNATIONAL COMPETITIVENESS

Our wage structure has lowered industry's international competitive position and caused imports to climb faster than exports. The resulting unfavorable balance of international payments—which seems impervious to persuasive pleas of government officials—the heavy loss of gold, and the danger of a loss of foreign confidence have raised the specter of a run on the dollar and possible devaluation. This threat is gradually impressing the need for a change in our labor policy (support of wage demands), fiscal policy (size of budgetary deficits) and monetary policy (interest rates and reserve rates) upon many who used to face domestic inflation with remarkable equanimity.

PRIORITIES IN LABOR POLICY

The first priority in labor policy is for government at all levels to remain impartial in the economic struggle over wages between management and labor. This means the repeal of discriminatory legislation which exempts labor from laws that must be observed by everybody else. It applies to the exercise of rule-making powers by regulatory bodies. And it definitely includes reconsideration of state or federal benefits for strikers and adequate maintenance of public order by law enforcement officials at the local level.

Unemployment is unlikely to persist when wage rates correspond to relative levels of productivity and are set by market forces rather than by political pressures which claim that the law of supply and demand can be repealed by an act of Congress.

DO DEFICITS MATTER?

by Raymond J. Saulnier

Dr. Raymond J. Saulnier is Professor of Economics at Barnard College, Columbia University, and is a member of the Graduate Faculty of Political Science at Columbia. He was Chairman of President Eisenhower's Council of Economic Advisers from December 1956 to January 1961. Four lectures given by Dr. Saulnier at Fordham University in the fall of 1962 under the Millar Foundation have been published under the title of *The Strategy of Economic Policy* (1963).

I

I do not mean to suggest by the title "Do Deficits Matter?" that there is any widespread belief that deficits in the budgetary accounts of the federal government are of no consequence whatever, regardless of how large they are, under what conditions they occur, or how long they persist. There are things said or written now and then that may suggest some such attitude, and I think it is fair to say that the Administration's budget proposals for fiscal 1964 hardly reflected an abhorrence of deficits, but actually no one would quarrel with the assertion that federal deficits—indeed, deficits arising in any sector of the economy—can be carried to excess. A recognition of this possibility was implicit in President Kennedy's January 1963 Tax Message to the Congress in which, while he asserted that a planned deficit of nearly $12 billion for the fiscal year 1964 was quite perfectly calibrated to fit the needs of the economy in 1963 and for two years thereafter, he conceded that anything larger would be excessive. In a similar vein, the Secretary of the Treasury indicated that a deficit larger than that budgeted for fiscal 1964 (though presumably not one of the planned size) would upset confidence abroad in the U.S. dollar and significantly increase the imbalance in our international payments.

Thus, although some have argued that the deficit planned for 1964 does not go far enough, the accepted wisdom on these matters—whether we take the view that the budget should be brought to balance only at full employment, which may be said to be the new doctrine of fiscal planning, or that it should be balanced over the cycle, which is the more traditional view—is that deficits do have a harmful effect at some point. The question is: at what point; under what circumstances; and in what way?

II

Unfortunately, the answers to most of the really interesting questions in economics begin with the clause "it depends," and so it is with the questions just posed. The fact is that the effect on the economy of a federal deficit depends in good part on how it is financed. There are three alternative methods to be noted.

1. The deficit may be financed out of current saving, in which case the securities must be sold directly to individuals or nonfinancial agencies (e.g., business concerns) or must be placed with financial institutions (e.g., life insurance companies, pension funds, savings banks, and other thrift institutions) which serve as their intermediaries in channeling savings into investment. In either case there is no increase in the money supply as it is commonly understood. But neither is there likely to be any increase in the over-all flow of demand onto the market for goods and services, nor any significant stimulus given to the economy.

One must use the expression "neither is there likely to be" in these connections, because it is possible that the sale of government securities in the indicated manner may activate balances that would otherwise have been held idle and, to the extent that they do so, there would be an increase in aggregate demand and some stimulus given to the economy, even in the absence of any increase in the money supply. But, except under conditions of deep depression, when there may be large amounts of idle funds (i.e., high liquidity preference), this possibility is of relatively little practical importance. Thus we may say that when a federal deficit is financed out of current saving there is not likely to be any increase in aggregate demand nor any stimulus given to the economy.

There will, however, be a change in the composition of demand; here we may distinguish two cases. First, if the federal securities are purchased out of an unchanged flow of voluntary savings there will of necessity be less savings available for investment in other forms. Whether the cost of funds to non-federal users, or to the Treasury for that matter, will rise as a consequence of the federal government's additional demands on the capital market will depend on how heavy these demands are and the strength of capital and credit demands from other sources. But it is inevitable that the federal financing will reduce the availability, as distinct from the interest cost, of funds for non-federal borrowers and will change the distribution of use of savings as between federal and non-federal users. In other words, the Treasury in this case pre-empts a larger share of an unchanged flow of savings; private users of savings and state and local governments in need of financing will of necessity get less.

Second, if the flow of savings is increased, e.g., if purchases of government bonds are made a matter of patriotic duty, with favorable response, then money that would otherwise have been expended on consumer goods is turned over to the government to finance its expenditures, and the ratio of private consumption expenditures to total expenditures is altered. Thus, although the financing of a federal deficit out of savings will redirect investible funds and will redirect demand so as to favor the government's uses, there is nothing in this case arising from the side of aggregate demand that may be said to be inflationary except where hitherto idle balances are activated.

However, some possible price-increasing influences must

be noted. As has been suggested, federal financing on the basis indicated may raise interest rates and thus exert a kind of cost-push on prices. But what can be much more important is that the government's use of funds may be concentrated in a relatively few industries (a rather common case) and as a consequence may push up the prices of selected materials and of labor. These cost and price increases, in turn, may be transmitted as a cost-push type of inflationary force to the rest of the economy. It is unlikely that this will happen except when federal expenditures are increasing rapidly (which may or may not involve deficit financing), but it is a very likely development when spending is rising rapidly, when the budget shows a substantial deficit, and when, as at present, much of the additional spending is concentrated in limited areas (defense and space industries) where resources are in fact already overemployed. In short, federal financing which is non-inflationary in the strictly monetary sense, because it is financed out of new, voluntary savings, may be inflationary in its cost-increasing effect.

2. The situation is much more serious, of course, when the deficit is financed by selling securities to the commercial banking system, or indeed when they are sold in any way that will, in and of itself, require an increase in bank credit either at once or at a later date. In this case, there is an increase in bank deposits and thus, by the usual definition of these things, an increase in the money supply. Other things being equal, there is also an increase in the flow of spending, that is, in aggregate demand. This is, in fact, the reason why bank-type financing is preferred by those who want to be quite sure that a deficit increases aggregate demand over what it would otherwise be. Indeed, some would say that if a deficit is not financed in this manner it can be of little or no good at all. In any case, a clearly inflationary pressure is exerted on the economy, as far as money supply and spending are concerned, by this type of deficit financing. Whether prices rise or not is a question we may defer for a moment.

3. Finally, a federal deficit can be financed by the absorption of federal securities by the central bank, in our

case by the Federal reserve banks. Under a fractional reserve system such as we have in the United States, this will not only increase both the money supply and aggregate demand directly, by an amount approximating the amount of the securities absorbed, but it creates the possibility of much larger increases in money supply and in aggregate demand by expanding commercial bank reserves and creating a basis for a multiple expansion of bank credit.

Without a doubt, this is the method of deficit financing most expansionary of money supply and aggregate demand and potentially the most inflationary. And it is precisely for this reason that it is in generally bad repute. Still, it is used now and then by governments in financial straits.

True, the laws and customs of central banking vary a good deal around the world with respect to the accessibility of the central bank as a source of credit or as to the availability of central bank resources as a means of holding down interest rate levels, but it is safe to say that the accessibility of its credit-extending facilities or of its general financial support to the central government of a country is unique. Other financial institutions may say "no" to federal financing in the sense that they may abstain from buying federal securities. And the central bank can say "no" to almost any borrower other than the central government. But the result of saying "no" to the central government in any really critical situation is necessarily a head-on disagreement and political struggle in which the central bank will almost certainly be at a disadvantage.

This difference is one of the main reasons why it is naïve not to distinguish among deficits according to their source or to ask, as it frequently is, "If it is sound for a business concern to go into debt, or to increase its borrowings, why isn't it equally sound for the federal government to do so?" The reason why this is a false analogy lies in the uniqueness of the central government's power position vis-à-vis the financial system generally (in this particular case, its position vis-à-vis the central bank) and in the corresponding uniqueness of its responsibility for financial self-discipline.

To summarize: whether a deficit is inflationary or not

will depend in large measure on how it is financed; but
the only deficit that is likely to stimulate the economy is
the deficit that is financed in a manner that is at least potentially inflationary.

III

So much for the relation of deficit financing to the money
supply and to the aggregate demand for goods and services. What about its effect on prices? Clearly, whatever
its impact on the money supply, deficit financing must, as
indicated, increase aggregate demand if it is to do what
it is expected to do. Accordingly, the question is: will an
increase in aggregate demand, if achieved, cause prices to
rise?

The usual responses to this question have it that an increase in aggregate demand will have no price-inflating
effect so long as a significant margin of economic resources
is unused. But it is far from agreed how narrow this margin must become before a price-inflating effect begins to
be felt. The question is often dealt with in a way that
assumes, at least implicitly, that the underutilization of
resources which it is hoped the deficit will correct is more
or less equal throughout the economy—geographically, in-
dustrially, and occupationally. In any case, it seems to be
taken more or less for granted that resources are sufficiently
homogeneous and fluid that unemployed portions can be
drawn into use whenever and wherever they are needed,
with little if any increase in unit production cost.

There is ample evidence, however, that this is far from
characteristic of our economy. The experience of virtually
every employer and even a casual inspection of the "help
wanted" columns shows that there are urgent needs for
certain skills side by side with high rates of unemployment
among the unskilled. What this means is that an increase
in aggregate demand sufficiently strong and sufficiently
prolonged to draw a significant percentage of unemployed
resources into work would be inflationary in its cost and
price effects, to say nothing of its monetary effects, long
before the desired absorption of resources was accom-

plished. Furthermore, a priori considerations suggest that because it is the high-cost capacity that would tend to be unused, an expansion of output would almost certainly involve an increase in unit production costs.

And we can be misled in these matters by averages. Because the impact of an increase in demand is likely to be widespread, and because there are many parts of the economy in which resources are by no means underemployed, even when average utilization rates are low, i.e., at the so-called "bottleneck" points, selective cost and price increases can appear rather quickly. This can lead to a more general price-level increase because many products and services are components of others, and as their prices rise a cost-push effect, which monetary policy will find itself under strong pressure to accommodate, begins to operate throughout the economy even when over-all utilization rates are still relatively low. In short, directly or indirectly, an increase in aggregate demand vigorous enough to draw into employment all, or reasonably close to all, resources would almost certainly entail substantial increases in costs and prices.

It may well make some difference in this connection whether the deficit occurs because of an increase in federal spending or from a reduction in taxes. In the latter case, and especially if the tax cut is concentrated in the bottom brackets of taxable income, the increase in aggregate demand is likely to be widely distributed and for this reason less likely than an expenditure increase to induce prompt cost and price increases. In the former case, an increase in demand arising from an increase in expenditures may, as indicated above, be concentrated on economic resources in relatively limited areas of the economy and inflate costs and prices rather promptly, if only selectively. In both cases, however, though more in the second than in the first, the non-substitutability of economic resources and their relative immobility suggests the emergence of cost and price increases considerably in advance of the appearance of "full employment," even where the latter is not too severely defined.

IV

But there is more to the story than this. Suppose there has been a sizable expansion in the money supply that has not induced significant cost or price increases. Can we count on avoiding inflationary effects indefinitely? Or has the inflationary threat been merely deferred?

The answer would seem to run as follows: first, if the freedom from cost and price inflation is due to the utilization of additional resources at no increase in costs, or at negligible increase, then the game is up as soon as we run out of resources at unchanged costs. Second, if the freedom from cost and price inflation has been accompanied by a build-up of the money supply that was prevented from having an inflationary impact because of a declining rate of money turnover, then the game is up whenever the rate of money turnover ceases to decline.

The potential inflationary effect is the greater, of course, the larger the increase in the money supply, that is, in liquidity, that has been incident to the deficit financing. In a sense, we may think of this as a kind of stored-up or pent-up inflationary force, as a kind of "inflation time-bomb." And the more impervious the unemployment that the deficit financing is intended to alleviate, the larger, and ultimately more explosive the inflation time-bomb that may be deposited in the economy.

The possibility of this type of development occurring is recognized in the January 1963 Economic Report, though a confident attitude is taken there toward the chances of success in coping with it. According to the report, the problem can be handled adequately merely by reversing the policies which in the first place led to the increases in money supply and in demand. This may be read as saying that the thing to do is to raise taxes and tighten money and to go as far with this mixture of policy as the situation requires.

This is a perfectly correct approach as a logical matter, but it raises a number of practical questions. First, if the need to reverse policy arises when there is still considerable unemployment of resources there will be strong pressure to continue the expansionist policy even at the expense of further cost and price inflation. How heavily you weigh this possibility will depend in part on how readily you think unemployed resources will be absorbed as aggregate demand increases. Because I believe that much of our present unemployment will require selective measures for its elimination, I doubt that it is likely to be reduced by over-all increases in demand. Accordingly, I would assign a high probability to the emergence of inflationary cost and price tendencies at an early point. And because pressure to continue the policy which produced them may well continue as long as a significant margin of unemployed resources continues, a genuinely inflationary outcome is well nigh inevitable.

Second, it would in any case be far from easy to apply the brakes, as the council suggests they should be, without producing a downturn. A fear, which would be far from unjustified, of producing this result would support a continuation of the demand-increasing and, by this time, inflationary deficit-financing policy. In any case, the inflation is almost certain to have continued for some time before the needed action, especially the needed fiscal action, is taken. And the longer the delay the more potentially disruptive the reversal.

Third, it must be recognized that there is a certain compulsion to continue an inflationary policy, once it has been started, and once it has had an inflationary effect. This derives from the fact that inflation's reflection in costs and prices is invariably uneven, and, as a result, relationships among costs and prices, vertically and horizontally, tend to get out of proper alignment. Thus, the typical temptation is to extend inflation "a little bit more" in order, hopefully, to correct the remaining maladjustments. But the characteristic experience is that there is always a residue to be corrected and that the corrective process itself tends to raise the average level of prices. The typically futile effort of "allowing wages to catch up with prices" is a case in point.

Fourth, government may be unwilling, for still other

reasons, to apply the brakes. The authorities must be prepared to call a halt to credit expansion even though credit tightening involves a squeeze on parts of the economy that are notoriously sensitive politically as well as economically, namely, small business and the home-building and -financing industries. The authorities may also find that an increase in the tax burden is called for when living costs are already high and rising. And they will certainly be called on, at least by the logic of the situation, to practice a significant degree of economy in public spending, which is rarely an agreeable political program.

In short, an inflationary process tends to perpetuate itself and to produce its effects on a kind of lagged or deferred time schedule. And to check the process may require an austerity program of the kind that calls for a high degree of self-denial. All things considered, we will be well-advised not to test our political system too severely on this point.

V

So far I have dealt with what might be called the mechanical or objective effects of federal budgetary deficits and their financing: effects on the money supply; on the volume and composition of demand; on interest rates; and on costs and prices. What has been said may suggest that people in their thinking about the economy and in the planning of their business or personal affairs are not much influenced by governmental policy. But they are. Let us consider, therefore, the subjective or psychological effects of a succession of budgetary deficits.

Here we must remember that the budget is, in a real sense, the mirror of government and that a failure of budget policy represents a failure of government itself. If a large planned deficit works out favorably; that is, if revenues increase, for whatever reason, sufficiently to reduce the deficit substantially or to eliminate it, or even to provide reasonable promise of its elimination in the not too distant future, then all may be well.

But if it does not work out well, it is government that has failed. This makes the difference. Individuals may get hopelessly into debt and businesses go into bankruptcy, but while this is serious in its way, our economy normally absorbs the shock. We can put aside at once any thought of governmental bankruptcy, just because the federal government has additional credit available to it under any circumstances, but we cannot put aside the thought of a failure of government's financial policies. And should these policies fail, the psychological consequences would be very serious. We would, in such a case, have to cope with the worst possible case of "inflation psychology"; but, even short of this, an inflation psychology—i.c., a widespread expectation that there will be, or will continue to be, an inflation of prices, costs, and asset values—may develop in an economy. And when it does, it is capable of producing all kinds of troublesome effects.

First, an inflation psychology tends to discourage saving. Even a relatively mild uptrend in prices is a deterrent to the purchase of fixed-income securities and to the holding, let alone the accumulation, of fixed-return deposits; and a substantial uptrend makes a mockery out of what would normally be regarded as prudent financial management. But saving, by the purchase of bonds or through the accumulation of fixed-income claims such as savings deposits or shares, is an expression of thrift which is practiced so widely by persons and families of limited means and is a species of saving on which our economy depends so heavily that any discouragement of it would have a demoralizing and crippling effect. And the outlook for the longer run so clearly indicates an excess of demand for capital over the supply of savings that a federal deficit-financing strategy which gave encouragement to an inflation psychology and tended to discourage thrift would be a serious hindrance to economic growth.

Second, an inflation psychology tends to turn investment preferences from fixed-income securities to equities and, more than that, toward the more speculative forms of real estate and equity investment and in general to invite financial excesses and resultant losses. There is no a priori reason for saying that this type of saving and investment, apart from very speculative varieties, is necessarily less

productive of economic benefit than is saving and investment of the less speculative types. But it is capable of
fitting this description. It may, for example, serve merely
to bid up stock prices or inflate land and real estate values.
And in its most speculative forms it may direct savings into
"get rich quick" schemes of whatever type the law permits. Certainly, such investment is more precarious for the
investor and potentially more disruptive for the economy.

Third, an inflation psychology tends to make the economy less stable. It encourages buying beyond foreseeable
needs by business concerns and consumers. It similarly
encourages the initiation of construction projects beyond
even foreseeable requirements. Investing and speculating
of this type may validate itself for a time by raising the
pitch of economic activity and lifting asset prices, but it
can overreach itself and leave the economy at some point
with inventories too high, plant capacity expanded beyond
foreseeable limits, with critical areas of postponable consumer and business demand saturated, and, all in all, with
the economy in need of, and in a mood for, readjustment.

Inevitably, the adjustment which follows will involve a
slowing down in the rate of growth of the economy, and
there is always the possibility that it may involve a serious
economic disturbance. Certainly the possibility of the latter is the greater, the deeper and more far reaching the
inflation psychology. It is, in short, a dangerous game.

VI

The domestic economic problems created by an inflation
psychology are serious enough, but even more troublesome
ones can develop in a nation's international economic and
financial relations. Unless the world trading community
as a whole is on an inflationary tangent, the effect of cost
and price inflation in one country is to undermine a nation's competitiveness in export markets, to prompt a net
outflow of capital beyond what would be involved in normal investment transactions, to encourage imports beyond
the country's exchange-generating capabilities and to promote a deficit in its balance of international payments. If,

as in the United States economy today, a substantial deficit in the balance of payments already exists and gold is
flowing out more or less regularly, a rising imbalance may
induce a still larger outflow of funds on the theory that an
acceleration of the gold outflow will induce corrective
measures prejudicial to outside capital. If this happens, the
imbalance in payments could, of course, be seriously
worsened.

At some point, a chronic balance of payments deficit
requires corrective or at least defensive action, and suggestions looking to such steps have already been expressed
in the United States. At least one prominent leader in the
banking community has suggested that the gold requirement against Federal reserve notes and deposits should be
eliminated in order to escape, or at least to defer, the em-
barrassment of not being able to supply gold as now legally
required. And one member of the Board of Governors of
the Federal Reserve System has suggested (see *Federal
Reserve Bulletin*, February 1963, especially page 136) that
if the balance of payments deficit is not corrected soon we
should explore the possibility of using tax measures to encourage exports and to discourage capital movements to
countries already "capital-rich." (A proposal for just such
a tax—up to 15 per cent on purchases of intermediate and
long-term foreign securities—was made by President Kennedy on July 18, 1963.)

There is a further and much more drastic corrective
measure available to a nation with a large balance of international payments deficit, namely, the devaluation of
its currency. In my judgment, this is not only unnecessary
at this point in the United States but would be unnecessary in any currently foreseeable circumstance. We must
realize, however, that a persistently inflationist policy could
lead us to such a measure.

So far, our balance of payments deficit has not required
us to take measures even of the first two types (correction:
very much sooner than expected, it did lead to the tax
proposal noted above), but it has forced us to take steps
in the handling of our foreign-aid programs and in our
federal procurement practices that violate certain basic

tenets of liberal commercial trade policy. Specifically, it
has forced us to tie foreign-assistance loans and grants to
purchases in the United States, even though goods purchased here are distinctly more expensive than when
bought abroad; it has prompted a more widespread use of
the "Buy American" principle in federal procurement,
again at higher cost than would otherwise be necessary;
and it has brought about the adoption of a military-pro-
curement policy that buys at home for use abroad even
where the home price is half again as high as the foreign
price. Beyond that, the deficit in our balance of payments
is prompting a reduction in the volume of our foreign assistance and suggests the need for greater reliance in the
future on unilateral (i.e., U.S.) than on multilateral (e.g.,
UN) assistance programs.

These are some of the costs in the area of international
relations of a chronic imbalance in international payments.
They are heavy costs, but they are light compared to what
they would be if our foreign-payments situation were to
deteriorate as a result of a return of an inflation psychology,
brought about by an essentially inflationary budgetary and
debt-financing policy.

VII

And the result of an inflation psychology is no fancied
fear. Developments in the mid-1950s illustrate how such a
psychology can start. Beginning in mid-1956, the consumer price index, after four years of comparative stability,
began an increase which for about two and a half years
averaged 3.3 per cent a year. The price increases were
clearly supported, when they were not initiated, by cost
increases. Average hourly compensation for production
workers in manufacturing rose by more than 6 per cent a
year in 1955–57. Construction costs rose by about 6 per
cent in 1956 and by nearly 5 per cent in 1957. The SEC
index of common-stock prices rose from 52 in 1953 to 117
in 1956, an average increase of about 20 per cent a year;
and in the process the ratio of stock prices to corporate
earnings about doubled. We have no reliable measures of

the increase in urban property values, but we do know that the price of farm land, which had doubled in the 1940s, rose about 30 per cent in the first half of the 1950s and still another 30 per cent in the second half of that decade.

It is no wonder that in these circumstances people began to talk of the inevitability of inflation and that a kind of inflation psychology became prevalent. The spread of this psychology would have been greater, of course, and would have left deeper marks on the economy if it had not been resisted by fiscal and monetary policy. Indeed, anything other than a policy of monetary and fiscal restraint would have aggravated the inflation psychology that existed and would have been a basis for even more widespread, rapid, and extended increases in costs and prices.

What we encountered in those years, and had to resist through economic, financial, and monetary policies that continued even after the cost and price increases had moderated, was a real case of an inflation psychology. And it must not be forgotten, much less denied, that our economy is the stronger today because that encounter was successfully concluded.

VIII

So far we have dealt with effects of budgetary deficits on costs, prices, and asset values and how these effects can be exacerbated in their domestic and international expression by an inflation psychology. Two additional matters must be considered, ones that are all too often overlooked or ignored. They are the effect of continuing budget deficits on the division in our economy between public and private activity and the tendency of inflation to deepen governmental intervention in the economy.

In the narrow economic sense the first of these is a matter of resource allocation; but in a broad political sense it involves the basic structure of our society—the question of the role that government is to play in our lives and specifically the question of how big the federal government is to be relative to everything else. The outcome will depend on whether the effect of the budgetary and debt-financing

policy pursued by government is to draw previously unemployed resources into use or to shift resources from one
use to another. To the extent that the former is the case,
the effect of the deficit on the allocation of resources will
depend, of course, on how the previously unused resources
are employed and will differ in ways that need not be
spelled out as between a deficit produced by tax cuts and
one produced by expenditure increases.

But it is unlikely that a deficit will serve merely to bring
previously idle resources into use. To some extent it will
shift employed resources from one use to another, either
by inflation (i.e., forced saving) or by voluntary saving,
and in so doing will shift the pattern of resource use and
capital formation more and more toward the public sector.
Certainly one would expect this where the deficit arises
mainly from an increase in federal spending. Whether
inflation occurs or not, a rise in federal expenditures relative to total spending expands the role of the federal government at the expense of the role of individuals and private groups and of government at the state and local level.
And the unique and critical importance of an inflationary
deficit with rising federal spending is that it makes it possible for this transformation of the nation's economy to take
place subtly without having to pass the test of raising taxes
or obtaining the necessary voluntary savings to finance it.

On the other hand, there is nothing subtle in the way
inflationary tendencies—even the fear of them—nowadays
elicit direct intervention in the economy. President Kennedy's handling of the abortive steel-price increase in 1962
is a vivid case in point. Of late, more extensive and systematic programs of price fixing have been resorted to by
Western European countries, notably France, as cost and
price inflation has appeared in their economies and become
genuinely troublesome. What events of this character tell
us is that our conception of the inflationary process must
be revised. It is a mistake to think of it as resulting simply
in a general rise in prices, as is pictured in the characteristic
(and comfortable) view of the free market economy with
limited government. Unhappily, what it more often results

in today is a broad extension of controls affecting both capital and labor.

Whether one would approve of such a transformation of our society or not may be said to be a matter of individual taste and preference, and this may be true. Some would prefer to see the public sector of the economy, more particularly the federal sector, expanded relative to the remainder and to see the role of government extended and deepened. Others would not. The latter, among whom I include myself, oppose a trend to more and more central government because they believe that it threatens the system of individual liberty which is our traditional ideal and our strength. They believe that individual liberty and freedom thrive where power is diffused and that they survive only precariously, if at all, where power is concentrated.

Indeed, the greatest danger in a fiscal strategy that employs the deficit as a deliberate instrument of policy is that, by releasing itself from the requirement of matching expenditures with revenues over some reasonable period of time, it makes it possible to reshape the nation's social structure in a manner that is essentially undemocratic. What is needed, and what is clearly available for our use, is a strategy of policy that will help us achieve our economic objectives of high production, employment, and income in a truly democratic way, without recourse to governmental deficits and within the framework of free institutions. This is the tested, preferred, and traditional American formula.

CAN A CONTROLLED ECONOMY WORK?

by Milton Friedman

Dr. Milton Friedman is Paul S. Russell Distinguished Service Professor of Economics at the University of Chicago. He is author or co-author of many books, the most recent of which are *Essays in Positive Economics* (1953), *A Theory of the Consumption Function* (1957), *A Program for Monetary Stability* (1960), *Price Theory* (1962), *Capitalism and Freedom* (1962) and *A Monetary History of the United States, 1867–1960* (1963).

The answer to the question posed for this paper is clearly yes. There are many controlled economies in operation. And they do work—each after its own fashion. But this is hardly an adequate reply. A horse and buggy works as a means of transportation. But it is far less efficient than an automobile—when the automobile is working. The crucial questions are: How well and for what purposes can a controlled economy work? These questions cannot be answered so simply.

Every economy is controlled. In current use, however, the term refers to economies that are largely controlled by government officials who prepare central plans and seek to implement them by political control mechanisms—economies like Russia and India—rather than to economies that are largely controlled by the separate individuals or enterprises composing them, whose activities are co-ordinated primarily by an impersonal market—economies like Hong Kong, Japan, the United States.

In recent travels in Eastern Europe and Asia, mostly in the so-called underdeveloped nations, and in both controlled and uncontrolled economies, I have been greatly impressed by the sharp contrast between slogans and realities. The economies that have the most explicit and far-reaching central plans give the casual traveler the impression of being unplanned. The economies that either have no central plans or rudimentary ones give the casual traveler the impression of being well planned. A man from Mars who had never heard the ideological discussions of the past fifty years but had simply observed the several economies would surely conclude that Russia and India were far less effectively organized and planned than Hong Kong or Greece or Japan.

The two respects in which the contrast is most obvious to the casual traveler are in the efficiency of distribution of ordinary consumer goods and the discrepancy between the public and private sector. The inefficiency of distribution in the Soviet Union, with spotty over- and undersupplies, queues and shortages, has been repeatedly remarked by observers. The same thing is true to a lesser extent in India, lesser because there is far less central control; distribution of consumer goods is predominantly private. The same thing was true in all Western countries when price controls were imposed during and after the war. What struck us particularly was the obvious change as we passed from Russia to Yugoslavia. Though also a Socialist society, Yugoslavia has in the past decade moved sharply away from central control and has introduced a large measure of decentralization. It is still far from having a free-market economy, but even the degree of decentralization it has achieved has sufficed to produce a more orderly and efficient distribution of consumer goods than in the Soviet Union.

In both Russia and India, there is an extraordinary discrepancy between the public and the private sector. In either country, if one sees a magnificent building, it is almost certain to be for the public sector. The new building in the Kremlin to house congresses of the Communist Party is a magnificent aluminum and glass building, modern in design, attractive in appearance, and seemingly of excellent construction. It is well known that the opera and ballet and other institutions strongly supported by the

state are magnificent, extravagantly outfitted, and of high
quality. Space research and the military are in the same
category. By contrast, recently constructed hotels are un-
attractive, poorly built, and badly equipped; the residen-
tial housing program is remarkable both for the large quantity being built and for its poor quality; most consumer
products in the stores are drab and shoddy; beauty is
hardly to be found in the ordinary man's ordinary life. It
is as if there were two nations, one a small, select group
that has every modern convenience and lives in the twentieth century; the other, the masses, who live on a wholly
different level, in the seventeenth or eighteenth century.
To invert a phrase of Galbraith's, what impressed us was
public affluence in the midst of private squalor.

India shows the same contrast, perhaps to an even more
marked degree, because the private squalor is far worse.
The most marked change, since an earlier visit of mine to
India some eight years previous, was in New Delhi, with
its many new government buildings, luxury hotels, and resi-
dences. In the rest of the country, the new universities,
power plants, government factories were on a level of ex-
travagance and modernity in sharp contrast with the rest of
the economy.

There is such a discrepancy in every country. Everywhere, public buildings tend to be monuments—and the
United States is no exception. But elsewhere, the discrepancy is far less marked. In Athens or Hong Kong or
Tokyo, there are dramatic, soaring buildings to house the
citizens and their private businesses; the stores are full of a
wide variety of high-quality goods for the run-of-the-mill
citizens; it is more difficult to tell by looking at a man on
the street whether he is a manual laborer, a clerk, or a
member of the political or economic upper classes; and
above all, there is some beauty and variety in the life of
the ordinary citizen.

What is true of different countries at a moment of time
is equally true over time. If one goes back to the nineteenth
century, what were the great success stories of economic
development? Britain, the United States, Western Europe,
Japan. Each of these succeeded in achieving a dramatic

increase in economic output and equally in the standard of life of its ordinary citizens. In none was there anything approaching a controlled economy. In each, there were numerous acts of government. Mostly, the governmental measures were devoted to providing for law and order, the sanctity of private property, and the enforcement of contracts—all necessary as a framework for the market. But even when they went beyond this, as in Japan after the Meiji restoration, they were detailed interventions to subsidize an industry here or there, or to achieve a particular objective. There was no attempt to develop a comprehensive "plan," to determine the structure of the economy, or to control its development in detail. It was taken for granted everywhere that private enterprise and the market were to be the main method of economic organization. And many of the specific interventions were harmful, hindering economic development rather than helping it. That was certainly true in Japan, where subsidization of industries like the iron and steel industry probably wasted scarce capital that could have been used more effectively elsewhere. Fortunately for Japan, international treaties debarred it for thirty years from imposing a tariff of more than 5 per cent, so it had the great advantage of free trade in weeding out its inefficient industries and promoting its efficient ones. In the United States, by contrast, development was hindered by protective trade policies.

The record is the same in the more recent period. Since World War II, economies like Japan, Hong Kong, Israel, Greece, and Formosa have turned in the most impressive performance—to leave out of consideration the more highly developed countries of the West. Each of these has had some degree of governmental intervention but none has had detailed centralized control of economic activity; all have relied primarily on free enterprise and the market. By contrast, India, which of all the free-world countries has gone in most extensively for centralized economic planning, has turned in a much poorer performance, showing disappointingly small gains in aggregate output, despite large assistance from outside. Indonesia is another example of centralized planning and disappointing economic performance, in its case probably actually retrogression.

Hong Kong is in many ways the clearest and most striking case. Here is an economy that has almost no natural resources, that has had to absorb a large influx of penniless refugees, and that has received relatively little aid from abroad. It has had complete free trade, with neither duties nor quantitative restrictions on imports and no subsidies on exports, no central planning, no central bank, a fixed rate of exchange of its money with the pound sterling, few detailed interventions, and not even very many statistics—that hallmark of the modern administered state. Yet—or I would say therefore—it has experienced an extraordinarily rapid rate of growth and its residents have a standard of living that is the envy of most of Asia.

The Soviet Union appears to be the one exception to the generalization that controlled economies have been less effective in achieving economic development than the uncontrolled economies. It has clearly been a controlled economy and it has clearly experienced a large measure of economic growth. However, the Soviet Union is not truly an exception. Rather it illustrates the use of the one term "economic growth" to cover two very different kinds of growth, one of which has often been achieved by controlled economies, the other of which has not been. One meaning of growth is a rise in aggregate physical output, regardless of its composition or the objectives it serves; the other is a self-sustaining rise in the standard of life of the ordinary people.

An ancient example of the first kind of growth is provided by Egypt at the time when the Pharaohs built the pyramids. Had any modern statistician been measuring the gross national product of Egypt at the time, he would have entered the pyramids at their cost, and there is little doubt that the aggregate so estimated would have shown a rapid rise. But this rise did not mean the production of goods and services of significance to the ordinary man. On the contrary, it involved a drain on the resources available to him; it was at his cost, not to his benefit. Similarly, a strong central government has always been able to extract a large fraction of the income of its people for its purposes, whether that be to build pyramids, or the monuments of the Mogul empire in India, or the military power created by the Nazis. This is the case with Russia. The growth of which it boasts, and with firm basis, is in the modern monuments of steel mills and great dams, sputniks, orbiting satellites, and military power. These are the purposes for which it has used the great resources it has extracted from its people. As a means of extracting such resources and converting them to governmental purposes, a controlled economy can work very effectively.

The second kind of growth is something else again. The rise in the standard of life of the ordinary people of Russia is far less dramatic than the rise in the gross national product or in the index of industrial production. It is not easy to measure, and there is much disagreement among Russian experts about whether there has been any and, if so, how much. But nearly all agree that whatever growth there has been in this respect has been at a slower rate than in Western uncontrolled economies, and, for that matter, than in Russia from 1890 to 1914, when the industrial revolution had just begun to take hold in an economy that was uncontrolled. Of course, the Russians claim that they are laying the groundwork for a future rapid rise in the standard of living. That may be. The proof of that pudding is in the eating. It remains true that, to date, Russia is no exception to the generalization that controlled economies have not been successful in achieving a rapid and sustained rise in the standard of life of the masses.

The facts I have been citing run counter to widely held beliefs. Many intellectuals in the West and probably the great majority of the intellectuals in the underdeveloped countries are firmly convinced that central planning by government is an essential requisite for rapid economic development, by which they mean a self-sustaining rise in the standard of living of the masses. It is an extraordinary testament to the power of words over facts, of ideas over evidence, that these views should be so strongly held. I have again and again asked groups in various countries with whom I have talked to name a single example of any country that had successfully promoted a rapid rise in the standard of life of its people by the techniques of central economic planning. If I leave the question in this form, Russia is the invariable answer. If I add, "and has also been characterized by a substantial measure of political and civil freedom," I get no answer whatsoever. Of course, the absence of any example to date does not demonstrate that none will occur. The future need not repeat the past. But the absence of any example should surely give rise to some skepticism, some doubt, some modesty of claims. Yet the belief in central planning is frequently held with a blind faith that seems religious rather than rational in character.

Why is it that controlled economies work so much less well than uncontrolled economies in achieving a rapid and sustained rise in the standard of life of the masses? The main reason is that the so-called uncontrolled economy is in fact a far more efficient system than the so-called controlled economy for harnessing the knowledge, the energy, and the will of the people of a society for achieving their own separate objectives. The so-called uncontrolled economy is controlled too; by the right people, by the millions of separate individuals who collectively make up the society, and whose separate aims and objectives collectively make up the true goal of society.

The most valuable resource of any nation is the detailed knowledge and specialized skills possessed by its citizens. The major advantage of the decentralized market economy is that it enables this knowledge and these skills to be used effectively. Because each individual is free to pursue his interests, he has a strong incentive to use his own resources effectively. But the separate activity of the individuals must be co-ordinated. In a modern economy, literally millions of individuals must co-operate with one another to produce our daily bread. In a decentralized economy this is done through the market, a system of voluntary co-operation that is the most effective system of co-ordinating the economic activities of many people yet developed. Through the market, each person is in a position to co-operate effectively with people whom he has never seen, whose names he does not know, who may live in places he has never heard of. Through the market, the information required to enable people to co-operate effectively is speedily transmitted, and just that information relevant to each person is brought to his attention. Let there be a revolution in Cuba together with crop failures which combine to produce a reduction in the quantity of sugar produced. The resulting higher price of sugar rapidly informs people throughout the world that economy in the use of sugar is called for. It gives millions and millions of individuals an incentive to dispense with the least essential uses of sugar and to reserve sugar for the most essential—the essentiality of the use being judged by each individual separately in accordance with his tastes. And it does so whether the people involved know the cause of the higher price or not; it leaves them no alternative, no way of shifting the adjustment to still others; but, in the process, it minimizes the costs of adjustment. Compare this rapid transmission of information and effective mechanism for rationing sugar with any administrative system operated through political channels that has yet been developed.

The central planners in a controlled economy may individually be far better informed and far more intelligent than the average participant in the economic process. Yet they are necessarily few. Their combined knowledge cannot come close to matching the aggregate knowledge of the many people spread throughout the economy. And they have no system of transmitting information or co-ordinating the actions of millions of individuals that is anything like the efficiency of the market. The result is clearly seen in the lack of co-ordination and apparent disorder that is so prominent in every controlled economy. It is seen also in the fact that no economy, however much controlled, has in fact been able to dispense with the market as a major means of organizing resources. Russia employs the market as the main means for directing labor; it permits farmers to keep small plots and sell the produce in relatively free markets, and these tiny bits of land provide a major part of the vegetables and of the meat consumed in the cities;

and there are many other sections of the economy in which the market operates either legally or illegally.

The controlled economy necessarily substitutes the values and objectives of the central planners for those of the people. That is the main explanation for the sharp gap between the public sector and the private sector referred to earlier. But even where the central planners seriously seek to use their powers to promote the interests of the people—as has been to a considerable extent the case in India—they have not been able to succeed. The reason is partly because of the inefficiency of the central planning mechanism already referred to. It is partly also because of the inevitable parochialism of all of us. We are all more aware of problems with which we are personally familiar, and take them more seriously, than problems we know about only by tale. With the best will in the world, the central planners are inevitably biased. One example is their tendency to favor projects that carry prestige and are newsworthy in preference to the many small projects that are individually trivial but may collectively be more important.

But there are also still more fundamental reasons for the inability of the controlled economy to promote a rapid and self-sustaining rise in the standard of life of the masses. The process of growth inevitably involves trial and error. Experimentation is necessary, and most experiments are likely to be unsuccessful. An effective system for fostering growth must contain a method of separating the successful from the unsuccessful experiments and, equally important, for terminating the unsuccessful experiments and backing the successful ones. This is one of the great strengths of the market, when it is allowed to operate. The so-called profit system is really a profit and *loss* system and the *loss* part is at least as important as the profit part. The discipline of the market is impersonal and inescapable. The enterprise that engages in an unsuccessful experiment loses money, and, whatever it may want to do, it has no choice but to call a halt. The enterprise that engages in a successful experiment makes money and has both the incentive and the resources to push the experiment further.

In a controlled economy, the situation is very different.

There may be no clear indicator of success or failure. More important, there is no such inescapable discipline. It is human to find it difficult to admit error, natural to plead that setbacks are temporary and the project will yet succeed, to cover up. And with the aid of the coercive power of the state, it is possible to do so. A factory established by the state may be an unsuccessful experiment in the sense that it produces a product at unduly high costs, or a low-quality product, or the wrong product. But unless it is unsuccessful in some extreme and dramatic way, it will seldom be abandoned or allowed to close. It will be coddled, subsidized, protected by tariffs, and by one means or another made to appear a success. Examples are plentiful in the United States, let alone in a country like India. Governmental steel mills are pointed to with pride in India, despite the fact that costs of production are much higher in their new modern plants than in the much older private plants. They can continue because tariffs and quantitative restrictions keep out foreign steel and enable public plants to charge a price covering their costs and decidedly higher than the net price private plants are permitted to retain. Small private but governmentally sponsored automobile plants can survive although producing cars at incredibly high costs, because all imports are prohibited. Rough estimates suggest that India annually wastes an amount equal to about one tenth of U.S. government aid by getting its motor vehicles in this way rather than through imports. I believe that central planners are less likely to pick the right experiments than private individuals risking their own capital. But this difference is far less important than the absence of any effective mechanism for terminating the unsuccessful experiments.

It is, of course, naïve to speak of the objectives of the central planners as if they were given independently of the existence of a controlled economy. The power concentrated in governmental hands is a magnet. Those who are most hungry for power, or can benefit most from the use of power, and are most unscrupulous in the methods they use to acquire power have an advantage in the struggle. And, unfortunately, once they get entrenched, it is difficult to dislodge them. The concentration of economic and political power in a single place leaves all too few effective independent foci of power to serve as a check on the irresponsible exercise of political power. That is, of course, one major reason why a controlled economy is antithetic to political freedom. But it also means that the powers of the controlled economy are not likely for long to be exercised in the interests of the public at large. I referred to India as a country in which the central planners were to a considerable extent seeking to promote the interests of the people. Yet even in India, that is only part of the story and, I fear, a diminishing part. Bribery, corruption and the use of political influence are rife. The public image of India is that of a strong central government which is shaping private actions to promote what the government regards as in the social interest. It is no less accurate to describe the situation as one in which private vested interests are able to use the controlled economy for their own purposes. That is one reason why more than a decade of planning has been accompanied by a still further widening in an already incredibly unequal distribution of income and wealth.

These tendencies operate in every economy. In the United States as in India, private interests naturally seek to use government for their own purposes. The gradual weakening of belief in the general principle that government should not intervene in economic affairs has enabled them increasingly to succeed.

Historically, in the United States, the tariff has always been a breach in that principle, and a most unfortunate breach. Free trade would always have been in the true interests of the people of the United States. Steady adherence to free trade would have forced enterprises to stand or fall on their productive efficiency rather than on their skill in bringing political pressure to bear. In the postwar period it would have provided a stimulus to the development of the backward countries along free enterprise lines. Instead, we have set them all a bad example and encouraged them to develop controlled economies.

Numerous other interventions have been added to the tariff. The Interstate Commerce Commission, initially established to protect the public against allegedly monopolistic railroads, rapidly became a means whereby the railroads could protect themselves against the competition of trucks and airlines. If it ever had a function, it has none now and should be abolished. The oil industry is loud in its vocal support of free enterprise. But it has supported and promoted governmental control over the domestic production of oil, has fought tenaciously to obtain and keep oil depletion allowances under the tax laws that are grossly discriminatory and indefensible, and more recently at least part of the industry has been heartily in favor of quotas on the import of oil—all measures that involve a departure from free enterprise. The list can be extended *ad nauseum:* control over agricultural prices and production is an infamous example of monumental waste and inefficiency and interference with freedom; the numerous special subsidies in the housing industry in a variety of ingenious forms deserve to be no less infamous; occupational licensure arrangements in many of our states, governmental control of radio and television—these are a few other examples.

To return to the question to which this paper is directed. A centrally controlled economy can work—to further the special interests of those in control of it. But it is a most ineffective system for promoting the interests of the public at large. It involves a concentration of power that is adverse to personal and political freedom. A decentralized system in which individuals pursue their own interests in accordance with their own objectives through voluntary exchange and voluntary groups works far better as a system for improving the lot of the masses of the people and for promoting and preserving political and civil freedom.

Unfortunately, the United States has in recent decades moved increasingly toward a controlled economy. We have become prosperous enough so that we can afford the economic waste involved. Had the central government played as large a role in the economic system a century ago as it does now, I very much doubt that we would have attained our present enviable position. But though we can afford the waste today, we gain nothing from it. It would be far better to move in the opposite direction, to remove present interventions, to extend the range of economic freedom. No other set of measures would do as much to promote both a further increase in our economic well-being and a further extension of political freedom. No other set of measures would do as much to set a good example for the rest of the world.

INFLATION[1]

by Gottfried Haberler

Dr. Gottfried Haberler, a professor of economics, also is a member of the faculty of Public Administration and Galen L. Stone Professor of International Trade at Harvard University. He has been Chairman of the Board of the National Bureau of Economic Research and President of the Economic Association.

Part I

America's capitalist economy has shown tremendous recuperative power. The two war inflations have brought about some changes, but our productive capacity and social fabric have remained undamaged. The war experience does not, however, in the least contradict the statement that a peacetime inflation of 4 per cent or more per year would soon become intolerable. Before it brought about radical changes, it surely would accelerate. It would start a flight from monetary assets, raise interest rates, and lead to the introduction of escalator clauses in wages, salaries, and later in debt contracts.

[1] The first part of the present paper has been adapted from the second edition of my pamphlet, *Inflation: Its Causes and Cures*, which was published the first time by the American Enterprise Institute, Washington, D.C. in 1960.
Since 1960, the danger of inflation has receded into the background. Wholesale prices have now remained stable for more than five years while consumer prices have risen only slightly. There has, however, been little improvement in the balance of payments and the basic principles and problems of containing inflation, as developed in Part I of the present essay, are in 1963 the same as in 1960. Part II was written in May 1963 and briefly sketches the development of the inflation problem since 1960.

So far, the United States has been spared that type of inflation. The inflations we have had were war inflation, short-run cyclical inflations, and recently chronic, though intermittent, creeping inflation. Rapid, prolonged inflation is, however, rampant in many underdeveloped countries, especially in Latin America. There can be no doubt, I believe, that it retards economic growth.

Chronic inflation in underdeveloped countries discourages thrift and makes the development of a capital market well-nigh impossible. It is a constant complaint in underdeveloped countries that they are handicapped by the absence of a well-functioning capital market. But how could it be otherwise? It is true, a poor country cannot hope, even without inflation, to develop a capital market that distributes more capital—or, to look at it from the other side, which absorbs more securities—than the meager savings plus the funds that may be attracted from abroad permit. Inflation does not only discourage saving, it also drives savings abroad, i.e., it encourages capital flight and impedes capital imports. Without inflation there is no reason why small and poor countries should not have well-functioning capital markets which efficiently and economically distribute the limited amounts of capital available among competing uses.

Furthermore, inflation not only dries up the sources of capital funds but also misdirects capital funds that become available. It may not discourage global investment, but it encourages the wrong kind of investment—excessive merchandising, building, and inventories. Open inflation stimulates excessive investment in inventories. Controlled or repressed inflation—if it is really effectively controlled—sometimes does the opposite. Thus, the British economy in 1946 and 1947 under repressed inflation was denuded of commodity reserves, which greatly contributed to its brittleness and lack of adaptability.

Even in underdeveloped countries prices are not entirely uncontrolled. The existence side by side of controlled and uncontrolled prices and areas creates very serious distortions. A glaring example is public-utility rates. The prices of telephone and telegraph services, railroad fares, and electricity rates are subject to control. These prices then lag far behind in the general rise and the consequence is serious undermaintenance and underinvestment in these vital services. The problem becomes especially acute if these services are provided by foreign companies. Inflation, "planning," and government intervention thus lead to a deficiency in social overhead capital, the importance of which for economic development the advocates of government planning never get tired of emphasizing.

The modern form of repressed inflation and semi-repressed inflation causes or implies a poliferation of controls and interventions—price control, import controls, exchange control, rationing, allocation, etc. This overtaxes and corrupts the administrative apparatus and diverts government energies and know-how from more important functions. This is a serious matter for any country, but especially for underdeveloped countries which are poorly endowed with the precious resource of governmental know-how, administrative efficiency, and political honesty; it involves a great waste of scarce manpower and brainpower which underdeveloped countries can ill afford.

Professor Theodore W. Schultz, of the University of Chicago, comes to the conclusion that "today Chile is operating about 20 or 25 percent below its normal output simply because of the way it is trying to live with its chronic inflation. If you go around in Chile and just assess the resources in agriculture, and in the shops in the cities, and so forth, you have rather a firm basis that if for a few years, there were to be a stable price level, and expectations got adjusted one would see that economy produce about 20 or 25 percent more than is now the case. There is that much slack in the economy, and the slack comes from the fact that there are price rigidities, price controls . . . . foreign exchanges are regulated . . . and each distorts the economy a bit."

If a country grows despite inflation, this may be deemed better than no growth at all. And governments sometimes manage to maneuver themselves into a position where this is the only alternative. If wage rates of industrial workers are raised exorbitantly by minimum-wage legislation—50 or

100 per cent jumps of statutory minimum wages are no rarity in Latin America—or by government-coddled labor unions, massive inflation may be the only way to prevent disaster. Or if governments by means of deficit financing continuously try to capture a larger and larger fraction of the national product for unproductive purposes, it may well be the lesser evil to top the government inflation by private credit inflation, i.e., to intensify inflation, in order to prevent the government from bidding away for its wasteful purposes too large a portion of available resources from productive investment. But there is no intrinsic economic reason, even in underdeveloped countries, why they should not develop without inflation—and without the continuous sapping of economic strength which the losses and wastes of inflation entail.

Let us turn our attention now to the slow, creeping type of inflation with which the United States and other industrial countries are confronted.

An annual price rise of 2 to 3 per cent is, of course, a lesser evil than one of 5 per cent or more. Some people may argue that if the alternative to such inflation is permanent unemployment of, say, 5 or 6 per cent of the labor force (on the average over good and bad years) with the corresponding annual loss of output and income, this condition would still be preferable to the injustices and evils of an inflation of 5 per cent per year or more; in other words, they would accept a 2 to 3 per cent inflation as the price for reducing unemployment by 3 or 4 percentage points and for avoiding the annual income loss that the unemployment entails.

The crucial fact is that in reality there exists no such choice. A continuous creeping inflation of 2 to 3 per cent a year could not go on indefinitely without causing unemployment. After a while the creeping inflation would accelerate, or, if it were kept at the creeping pace by restrictive financial policies, unemployment would emerge which the creeping inflation was supposed to forestall. I am speaking now of *continuous* creeping inflation.

That the pace of continuous creeping inflation will inevitably tend to quicken if it is not halted or reversed follows from the fact that as creeping inflation continues, more and more people will expect a further rise in prices and will take steps to protect themselves. Interest rates will go up because the lender wants protection from the depreciation of the value of money and the borrower thinks he can afford to pay higher rates because the price of his products will go up; labor unions will ask for high wage increases in order to secure real improvement; the frequency of wage and salary adjustments will increase, and cost-of-living escalators will be built into more and more contracts; and eventually "fixed" incomes will be regularly adjusted.

It is, therefore, an illusion to believe that a creeping inflation can remain so indefinitely. How long it takes before it starts to accelerate and the rate of acceleration depend on many factors, among them past history. People in Europe who have gone through a disastrous inflation react quicker than those, like Americans, who have had less experience with inflation.

Some proponents of the theory that creeping inflation is no serious menace take the position that the monetary authorities always have it in their power to prevent creeping inflation from accelerating. The late Professor Sumner Slichter, for example, called upon the Federal Reserve to keep money sufficiently tight to prevent prices from rising by something like 5 per cent a year, but to make sure that prices are allowed to go up by 2 to 3 per cent. An annual price rise of more than 4 or 5 per cent would be dangerous inflation. Less than 2 or 3 per cent would create unemployment because of the irresistible wage push exerted by labor unions.

It is, of course, true that sufficiently tight money can prevent prices from rising faster than 5 per cent annually —or any other pre-assigned rate. But once a creeping inflation tends to accelerate—because wages, interest, and other cost items are increased in anticipation of rising prices —the policy of keeping the price rise to a creep by tight money must have the same results, i.e., unemployment, as would prevention of the price creep in the first place. Creeping inflation is only a temporary stopgap if Professor Slichter were right in saying that labor unions will always insist on, and have the power to obtain, wage increases in excess of the general rise in average productivity.

If the dilemma of the wage push does in fact exist, inflation cannot avoid but only postpone it. Moreover, if a wage push did not exist in the first place, that is to say, if demand pull were the original cause of inflation, prolonged inflation is likely to create wage push, because inflation fosters the emergence of labor unions, it gives them prestige and power by offering them unending opportunities for easy (though under those circumstances largely phony) successes in the form of wage increases which would have come anyway, but for which the unions take credit. This will accustom them to annual wage increases, which they then will try to continue when the demand pull has come to a halt.

The United States has never before gone through a period of chronic inflation, continuous or intermittent, resembling the inflation of the last twenty-seven years. The same holds true of Western Europe. The inflations that the country experienced before 1940 were war inflations or cyclical inflations which almost always characterize the upward phase of the short-run business cycle.

However, many prominent economists (not to mention scores of lesser writers and outright cranks) have linked inflation and growth, or pictured inflation in one form or other as a helping or even an indispensable condition of economic growth. Keynes has devoted much space to the discussion of inflation in almost every one of his economic writings. In one of his first books, *The Economic Consequences of the Peace* (of Versailles), he had this to say:

> Lenin is said to have declared that the best way to destroy the Capitalist System was to debauch the currency. . . . Lenin was certainly right. There is no subtler, no surer means of overturning the existing basis of society than to debauch the currency. The process engages all the hidden forces of economic law on the side of destruction, and does it in a manner which not one in a million is able to diagnose.

This sounds like an indictment of the slow, creeping

inflation, but was actually directed against open war inflation which makes the description of the process as "subtle" somewhat inappropriate.

In the 1930s Keynes became understandably more and more preoccupied with the dangers of deflation and, by comparison, inflation lost in Keynes's mind much of its dread and ominous qualities. But it is incorrect and unfair to call Keynes, as is done so often, an out-and-out inflationist. Keynes made it quite clear that he was not speaking of inflations resembling the present creeping type. "It is the teaching of this Treatise," he said, "that the wealth of nations is enriched, not during Income Inflations but during Profit Inflations—at times, that is to say, when prices are running away from costs," i.e., from wages, and hence real wages are falling.

The clear implication is that Keynes would have looked with great concern on the present kind of inflation, no matter whether it is of the pure wage-push type in the sense that wages are pushed up and prices follow, or whether prices forge ahead and wages follow without delay, quickly annihilating the profits produced by the price rise. What matters from Keynes's standpoint was that wages (and other non-profit incomes) should lag substantially behind prices so as to leave a large and long-lasting margin for profits. This is clearly out of the question under present-day conditions. It is probably for this reason that Keynes, despite all that he said in favor of profit inflation, summed up his position as follows: "I am not yet converted, taking everything into account, from a preference for a policy to-day which, whilst avoiding Deflation at all costs, aims at the stability of purchasing power as its ideal objective." There is no reason to believe that he ever changed his position. During World War II he became again concerned with the problem of inflation.

Joseph Schumpeter, too, attributed to inflation an important role for economic growth under the capitalist system, of whose capacity to increase output and to raise the economic welfare of the masses he had the highest opinion. According to him, the capitalist free-enterprise economy necessarily develops and grows in cycles. Mild fluctuations of business activity are an essential part of the capitalist growth mechanism and credit inflation is an essential ingredient of the business cycle upswing. The prosperity phase of the cycle is the time when the innovating entrepreneurs introduce new ventures (new products, new markets, new methods of production, etc.) into the economic system. These innovations require large investments, which are partly financed by inflation. Inflation and the forced saving which it entails, are the method by which the innovating entrepreneurs draw resources away from the more stagnant or routine parts of the economy.

Like Keynes, Schumpeter regards only profit inflation—inflation which is not too quickly followed by wage rises—as potentially productive. He makes it clearer than Keynes that in the nature of the case this productive inflation can be no more than a passing phase of limited duration and must be unforeseen and unanticipated. In fact, he was of the opinion that in a well-functioning capitalist economy the "natural" *long-run* trend of the price level is downward rather than upward, because during the depression phase of the cycle, when the new innovating investments undertaken during the upswing begin to bear fruit, prices normally would fall more than they rose during the preceding boom. Without necessarily accepting every detail of Schumpeter's theory, I find it difficult to believe that it does not contain a good measure of truth.

Another conclusion is also clear, namely, that the current type of chronic inflation in which wage push plays an important role, either as an initiator or as a quick-acting intensifier of a demand-initiated inflation, cannot possibly be justified on Schumpeterian grounds.

Otto Eckstein has correlated price changes and growth rates. Using Simon Kuznets' data, he gives rates of growth of output per decade and rates of change of price per decade for the United States, the United Kingdom, and several other advanced countries covering the period of 1870 to 1954. It is highly important that during "the late decades of the 19th century, which saw some of the most rapid growth of Western countries, prices generally were falling." It is, of course, not surprising that there exist periods of falling prices associated with very low growth rates (e.g., in the United States in 1929–38) and decades of rapidly rising prices (mainly war inflation) that also were periods of exceptionally slow growth. That destructive wars and deflation retard economic growth is to be expected, but I should like to recall that falling prices, when the price decline is due to rising output (as in the late decades of the nineteenth century) are radically different from falling prices that are due to the contraction of the monetary demand. Also recorded are decades of rising prices associated with rapid growth (e.g., in the United States in 1904–13 and 1939–48). This checkered statistical picture has induced some investigators to throw up their hands in despair and to conclude that nothing general can be said on whether inflation is good or bad for economic growth. In my opinion, this conclusion is much too defeatist. Surely decadal figures (the only ones available for earlier periods) are too crude, because they overlap cycles and war periods. But it does not follow that a more careful historical-statistical investigation, which pays attention to the cyclical phases and other special conditions of each period and country, would not lead to useful generalization.

It seems to me clear that in our times in both respects little margin is left for "creative" inflation à la Schumpeter and Keynes. Wages have become very flexible in the *upward* direction (while remaining rigid downward) and inflation psychology has become widespread and is ready to re-emerge quickly even when allayed by a lull in the price rise.

The stimulus to investment and growth, which inflation can temporarily afford, can also be provided by non-inflationary policies without the same limitation and detrimental side effects. If it is true (as Schumpeter and Keynes say) that inflation promotes growth by creating profits which serve both as incentives and as financial sources of investment, it is also clear that the same incentives can be provided at stable or even at slightly falling prices, if only the increase in wages (and other cost) is kept in bounds. I refrain from trying to specify what kind of wage rise would be compatible with non-inflationary growth. Depending on the circumstances it may be a little more or a little less than the average rise in labor productivity. But it should be stressed that under non-inflationary growth *real* wages will rise just as much, and in the long run faster than under inflationary conditions. That rapid growth is possible with stable or even falling prices is confirmed by the experience of the last decades of the nineteenth century and during the postwar period by the phenomenal growth of Western Germany and Switzerland. (The latter looks less impressive only because it started from a much higher base.)

Only a few years ago it would have been difficult to find anyone, economist or not, who would have thought that the state of the balance of payments could in the foreseeable future become an important factor in the choice between a "little" inflation and no inflation.

It is generally agreed that it would be dangerous if the deficit in the U.S. balance of payments were allowed to continue for much longer at the present level, because it might undermine the confidence of the world in the soundness of the U.S. dollar and lead to a withdrawal of foreign balances in the form of gold. In view of the fact that the law requires that the currency in circulation be covered 25 per cent by gold, large withdrawals of gold would be a serious matter.

The question that primarily interests us in this study is —what has been the role of inflation in the deterioration of the U.S. balance of payments? It is true that since the early 1950s the U.S. indices of wholesale prices, consumer prices, wage rates, and wage costs have not risen more than the corresponding indices in most foreign countries. But for certain important commodities U.S. prices have risen much faster than those in competing countries. This is especially true of steel where wage push has been especially strong. Moreover, U.S. export prices (as distinguished from the price level in general) have definitely risen substantially more from 1953 to 1959 than European or Japanese export prices.

The rapid deterioration in the U.S. trade and payments

position since 1957 has to be attributed mainly to the
rapid recovery of industrial Europe and Japan from war
destruction and dislocation and to the fact that these countries have increasingly adopted sound financial policies
which have greatly improved their competitive positions
vis-à-vis the United States.

From this it does not follow, however, that U.S. inflation
has nothing to do with our payments position. On the contrary, it means that in view of the changed competitive
position the United States can no longer afford even a
"little" inflation without losing gold. Moreover, disinflation
or at least holding the pace of inflation below that of our
principal competitors is the main prerequisite for a correction of the imbalance.

The position of the United States as the world's fore-
most banker and of the dollar as the world's principal
reserve currency greatly increases our responsibilities. At
the same time, it excludes easy solutions which would be
open to others. Thus if a small country is confronted with
a large deficit in its international balance it could let its
currency drop a few points and that would take care of
the problem. The United States cannot tamper with the
gold value of the dollar without committing a crass breach
of the confidence of all those who have entrusted us with
keeping their international reserves and without provoking
an international financial crisis which would greatly weaken
American leadership in the free world. Only a radical
change in the existing international payments methods and
arrangements could alter this situation.

The conclusion is that from now on not only considerations of international stability and sustained growth but
also the international position of the United States impera-
tively require that inflation be stopped. The U.S. monetary
policy is no longer exempt, as it was or many thought it
was, from external restraints. Every effort must be made
to avoid a serious clash between the requirements of external and internal stability. If, for example, excessive wage
push and downward rigidity of wages put us in a position
where only an inflationary price rise could prevent serious
unemployment, we would find ourselves in a dangerous

spot in view of our external vulnerability. Or, as E. M. Bernstein has pointed out, if the United States entered the next recession with a large deficit in the balance of payments, vigorous anti-depression policy by means of easy money, as it was practiced rather successfully in earlier postwar recessions, may be seriously hampered; for low interest rates may well induce large withdrawal of foreign funds in search of higher yields elsewhere.

One conclusion is certain and cannot be stressed too strongly: in principle, it is always possible, in developed as well as underdeveloped countries, to manage in such a way that chronic inflation is avoided without creating prolonged and serious lapses from full employment and without endangering economic growth. This follows from classical equilibrium theory as well as from Keynesian economics. If inflation seems to become unavoidable, or if, compared with practical alternatives, a policy of letting prices rise appears as the lesser evil, it is always due to faulty monetary, fiscal, and wage policies. These include: excessive government spending; inability to tax sufficiently; impotence or unwillingness to curb labor unions and to prevent them from pressing for wage increases in excess of the average rise in labor productivity; and last but emphatically not least, lack of monetary discipline which either produces demand pull of its own or gives way to cost push and provides inflationary finance for government deficits.

The type of measure used for preventing inflation or stopping it once under way must, of course, to some extent depend on the diagnosis of what kind of inflation it is. Especially relevant is the question of whether demand pull or cost push is responsible, and, if both are involved, their relative strength.

Demand pull is more basic than cost push, because a cost-push inflation could not develop without an increase in aggregate demand. Hence what is said about dealing with pure demand inflation applies also, although with certain qualifications, to cost-push inflation. These qualifications, which will be taken up presently concern the desirability or necessity that measures to control or to cut back aggregate demand be accompanied or preceded by measures designed to prevent wage push and possibly to control monopoly power of firms in oligopolistic industries.

Aggregate demand depends on the quantity of money (M) and the velocity of its circulation (V). It can be controlled and, if necessary, cut back, and the quantity of money can be regulated, either by monetary or fiscal policy. *Monetary* policy comprises discount rates, open-market operations, and changes in reserve requirements of private banks as well as more specialized measures dealing with particular types of credit—such as stock-exchange credit, real estate credit, and consumer credit. By *fiscal* policy, we mean variations in government expenditures and government revenues. Through developing a deficit or surplus, the government can add to or subtract from the expenditure stream and increase or decrease the privately held quantity of money (money held by the government is usually not counted as money in circulation).

Monetary policy has the great advantage that measures can be initiated and changed quickly in case of need, while fiscal-policy changes are subject to long delays because they have to go through lengthy parliamentary procedures. Moreover, in countries where the monetary authorities have some political independence—and to some extent this is still the case even in those Western countries where the central bank has been formally nationalized—monetary policy is less subject to demagogic political pressures than fiscal policy.

On the other hand, it is probably true that measures of monetary policy (changes in interest rates and availability of credit brought about by discount and open-market policies) unless applied sharply and abruptly in large doses influence expenditure streams and prices slowly, with a lag, while fiscal policy measures, on the expenditure and revenue side, once they are taken, exert their influence more quickly. However, this advantage of quicker effect, of fiscal policy over monetary policy, establishes a superiority of fiscal policy only if the handicap of legislative and administrative delays in taking the respective measures has been overcome—a most serious handicap indeed.

If the battle against inflation is to be won, monetary

and fiscal policy should be co-ordinated. At the very least they must not be operated at cross purposes. Clearly, the anti-inflationary effect of a tight money policy can be off-set by a loose fiscal policy (budget deficit), and a firm fiscal policy (a balanced or overbalanced budget) will not stop or prevent inflation if it is accompanied by a flabby monetary policy.

The inflationary effects of an easy-credit policy offset by a tight budget are rarely encountered nowadays. If the budget surplus were produced by taxes on consumption or still better by reducing government expenditures for useless purposes, this procedure would amount to a policy of forced saving or transfer of resources from unproductive to productive purposes, which could become a potent weapon of economic development and accelerating growth, applicable in developed as well as underdeveloped countries. It is a pity that it is so rarely practiced.

Monetary policy, fiscal policy, or any combination of the two that prevents expansion of demand will also prevent a price rise resulting from or intensified by wage (or other cost) increases. But it must be admitted that it will do so only at the price of permitting a certain amount of unemployment—how much depending upon the strength of the wage push. It should be observed that in this respect fiscal policy is in precisely the same position as monetary policy, which is often ignored or overlooked by the critics of monetary policy.

The ideal policy would, of course, be to remove the cost push at the source while keeping a tight rein on aggregate demand by means of financial policies.

In the meantime, monetary and fiscal policies must remain the first line of defense against inflation even if wage push is unquestionably present. The reasons for this statement are the following.

We cannot be sure how strong the wage push really is. Maybe only a little unemployment will stop it. Moreover, once inflation has proceeded for a while, some transitional unemployment will result when inflation is stopped, even in the absence of a real wage push. Hence, the monetary brakes on inflation must not be released immediately when some unemployment appears. The monetary medicine must be allowed to work for a sufficient period. In addition, whatever the basic strength of the wage push, we can be sure that it is intensified (if not originally brought about) by the inflation, which it may have helped to create or at least to accelerate. Concretely, a prolonged inflation cannot fail to strengthen labor unions by giving them endless opportunities of easy though partly spurious and illusory successes. They will want to continue the wage increases after inflation has been stopped or slowed down—a habit from which they can be disabused only gradually.

But to repeat, the ideal, least painful, and least costly method of stopping a wage-push inflation—or more precisely an inflation which contains an element of wage push —is to remove the wage push at the source or at least to reduce it to innocuous proportions. If there were competition in the labor market, it would be easy to prevent inflation by monetary and fiscal policy, and with a stable price level the wage level would rise roughly in proportion to the gradual rise in average labor productivity. Or, if the wage level could somehow be so manipulated as to rise in proportion to the gradual increase in average labor productivity, the price level could be maintained roughly stable without causing unemployment.

The fact that over many years the share of labor income in total national income has been fairly stable, a phenomenon that has often been observed and commented upon, would seem to warrant the conclusion that only slight deviations between the rise in the wage level and the level of average productivity are required to maintain equilibrium at full employment. It is for this reason that we can regard a wage level which rises parallel with average labor productivity as a rough yardstick for non-inflationary wage policy.

How can the wage level be prevented from outrunning the average productivity of labor? The wage level is, of course, a highly abstract concept. It is not a policy variable, at least not in a free enterprise economy. This does not mean, however, that the problem is in any sense unreal. In practice, it reduces to the question of whether and how the power of the big labor unions can be curbed, because the big labor unions are the spearhead of the wage push. Wages and salaries of non-unionized workers and employees follow the road bulldozed by union pressure. Naturally, there are delays, but in a prolonged inflationary climate these lags tend to become shorter and shorter.

If union pressure on the wages of unionized workers is kept under control, no inflationary wage movements need be expected to emanate from the non-unionized employees. Wages and salaries are, of course, even then subject to demand pull. This means that in case demand is so controlled as to keep the price level stable, wages and salaries will be pulled up roughly parallel with average productivity; but we need not fear that an independent upward thrust from that quarter would imperil either employment or price stability.

But how can union power be curbed? Some of the leading experts on labor think it just cannot be done. Professor Slichter, who clearly saw the dilemma posed by union wage pressure, repeatedly said that nothing could be done to curb union power to raise wages except to create an intolerable amount of unemployment, and he therefore accepted slow creeping inflation as the lesser evil.

I find it difficult to believe that our society should be unable to curb union power without resorting to measures so drastic as to be difficult to reconcile with individual freedom and free enterprise. Such drastic measures would be compulsory arbitration, government wage fixing, or splitting or dissolution of unions. At any rate, there are less extreme reforms and changes in policy which have never been tried or at any rate not persistently applied; these should be given a trial before more drastic measures are contemplated.

First, unions have acquired over the years *de jure* or *de facto* numerous immunities and exceptions which go far beyond anything accorded to business and other private associations. It is difficult to believe that legal reforms restoring a more balanced power equilibrium between the parties in wage bargains and eliminating violence and other abuses would not have some effect in relieving inflationary wage pressure.

Secondly, and probably more basic and important than legal reform, is a change in the attitude of public opinion and of all branches of the government. It should be possible to arouse public opinion to the dangers of wage inflation and to bring its weight to bear on unions which by force of crippling strike and intimidation impose inflationary wage increases on the economy. Then the aroused public opinion could force the government in its executive as well as in its legislative branch to pick up some courage, instead of maintaining a studious neutrality in wage bargaining and issuing platitudinous appeals to everybody to behave, or outrightly capitulating to striking unions and bringing pressure on employers to capitulate. If instead unions were told in no uncertain words that their wage demands are inflationary and intolerable, one could expect to observe quickly a marked tendency for moderation in wage bargains.

But if monetary policy gives way as soon as a little unemployment appears, and the monetary authorities are ready to bail out by monetary expansion those who engage in inflationary wage policies, the battle of arguments cannot be won. It will not be easy to eliminate inflationary wage pressure. But experience in foreign countries, notably in West Germany and now also in Great Britain and France, shows that it is not a hopeless task to prevent wage inflation without creating much unemployment and checking growth. Though the task is not easy, neither should the magnitude of the problem be exaggerated. If wage inflation is prevented, real wages would increase just as much. In the long run they would rise even faster. For setbacks and interruptions, which are the consequences of inflation, would disappear, and cyclical depressions or recessions resulting from other causes than from stopping inflation in the face of wage pressure could be counteracted more quickly and vigorously by monetary and fiscal measures—if the authorities are relieved of the constant fear that by combating a cyclical depression they would give a fresh push to chronic inflation.

Fortunately, it would require only a small decrease in the rate of increase of money wages to eliminate inflationary wage pressure. It is understandable, however, that politicians are reluctant to grasp the nettle of labor-management relations in general and of labor union control in particular, that they seek refuge in side issues and hire experts to write tons of reports on all conceivable aspects and ramifications of the problem and propose minor reforms on hundreds of matters which do not go to the root of the problem but enable the politician to stay away from the disagreeable fact of wage push.

Clearly, any policy or measure that tends to increase output per head may be thought to that extent to relieve inflationary pressure by creating a larger margin for non-inflationary wage increases. Now there are many ways in which new policies, changes in policies, and last, but emphatically not least, abandonment and discontinuance of established policies can accelerate growth (output per head).

Control of profits and prices in "monopolistic" or "oligopolistic" industries will be demanded by many as a complement to a policy of curbing union power. Leaving aside questions of political strategy and expediency, nothing useful can be expected from such policies. Since there does not exist an independent continual cost push emanating from "administered" prices comparable to the wage push exerted by trade unions, there is no room in a rational anti-inflation policy for measures to prevent "mark-up inflation." Any move in that direction would only make things worse by multiplying red tape and diverting attention and effort of business managers away from the pressing problems of increasing efficiency of production and lowering costs.

Some measures in this area which have been proposed by economists as powerful antidotes for inflation and are actively sponsored by influential politicians would have effects opposite from those intended. For example, one plan starts from the theory that "inflation will be checked if the pricing policies of the [dominant] corporations are publicly reviewed before increased prices may be made effective" and a bill proposed in 1959, which has received serious

consideration, provides for public hearings and investiga-
tions of large corporations whenever they want to raise
prices. But a policy which makes price increases difficult
and highly embarrassing would provide the strongest possible inducement for the firms concerned to avoid price reduction. The long-run effect would be to freeze prices. In
view of the fact that stability of the general price *level* requires that prices of products of progressive industries and
firms be reduced and be flexible downward, any policy that
makes precisely these prices rigid is bound to have inflationary effects in the long run whatever may be the short-
run effect at the time when the policy is first introduced.

All this does not mean that the substitution of competition for monopoly, wherever the latter exists, would not be
desirable. But the rise in recent years of foreign industries
competing with a long list of American industries ("oligopolistic" as well as competitive) has increased healthy
competition and further weakened and made obsolete the
theory of administered prices and administered price inflation.

Instead of pursuing a policy of harassing business leaders in law courts and before congressional committees for
alleged "profiteering" and monopolistic practices, it would
be far better to subject them to still stronger competition
from abroad by reducing barriers to imports. Reductions
of tariffs and other obstacles to imports could and should
be bartered for similar reductions in trade barriers in foreign countries.

Let me finally ask what are the chances that the era of
postwar inflation is over? I am afraid I cannot quite share
Per Jacobsson's refreshing optimism. True, the resistance
to inflation has become stronger in many countries, and as
far as the United States is concerned, the increased foreign
competition has had a very salutary restraining influence
which is likely to continue. In a world of convertible cur-
rencies, it is difficult for any country to inflate faster than
the others. The small countries of Western Europe have
known for a long time that they have to stay in line. The
United States is in the process of learning this lesson. The
controversial question whether stable or flexible exchange

rates (both under convertibility) provide a stronger deterrence against inflationary escapades cannot be fully discussed here. Let me simply say this: under stable exchanges (gold standard) a deficit in the balance of payments exerts a depressive influence on the economy and thereby contributes an automatic brake on inflation which is absent in the case of flexible exchanges. But if a country is very unemployment-conscious and pursues a determined full-employment policy, the question as to the comparative inflation braking power of the two exchange systems turns on the motivations of the policy maker: will they be more impressed by the dwindling of the gold reserve or by the downslide of the international value of the currency? This question can hardly be answered once and for all. Much will depend, e.g., on the degree of reluctance to resort to all sorts of measures belonging to the armory of exchange control and similar factors.

However, the basic forces making for inflation are still conspicuously present in all industrial countries in varying degrees (not to mention the underdeveloped world where inflationary tendencies are much stronger): emphasis on very high levels of employment; low tolerance even for transitory unemployment; high and rising levels of public expenditures and correspondingly higher tax burdens; strong wage push and almost complete downward rigidity of wages; and to a much lesser degree downward stickiness of many prices.

As far as the industrial countries, especially the United States, are concerned, the most serious threat to tolerable price stability (in peacetime) comes from the wage front. If the wage push and wage rigidity could somehow be moderated, it would not be very difficult to manage financial policies, monetary and fiscal, so as to maintain tolerable price stability and a high level of employment at the same time.

The ideal would be to keep the rise in the level of money wages over the long run approximately at the rate of the gradual rise in labor productivity. Since prices practically always rise during business-cycle upswings, the rise in money wages should be a little less than the rise in productivity during business cycle downswings, so as to let prices fall in order to compensate for the rise during the upswing.

But since prices have hardly declined during any recent recessions and have even continued to rise a little during the last one, it is difficult to avoid the conclusion that we have to count at least on a slow though intermittent up-creep. All we can hope is that it will really be slow and will not get too much out of line with that in the principal rival industrial countries.

Recovery and growth policy will have to tread cautiously, and any unnecessary inflationary measures should be avoided. By "unnecessary" inflationary measures I mean such measures that do not serve to stimulate recovery or accelerate growth. During a period of widespread unemployment and slack, increasing government expenditures or reducing taxes and thus creating a budget deficit, though it may be called inflationary, may be necessary to stimulate recovery. It is, of course, another question, which cannot be discussed here, whether the numerous schemes involving additional expenditures, which are now under active consideration, do not add up to sums much larger than can be justified on grounds of recovery and whether they are all of such a nature as to make them qualify as growth-promoting measures. But raising minimum wages in the present situation must be characterized as an unnecessary and irresponsible inflationary step. Because of contractual obligations and the practical necessity, in the interest of labor morale and efficiency, to maintain wage differentials where wages are higher than the legal minimum, it is a much more powerful inflationary cost-raising measure than may appear at first blush. Raising farm price supports and restricting farm output is equally irresponsible, because it boosts the cost of living and is clearly detrimental to growth. So would be a government-decreed and forced shortening of the work week. The last-mentioned measure the President himself has rightly rejected for the right reasons. Is it too much to hope that the same reasoning be applied to other inflationary cost-raising and growth-stunting measures?

Part II

During the presidential election in 1960, the anti-inflation policy of the Eisenhower administration was under severe attack by the victorious candidate and his economic advisers. Especially the Federal Reserve Board was criticized on the ground that the kind of creeping inflation—"wage-push and administered price inflation"—from which the American economy was supposed to suffer, could not be counteracted by monetary measures. Tight money would only produce unemployment, but would not cure the inflation—it was said.

After the election was over, it became apparent that the new Administration would continue substantially the same policy of containing inflation by monetary policy. William McChesney Martin remained Chairman of the Board of Governors of the Federal Reserve System and when his term of office as Chairman expired early this year, he was reappointed—a symbol and guardian of monetary soundness.

Looking back over the last two years, we find that price stability has been maintained. The economy has recovered from the short recession in 1960–61 and is still moving upward at this time—May 1963. The Stock Exchange crash in May 1962 had surprisingly little influence on the economy as a whole. On the other hand, the balance of payments is still in deficit. In fact, 1962 had been very disappointing in that respect and the first quarter of 1963 was no better. Also, the unemployment situation has not improved. Unemployment is still between 5 and 6 per cent.

If it were not for the precarious balance of payments, it should be possible to bring about a more rapid expansion by easier money. Also, the proposed tax cut would be more palatable if our international balance were more favorable.

There is a chance that the U.S. balance of payments position may be eased by inflationary developments abroad. Wages have been rising very rapidly in Europe. Until now the influence of rising wage costs on prices has been largely offset by rising productivity and absorbed by high profits.

But prices have started to rise, and the Europeans find it more and more difficult to offset and absorb higher wages. If this goes on another year or two, and we manage to keep prices stable and restrain labor unions from pushing wages faster than is compatible with stable prices, the balance of payments will probably get back into equilibrium without any drastic measures such as the imposition of all sorts of direct controls or a devaluation of the dollar.

We cannot be sure, however, that we will in fact be let off the hook so easily. The Europeans may be able to control their inflation or they may overshoot the mark and get into a recession. In either case, there would be increased pressure on our balance and we would soon be faced with the disagreeable dilemma of either introducing controls or depreciating the dollar. This would be a most embarrassing dilemma indeed, and it should not be overlooked that we have already traveled the road of controls and restrictions some distance. But if we ever were faced with a clear choice—comprehensive import and payment control or devaluation of the dollar—it is to be hoped that we cut our loss and choose the latter.

We can escape the dilemma only if we are able to restrain the wage push. It is increasingly being recognized, both here and on the other side of the Atlantic, that preventing wage costs from outrunning the annual rise in labor productivity is the basic and most difficult problem faced by the Western democracies. On its solution depends the maintenance of internal and external equilibrium.

This has been forcefully stated by Per Jacobsson, the highly respected Managing Director of the International Monetary Fund in several speeches just before his untimely death in May 1963. It has also found unexpected support from another Swedish economist, Professor Gunnar Myrdal, who in the political spectrum stands well to the left of center. (See *The New Republic,* January 26, 1963, p. 19.)

Jacobsson called for a temporary wage freeze. Suppose labor unions could be persuaded to forego the customary annual wage hike for a year or two. This would relieve the financial authorities of the constant worry about inflation and the balance of payments. Hence more expansionary

policies could be pursued; employment would rise and unemployment decline. The wage bill—aggregate income of
labor as a whole—would rise. Even real wage rates would
increase because with stable money wages prices could
gradually decline as labor productivity (output per man-
hour) would continue to increase. All that would be needed
to bring about these results is a little money wage discipline.

It almost sounds too easy and too good to be true—but
as Jacobsson has pointed out, precisely this policy of wage
restraint was actually followed by Sweden during the Great
Depression of the 1930s. They even went a little further
and reduced money wages somewhat. This enabled them
to mount successfully an expansionary policy, and Sweden
thus escaped the horrors of the Great Depression. There is
no reason to doubt that a policy which succeeded under
the much more difficult conditions of the 1930s would
again succeed in the 1960s.

The *Annual Report of the Council of Economic Advisers*
for 1961 grappled with the problem and produced "Guide-
posts for Noninflationary Wage and Price Behavior." (Pp.
185–90.) The council's suggestion was that, subject to certain qualifications, wages should rise in proportion to the
rise in average labor productivity. Such a policy would aim
at a roughly stable price level.

In my opinion, this would be acceptable, if we had no
balance of payments problem and if the economy operated
close to a full employment level. (It goes without saying
that "full employment" does not mean literally zero or almost zero unemployment. The new Administration, soon
after the election, lowered its sights; full employment is
now usually defined as 4 per cent unemployment.) With
the balance of payments situation as it is, the 1961 guide-
lines are insufficient. Until the balance of payments has improved and the unemployment percentage has gone down
to a more acceptable level, the norm for equilibrium wage
increases should be definitely less than the rise in average
labor productivity. Needless to add, if it were possible to
raise the rate of growth of labor productivity, there would
be more scope for wage increases. But to bring about a sus-

tained rise in labor productivity is necessarily a slow process. Growth, that is to say a sustained rise in labor productivity (output per man-hour), should be carefully distinguished from cyclical recovery, that is, a rise in overall GNP following a cyclical recession. The latter can come rather quickly and spectacularly within a year or two, while the former is a matter of many years.

Let me formulate the available alternatives as follows: if we are not able to restrain labor unions from pushing up money wages faster than the gradual rise of labor productivity, we shall again be faced with creeping price inflation as soon as the economy goes into higher gear either by its own momentum or spurred by a tax cut. The balance of payments will then go deeper into the red unless inflation abroad enabled us to inflate at home without impunity. But even in that favorable case, on which we cannot count, domestic reactions to rising prices would force us sooner or later, whether we like it or not, to damp down economic activity by tight monetary or fiscal policies.

If, on the other hand, we are able to keep the rise in the money-wage level for some time below the rise in average productivity, the economy will be able to expand faster. The business cycle presumably would be still with us, that is to say there would be mild fluctuations. But the cycle would play around a more steeply rising trend and would be even milder than it was in the postwar period.

THE USES OF NUCLEAR ENERGY

by Edward Teller

Dr. Edward Teller, nuclear physicist, has made significant contributions to the development of atomic weapons and to the design of the world's first hydrogen bomb. He is currently at the Lawrence Radiation Laboratory at the University of California at Berkeley and is the co-author of two books, *The Structure of Matter* (1948) and *Our Nuclear Future* (1958), and the author of *The Legacy of Hiroshima* (1962). His current research is concerned chiefly with peaceful applications of nuclear energy.

Introduction

The dramatic end of World War II focused the attention of the world on nuclear energy. But the first eighteen years of what we sometimes call the "Nuclear Age" did not see any revolutionary changes which can be concretely ascribed to this important new source of power. The influence of the atomic nucleus is with us. But it is much more so in our minds than in the physical realities by which we are surrounded.

Many had expected that in the Nuclear Age power could become cheap and freely available, like air and water. This prediction unfortunately has not been realized. In fact, nuclear energy is not yet competitive with older sources of power such as coal, oil, and hydroelectricity.

Even more radical predictions have been made in connection with the wartime use of nuclear energy. The nuclear bomb has been called the absolute weapon. It was freely predicted that nuclear weapons will make all other arms obsolete. It was also predicted that the existence of these devastating tools will make an end of war itself. What has happened is rather different from these predictions. Wars are still with us, and we do not expect secure peace to be established in the immediate future. To the novelty of increasingly powerful atomic explosives there has been now added the revolutionary innovations of intercontinental missiles. At the same time, serious arguments have been raised for a return to conventional weapons. The simple fact is that our military spending remains massive and only a small fraction of this expenditure is devoted to the development or the production of nuclear explosives or other nuclear tools.

What we have said so far is what appears on the surface. In reality the influence of nuclear energy is pervasive. If we look into the future we see the virtual certainty of an ever increasing influence of nuclear energy on the instruments of peace and the tools of war.

The Use of Isotopes

It is remarkable that the first profitable use of nuclear energy happens to be one which is applied in many places in an inconspicuous manner. This use is based on a by-product of nuclear energy, the radioactive isotopes.

Nuclear processes lead in a number of different ways to the plentiful formation of atomic species which are similar to well-known atoms but which nevertheless are different. In all of their chemical and in most of their physical properties these new elements are the same as the old ones. But they are radioactive, that is, they emit a strong and penetrating type of radiation which does not affect our senses. These new atoms are called the radioactive isotopes. They can be used in a variety of ways.

The radiations emitted by these isotopes can be easily measured by simple instruments. In big amounts these radiations are dangerous. Fortunately they can be detected even if present in amounts less than one thousandth of the danger limit. The strong radiation makes it possible to trace the presence of these atoms in very small quantities. This has been of importance in industrial processes where the detection of small amounts of material can be important. One obvious example is in measuring the rate at which bearings are worn out. Radioactive materials added to the surface layers of a bearing appear in the lubricating oil. In this way the slow erosion of these important surfaces can be quickly and quantitatively measured.

Radioactive isotopes can be important in a much more specific manner. Each of these elements behaves in its biological functions precisely in the same way as the better-known non-radioactive twin. The path and behavior of a radioactive isotope can be traced with ease and precision in a live plant, animal, or human being. In fact, it can be observed even in a cell or a virus. Because of the practical identity of the behavior of radioactive and non-radioactive elements, we can, therefore, find out most relevant pieces of information about the functioning of practically every chemical in almost any living system. This has proved most helpful in medicine, in agriculture, and in many branches of biological research.

Industry has used radiation in a much simpler and yet in a helpful fashion. Radiation is absorbed, according to simple and well-known laws, by various materials. This opens up the possibility to control in a simple and automatic way the thickness of sheets of paper or metal produced in our factories.

The above descriptions are crude, and the list is incomplete. It is, however, noteworthy that adding up all the many individual uses of isotopes this application of atomic energy is today estimated as a $100-million-per-year component in our industrial life.

Looking into the future we can expect that the cheap availability of radiation sources will bring about great changes particularly in connection with agriculture. Radiation from radioactive isotopes might be used on a massive scale to keep down infestation in our food stockpiles. It is well known that today and for quite a few years to come our problem is a surplus of food rather than a deficiency. In the long run it is likely that food surpluses will have to be handled as valuable assets. Ten or twenty years from today we probably will have the ability to have radioactive isotopes as by-products in sufficiently big quantities so that this resource can be used to conserve stored foodstuff. It is to be specifically noted that this can be done at a sufficiently low level of irradiation in which no harmful side effects are likely to result.

Artificially induced mutations in our crops and domestic animals have not as yet been used in order to improve our agricultural production. If such mutations are ever to be used in an effective manner, the procedure of trial and error will have to be used on a wide scale. The point is that one cannot define in clear-cut scientific terms what mutations happen to be useful. This is a question of judgment in which the individual educated farmer in many cases can make valuable contributions. The tool of radioactive isotopes in the hands of educated and responsible modern farmers may turn out to be one of the key factors contributing to the solution of the problem of food shortage throughout the world.

In developments of the kind that are mentioned above the dangerous nature of nuclear radiation must constantly be kept in mind. This danger is no reason to impede progress. The use of drugs was not held back by obvious risks. Radioactive isotopes can be more easily controlled than drugs for the simple reason that they are more easily detected and, if lost, more easily recovered because of the characteristic strong signals emitted by the radioactive isotopes. At the same time it is clear that the widespread use of radioactive isotopes must be regulated and kept under control in the same way as the disposition of drugs. The necessary legal restrictions will have to be kept up to date.

The Story of Nuclear Reactors

In 1945 we were told that nuclear energy will make a great contribution to our economy as soon as it can be produced for 7 mils (or 0.7 cents) per kilowatt hour. We are just about at the threshold of achieving this goal, but competitive production of electrical energy from nuclear sources is still not in sight. The reason is that in the intervening years big-scale production of electrical energy from conventional sources has become less expensive. Today, new, big electrical generating plants using fossil fuel deliver electricity for 5 mils per kilowatt hour. This is the more remarkable if we take into account the fact that since 1945 most other commodities—from cars and groceries to the expense of a telephone call—have doubled in price. In trying to make nuclear energy pay we are chasing a receding target.

It would be a mistake, however, to state that in this important field nuclear energy did not make its contribution. I believe that the present low price of electricity is in part due to the very fact that nuclear energy has appeared on the horizon as a powerful potential competitor.

It is even more important to state that nuclear reactors might indeed become quite competitive, providing one of two conditions should be established.

The production of nuclear energy is coupled in many cases with an important by-product: plutonium. Up to the recent past our government has bought commercial plutonium for $30 per gram (or a little more than $12,000 per pound) of plutonium. If our government needs plutonium then $30 is a reasonable price. If this price were indefinitely continued to be paid to any commercial producer whose reactor will deliver some plutonium, nuclear reactors would become the most economical way to produce electric power. Actually, the price paid to a private company producing plutonium is being reduced now and eventually will become a small fraction of the $30 quoted above, and it is expected that little encouragement will be given to plutonium production in the future.

The reason for this is the widespread and strongly held belief that we do not need much more plutonium for military purposes. At the same time we know that plutonium is a material which in reactors is hard to handle and so the non-military use of plutonium has been discounted. In a later section we shall discuss reasons why continued production of ample plutonium may well be in the interest of the defense of our country. One may look at the present situation as an artificial restriction on a natural joint development of private power together with needed military defense. This restrictive policy may turn out to have grave consequences in the 1970s.

There is another line of development which may lead to economic production of power by nuclear reactors. This is the possibility of using nuclear reactors in very large units. It has been proposed by Hammond at Los Alamos that nuclear reactors with an output of 25 million kilowatts of heat energy should be constructed. Such big power units, if fully and steadily utilized, could serve one of two purposes. They may deliver electrical energy at a price possibly as low as 2 mils per kilowatt hour. Alternatively, they may be used to convert sea water at a price possibly as low as $30 per acre-foot.

It should be noted that the figures quoted in the above paragraph have been obtained without any support price for plutonium. At the same time they cannot be considered as realities today. They presuppose difficult but probably feasible developments of big-scale facilities. Such a development is not likely to lead to success earlier than in 1970.

If and when success is achieved one still may ask whether an amount of almost 10 million kilowatts of electrical energy (which corresponds to 25 million kilowatts of heat energy) will ever be needed in a restricted area in which the cost of electric transmission can be held at a low level. With the growth of our industrial centers the answers to this question may well be positive. Specifically, the development of industries like the aluminum production, which require great amounts of electric power, may influence the construction of such gigantic electric generating plants.

On the other side of the question, one should remember that few of our agricultural districts are willing to pay more than $5 for an acre-foot of water. There is at least one striking exception. According to the plans of the Feather River Project in California, water in southern California will be delivered at a price of $60 per acre-foot. If the capital cost is estimated not according to the interest rate paid by the government but rather according to the interest rate paid by private enterprise, then the Feather River water in Los Angeles may actually cost as much as $100 an acre-foot. The amounts needed in southern California closely correspond to the amounts that Hammond's giant plants might produce.

There is another broad area in which development of nuclear power plants has been expected for many years. This is the area of mobile power. Nuclear submarines are being produced today in increasing numbers. Nuclear surface ships are being built. Many hundred million dollars have been spent on the development of a nuclear-powered airplane and there is continued discussion of nuclear-powered locomotives and even automobiles.

This field of mobile nuclear power does not show any real economic promise, and the application of this type of nuclear power should be properly restricted to military uses. There can be no doubt that the Polaris submarines and other nuclear submarines constitute a very important component of the defense of the United States. This is due to the fact that nuclear submarines can stay under water almost indefinitely, and therefore they remain practically invulnerable even in a nuclear conflict. A similar argument cannot be made for the nuclear surface navy, and there is some question whether construction of surface ships of this or any other type will become a useful component of our national defense. The answer may be "yes," but proof is still lacking.

I do not think that the *Savannah* or any of its commercial successors will turn out to be economical and useful in our lifetime. A nuclear ship does not need a particularly big power plant, and ships have access to relatively cheap oil. Under these conditions, in the field of ship propulsion oil will remain for many years to come cheaper than nuclear energy. In addition, a nuclear reactor in a mobile system such as a ship always represents a hazard. In the case of the nuclear submarine, this hazard must be accepted as a calculated risk and all possible steps must be taken to minimize it. In a commercial nuclear vessel this hazard can hardly be justified. The situation is even worse with respect to nuclear-propelled manned airplanes. Such planes have to carry such heavy shielding as to make their operation non-competitive and ineffective. In addition, a single unfortunately located crash by a nuclear plane near a big city could expose this city to radioactive fallout comparable to that which could be derived from a hydrogen explosion. This is due to the accumulation of many long-lived radioactive isotopes in the powerful nuclear engine of the airplane. For all these reasons it was a wise decision to cancel further attempts to develop nuclear propulsion of manned airplanes.

Similar arguments hold with even greater force for nuclear locomotives and nuclear cars. These instruments combine in them a maximum of hazard with a minimum of utility.

In space propulsion, however, nuclear energy may in the long run make valuable contributions. It seems to me that this is a field of great difficulty, and results so far have not been encouraging. In the long run, however, there are possibilities of real progress. Furthermore, the effective working of a space engine can occur at a sufficient distance from the earth as to eliminate any real possibility of a serious accident on earth. That the nuclear energy will have hazards for the astronauts is obvious. On the other hand, we must realize that exploration of space cannot be undertaken unless our explorers are willing to take risks. These risks must be kept to a minimum but cannot be eliminated.

Nuclear Weapons

We have stated that nuclear reactors unfortunately have not yet found their widespread economic usefulness. On the other hand, one may say that most fortunately nuclear bombs have not yet been widely used in wartime. This has not been due to the fact that development of nuclear explosives has lagged. The opposite is true.

Since Hiroshima, the yields of nuclear weapons have increased a thousandfold, and the ratio of yield to weight has also increased by a comparable factor. The reason why nuclear weapons have not been used is the simple fact that they are much too effective.

It is a belief which is widely held and which I share that the main purpose of the existence of our nuclear weapons is to prevent their use by our opponents. Many have drawn from this correct statement the conclusion, which I consider a dangerous fallacy, that the time has come to eliminate nuclear weapons or at any rate to restrict their further development. We shall be able to prevent the use of nuclear bombs that are in Russian hands only if we keep up with the Russians in this rapidly developing field.

During the negotiations for an end to nuclear testing, it was claimed that such an agreement could be effectively policed. Simple and universally accepted facts do not justify such a claim to a sufficient extent.

No objective method has been found to detect and identify small nuclear explosions. Secret atmospheric testing can be carried out by nuclear devices of under one kiloton (one thousand tons of TNT equivalent). Application of clean nuclear devices—that is, devices producing greatly reduced amounts of radioactivity—may make it possible to raise the limit to a few kilotons. The limit below which secret underground explosions are possible is higher still. Here it is very likely that tests under ten kilotons may be hidden and bigger explosions can be carried out in secrecy if care is taken to reduce the seismic signal. Tests in distant interplanetary space can be carried out in a manner useful for military development up to the megaton (million tons of TNT equivalent) range without serious danger of detection.

The possibility of space testing has been discounted. The reason for this is probably that we have not as yet carried out any tests in distant space. As long as a mode of testing is not actually executed by the United States, it appears extremely difficult to obtain agreement that such types of tests might be effectively practiced now or in the future by the Soviet Union. In such cases the wishful thinking that prefers our imagined safety to our actual danger has prevailed for years in the minds of our policy makers. This situation is the more remarkable because of the fact that the possibility of big secret tests in space has been discussed in detail by American, British, and Russian experts in June and July of 1959 in Geneva. We have explained to the Russians how such type of testing could be effectively executed and hidden, and they have agreed that this can be done. We have also proposed as the only cheap and effective method of checking such explosions to inspect every outgoing space rocket. This indeed would be a practicable control, since the firing of big rockets can be detected with a reasonable assurance. The Russians have refused to consider the inspection of outgoing space vehicles and we have not pressed the point. Therefore any system of policing nuclear tests is at present wide open, and violations could be carried out up to the biggest explosions.

The main argument that has been advanced in favor of test cessation is the alleged circumstance that we have enough nuclear explosives and that further testing is in fact superfluous. This argument is closely connected with the general important question of the aims of further development in the field of nuclear explosives. Starting from the discussions connected with the test ban we shall now give a general survey of the aims of such weapon developments.

During the discussion of a test moratorium from 1958 until 1961 proponents of a test ban laid great emphasis on the useless nature of two developments. They contended that big explosives can no longer be effectively improved and they completely discounted the need for nuclear testing in the development of missile defense. It is significant that by claims and actual execution the Russians have drawn our attention in 1961 to precisely these two fields. What our internal discussions could not settle, the Soviet test series and the boasts of Khrushchev have actually settled for us. We are faced with the real danger that the Russians may develop an effective missile defense while we lack such a defense. This would be as bad as if the Russians had the means of a strategic nuclear attack while we lacked such means. The difficulty is compounded by the fact that today the Russians seem to be clearly ahead of us in big nuclear explosives.

Correspondingly, we are now belatedly giving some attention to big nuclear explosions and to missile defense. Our efforts are impeded by continued attempts at arriving at test ban agreements. To test big bombs or to practice the art of missile defense atmospheric tests are needed. Our only atmospheric test series since 1958 was carried out with short preparation and in a hurried manner. These limitations were due to political rather than to technical reasons.

The all-important question of missile defense has been the subject of much work and even more discussion. The results of this discussion are inconclusive. In the end experience alone can decide. One must hope that mock experience will be sufficient and that we shall never be faced with the overwhelming danger of the situation where nuclear defenses must be tried out in earnest. While the upshot and the details are complex and classified, the general results of the discussion can be stated in reasonably simple terms.

It is obviously difficult to hit an incoming missile which is moving considerably faster than a bullet. The only real hope of an effective defense lies in the application of defensive nuclear explosives that can destroy the incoming missile even when the misdistance is sizable. At the same time the yield of the defensive missile and the altitude of its explosion can be so arranged as to produce no harmful effect on the defended territory which lies below.

Unfortunately such nuclear defenses can be countered in several ways. Of these, the ample application of decoys is the most effective. The result is a most intricate problem whereby decoys and other penetration aids have to be matched against radar detection, methods of discrimination, and eventually an ample and readily available supply of rockets carrying defensive nuclear warheads.

It has been correctly stated that the problem of missile defense has many components besides the development of defensive explosions and the observations of the effects of these defensive explosions. At the same time one must remember that in this intricate question all factors interact. It has been claimed that the problem of our nuclear defenses is mostly connected with the development of radar and that tests are not needed to make progress toward missile defense. This sounds to me almost as absurd as if someone claimed that good fencing requires only excellent eyesight and that actual training in the wielding of the foils is not a necessity. One must remember that in the match between an incoming nuclear explosive and a defensive nuclear explosive the properties of the explosive used are of decisive importance and that the relatively unexplored field of the effects of nuclear explosives at high altitude can produce surprises and can provide solutions to problems which arise from the continued change in our detection and discrimination techniques.

It would be a mistake, however, to believe that missile defense is the only important field in which further tests are essential. An example of another field is the development of clean and cheap explosives for tactical purposes.

By underground explosions we have made in recent years considerable progress toward the development of clean nuclear devices. Cleanliness is in fact of great importance in tactical applications. Great harm may be done to noncombatants, and even the safety of our own troops would be jeopardized by the fallout from our own explosives. On the other hand, if small, clean explosives become easily available, the effect of this firepower is the same as that of conventional artillery of an extreme mobility. One can apply one's nuclear explosions for the purpose of destroying concentrated armed forces of the enemy and one can deprive any Soviet aggressor of the use of his massive manpower equipped with conventional means of combat. To pursue this aim it would be necessary to decrease the cost of nuclear explosives and to produce plenty of the best nuclear explosive, which is plutonium. We have pursued the first aim to a limited extent and we have been remiss in the plentiful production of plutonium. In the balance of power as applied to limited nuclear conflicts, this omission may have fatal consequences in the coming years.

There exists the undeniable danger that a limited nuclear conflict may escalate. One must realize of course that a conventional conflict may also escalate. It is somewhat doubtful that the danger of escalation justifies our neglect of serious preparation for a limited nuclear conflict and is sufficient reason for our expensive alternative plan of preparation for conventional battle. A recently published Soviet book on military strategy edited by Soviet Marshal Sokolovsky contains no assurance that the Soviets will refrain from using nuclear weapons in a limited war, and it also fails to state that use of nuclear weapons on the battlefield of a limited conflict by our side will make escalation more likely.

Neither limited conventional war nor a limited nuclear conflict can be eliminated from our planning. In dispersed guerrilla-type activity as is now going on in Vietnam, there is no reason to use nuclear explosives. On the other hand, in case of a massive confrontation our conventional forces would have to be concentrated, which would make us particularly vulnerable to the nuclear weapons of the other side. If we have not prepared for limited nuclear war, the use of Russian tactical weapons would place us before the desperate choice of accepting massive defeat or initiating all-out intercontinental war by our own action. It is my conclusion that the development of the means of tactical war gives us one of the essential tools by which we can counter enemy action in an appropriate manner without escalation. Another equally essential tool is an ample stockpile of plutonium.

It has been stated above that the Russians are ahead of us in the development of the biggest nuclear explosives. They also claim to be ahead in missile defense. It should be added that it is in general hardly possible to compare the status of American and Russian development. No one on our side possesses adequate knowledge of the state of nuclear art in Russia. But there is one general argument which indicates that the Russians are probably ahead in a much more general and dangerous manner than is commonly realized.

Our methods of observation have been good enough to find out at what time the Russians conducted their first nuclear explosion and their first thermonuclear explosion. The speed with which they developed the atom bomb and the hydrogen bomb gives a clear indication of their technical competence. They have performed these difficult tasks rapidly and with little testing. In recent years they have tested in the atmosphere with greater frequency than we have. Assuming that they have not lost their technical competence we are led to the almost unavoidable conclusion that these tests, or rather experiments, must have told them many of the things that we wish to know. The Russian tests may in fact have opened up some problems connected with nuclear explosives which are not even suspected by our side.

Development of explosives for missile defense and for tactical nuclear warfare have been used to illustrate the importance of making further progress in nuclear weapons. There is a general reason of even greater importance why this development must not come to a standstill.

Nuclear explosives have developed rapidly, and the problems connected with them have changed radically every few years. Further research and development will open up unknown and unimagined possibilities. This may be connected with inflicting damage. It may also be connected with defense against damage. One thing seems virtually certain. If we stand still we are going to make no progress. On the Russian side even a moratorium will permit further progress because no one has claimed that small nuclear explosions can be policed. The claim that explosions under a few kilotons or under one kiloton will not lead to essential progress is completely unsupported. Such applications have led to the development of our clean weapons. Small and undetectable explosions in the atmosphere can be most powerful tools in developing missile defense, and small explosions can even be used as models on the basis of which big explosives can be designed. We know that we will be effectively bound by the test ban. On the other hand, we must assume that the Russians will exploit the loopholes which certainly exist for small kiloton explosions and which also exist in the field of space testing. Within a few years during a test ban we are likely to find ourselves at a fatal disadvantage vis-à-vis the Soviet Union.

It has been claimed that the recently negotiated test ban is essential to prevent proliferation of nuclear explosives. It is past experience that every nation that has come into possession of the raw materials for nuclear explosions did detonate a bomb within a few months. I do not believe that progress in this important field can be effectively limited. I rather believe that these difficult international problems have to be faced. The test ban will only serve to drive the problem underground and will give rise to a lawless situation as did the unenforceable law of prohibition in the United States. In case of a test ban lawlessness will become rampant in the international theater. Our overriding need is international co-operation and peace. In a lawless world we should find only chaos and catastrophe.

Plowshare

In most people's minds nuclear explosives are connected exclusively with the most destructive variety of war. In actual fact, these same tools hold the greatest promise of early, massive, and thoroughly economical peaceful applications. Active work on this subject has been going on for the last six years. Realistic plans are all but ready for a number of important and safe applications, and thinking is proceeding along many additional hopeful lines.

The main application of nuclear explosives for peaceful purposes is in a field best described as geographical engineering. The best example of this type of enterprise is a sea-level Isthmian canal.

Continued increase in shipping across the Panama Canal is likely to saturate available facilities in another decade. Needed improvements of the present locks will cost more than half a billion dollars and will be only a temporary solution requiring continued great expenditures for operation. Furthermore, the present canal as well as any successor of the kind here mentioned is extremely vulnerable to military attack. In case of a serious conflict we cannot count on the use of the canal.

It would be very much better to replace the Panama Canal by a sea-level waterway of great traffic-handling capacity which would require no operating expenditures and which could not be destroyed even by a nuclear attack. Unfortunately, such a canal constructed by conventional means on the present canal route is estimated to cost over $2 billion.

With the use of nuclear explosives the problem can be solved. A series of appropriately placed nuclear explosives could produce overlapping craters which would form a sea-level canal satisfying all the requirements stated above. Moreover, such a canal could be constructed according to detailed studies in any of five different places. The cost would range from $700 million for the shortest route to over $2 billion for the route cutting across Mexico. The fact that the canal can be constructed across one of several countries puts us in an excellent bargaining position.

Considering the widespread and exaggerated statements concerning fallout, the question naturally arises whether a massive job like the Panama Canal requiring a total explosive yield of many megatons could be excavated safely and whether such an enterprise would be politically acceptable even if safe operation were guaranteed. The development of clean explosives solves this problem. We have made considerable progress in this direction and the time is approaching when, according to our present hopes, a crater created by an appropriately buried clean nuclear explosive will be available for further engineering work immediately after the explosion. This could be done without exposing anyone to a radiation greater than the amount that has been permitted in the laboratories of the Atomic Energy Commission, and that has never produced any observable ill effects.

It must be realized, however, that massive excavation is connected with earth shocks and with some blast effect in the atmosphere. Massive excavations will require evacuation of the area within twenty miles at the time of the actual blast.

The Isthmian canal is only one of many examples. Other possible canal constructions within the United States are certain sections of the Tennessee Tombigbee canal and a canal that could be blasted across the western end of the Aleutian peninsula.

The building of canals may be the most impressive but not the most simple of the earth-moving jobs. We can create a harbor on almost any shoreline for the amount of money that it used to take merely to equip the harbor. These harbors dug by smaller explosions may require evacuation to a distance of 5 or 10 miles at the time of the event.

Straight earth-moving jobs may be useful in other branches of civil engineering such as the building of roads and the preparation of the terrain for the location of railroad tracks. Studies have indicated that in case of some such civil engineering jobs within the United States millions of dollars could be saved by the application of nuclear explosives.

In the exploitation of water resources nuclear explosives can play an extremely important role. We could use this concentrated form of energy to close canyons, to dig new river beds and to break up water-impermeable layers, to permit the recharging of underground water deposits. One also could create reservoirs that could store water on the surface in considerable amounts. Some plans of such important engineering jobs have been discussed within the United States, as, for instance, the location of a dam on the Yukon River. The resultant water reservoir would extend to the borders of Canada, and the production of electricity would be more than twice that obtained from the Grand Coulee Dam.

Use of nuclear explosives for aid in mining is a problem whose solution is less advanced but no less important than the examples discussed above. Nuclear explosives can be used to blast away overburden and expose valuable mineral deposits at a depth as great as several hundred feet or even a thousand feet. Nuclear explosives also could be used to change the consistency of underground deposits such as tar sands or oil shale. In this way the United States and Canada might become independent of foreign oil supplies for the next century.

The importance of all the foregoing might become more vivid if one imagines that we continue to neglect this great opportunity and permit the Russians to acquire leadership in this field. We know of big explosions used behind the iron curtain both for mining purposes and for the deflection of a river. The Russians have claimed that they have performed all this with conventional explosives. If they have done so, this still may be merely an introduction to later use of nuclear explosives. One must remember, however, that the Russians have refused to let us inspect the sites of these explosions and we had no chance to verify whether these explosions indeed were conducted by conventional or by nuclear means. Russian initiative in Plowshare on a national or international scale would be a great victory in the technological race. Its propaganda value may well exceed that of Sputnik and the economical importance would dwarf enterprises like that of the construction of the Aswan Dam.

The above list does not include many of the dreams connected with nuclear explosions whose realization is open to doubt. It may turn out that nuclear explosives will play a decisive role in space propulsion and in engineering enterprises on the surface of the moon. It may be that nuclear explosives hold the key to problems like the desalting of seawater. These examples are mentioned on the basis of concrete proposals that are far from proved but which also give some hope. Even if one discounts these possibilities and considers only the projects of proven feasibility one must conclude that nuclear explosives, properly applied, could become the earliest massive way in which nuclear energy can find a highly profitable application in our peaceful endeavors.

Conclusion

The above statements have been made with the intention of showing that the dangers and the opportunities due to nuclear energy have not been generally understood by the public nor even by those who are charged with making the most important decisions concerning the future economic development and the safety of the United States. In a technical sense much has been accomplished. This has been due to the fact that nuclear energy is a fertile and rapidly developing field and to the admirable and successful efforts of the Atomic Energy Commission. Even so, it may turn out that when future historians look back on the decades following the discovery of nuclear fission they will be particularly struck by the great number of opportunities the United States has missed.

We could use Plowshare first in the United States and then throughout all continents as a cheap and powerful tool to open up raw material resources and exploit water for agriculture for power and for transportation.

We could vitalize our nuclear power industry by a support-price for plutonium which would also insure our future strength to resist limited aggression in a limited way.

We could unite with our Allies in a mighty technical effort to regain leadership in missile defense and other fields of nuclear technology.

Instead of all this we see our nuclear policy determined not by imagination and hope but by caution and by fear. In an earlier phase of the industrial revolution American enterprise was often called crazy; in the nuclear age it may well be called timid.

LABOR POWER AND RESTRAINT

by Edward H. Chamberlin

Edward H. Chamberlin has been David A. Wells Professor of Political Economy at Harvard since 1951. Professor Chamberlin is known chiefly for his *Theory of Monopolistic Competition* (1933). He has served on various government committees and in recent years has concerned himself particularly with problems of collective bargaining. He is the author of "The Economic Analysis of Labor Union Power" and other essays in this field.

Terminology is important. Indeed, it has been said that if, in an argument, you can get your adversary to adopt your terminology, the battle is half won already. I am sure that few of us realize the extent to which we already use the Marxian language, either directly or indirectly in ordinary speech, and even officially. Few of us, too, realize the extent to which this language derives from the classical economics. Indeed, the first sentence of Adam Smith's *Wealth of Nations,* too long to quote in full, is to the effect that "the annual *labor* of every nation" supplies it with what it "annually consumes," with no explicit reference to capital or to management. It is well known that Ricardo had a *"labor* theory" of value, and Marx claimed to have got his theory from Ricardo!

It remains true that with Marx labor is "exploited": the capitalist income derives from a position of power whereby the "capitalist" keeps a part of what rightfully belongs to labor, whereas both Smith and Ricardo clearly recognized the contributions to production undoubtedly made by both management and capital. Yet both the classical ("liberal") and the socialist terminology make it easy and natural for us to speak of the "average productivity of *labor*" when what we really mean, whether in the individual firm or in the whole economy, is the average productivity of all the productive forces taken together.

The language makes it easy for labor to make—and in perfectly good faith—claims for wage increases on the basis that "labor" productivity has increased, no matter what the actual cause of the improvement. Since the concept for the economy as a whole is arrived at by the simple arithmetic of dividing the total national income by the number of man-hours worked, "labor" productivity will *always* increase with greater efficiency, even though the improvement may be entirely the result of superior equipment or of better management. To avoid misunderstanding, let me make perfectly clear that I am not here attempting to give a full answer to the difficult question of "justice" which is involved in the sharing of the fruits of technological progress—although there is much to be said for what would happen in a genuinely competitive regime—that they would be enjoyed, not by any particular interest, but by the community *as a whole* in the form of lower prices. I want only to point out that calling it "labor productivity" makes a major contribution, through the machinery of collective bargaining and the strike threat, to the setting of wage levels which are not unrelated to technological and structural unemployment.

Another bit of Marxian terminology which is widely used is "capitalism" as a description of Western economic society. There can be no doubt that it has a certain general acceptance, in spite of the fact that it carries with it the strong flavor of a class society in which all power is concentrated in the hands of a property-owning class. Evidently, the Communist cause has a major interest in labeling every form of organization which is non-Communist as capitalism. To the underdeveloped countries the word is poison—identified with *foreign* controls, especially of minerals and raw materials, and for us to talk with them at all in terms of the achievements of "capitalism" in modern America seems an incredible blunder.

To the European too, I have learned that capitalism means something very different from the system which has evolved in this country. In Europe there was a feudal past to break down. A strong tradition of status militated against that erosion of the social system which is a natural concomitant of active price competition. Cartels were a natural development, agreements in restraint of trade were not forbidden. In Europe there was naturally no attempt to "preserve" a type of competition which had never existed anyway.

As a result, the most effective way in Europe for labor to oppose established economic power was through the *political* machinery: working for change either through evolution on the one hand, or through the threat of revolution on the other. Strikes, and the threat of strikes, have on the whole been much more political in character—a method of political warfare—than as with us a "normal" part of the bargaining process. As a result it has been amply demonstrated that using the *machinery* of democracy, so-called "capitalism" may be transformed into a welfare state, in which the traditional goals of socialism are largely realized.

As a natural concomitant, labor organizations in Europe generally are more all-embracing and more centralized than here in America. To most people there, "capitalism" suggests the earlier period of greater power in the hands of owners before these more recent developments had taken place. It certainly does not carry with it the idea of competition, either in the product market—the selling of raw materials and goods as with us—or in the labor market—the recruiting and holding of a labor force.

The cynic—and the doctrinaire Marxian—will say that we have the same organized business power in the United States, and that labor should have complete freedom to oppose that power by any means whatsoever. But in America we have a different background. Our period of political unionism was short-lived. Radical unionism clearly had no future here, and Samuel Gompers was right when he decided in favor of—well, what has come more recently to be called business unionism.

We never had to cope with the feudal tradition. On the contrary, the leaven of expansion into new territory lying to the west provided so much opportunity over such an extended period of our early history, that something like equal opportunity for all became firmly established as a part of the American ideal. It has remained so even after the frontier was a thing of the past, right down to the present time. Thus, we make a brave attempt in industry to prevent or regulate monopoly—to "preserve competition" in the belief that great concentrations of economic power are incompatible with the ideal. Of course it is a much discussed question how successful this policy is. But in contrast with Europe, there can be no doubt that the spirit of industry in this country is a highly competitive one, and I think the anti-trust laws are an important part of the reason why this is so.

At the same time we have placed virtually no restrictions upon collective actions by laborers. Employers fought unionism from the first, and the concern of government was to protect laborers from this opposition. Such protection, however, in spite of some noble affirmations in earlier legislation, became really effective only with the Wagner Act in 1935. It became effective because not only did the act virtually eliminate employer interference, but it provided directly the administrative machinery through which collective bargaining was to be brought about. Its declared purpose was to "encourage the practice and procedure of collective bargaining," and in this it was eminently successful.

One cannot escape the conclusion that it went to the extremes that it did not only by reason of problems arising out of the Great Depression but as a natural reaction from the other extreme of employer insistence upon what was surely an antiquated conception of industrial relations. It is not surprising that this sudden and complete release from frustration in the organization of labor should lead to manifold excesses and to exaggerated conceptions of labor's position in the economy. Labor, having been held back for so long, was now presented with what seemed to be complete freedom of action.

But in a liberal society there must be a limit to *any* growth in power. What seems so strange in retrospect is the view held by so many in the early days and by so many even today that the labor "cause" is a movement, and one is either for it or against it. In the words of one labor leader testifying before Congress, even to *raise the question* of whether unions have too much power is to question their very right to exist. I am indeed raising the question, as I think any economist who takes his job seriously must. But I protest that this is *not* challenging the right of unions to exist.

Given this attitude, however, it is not surprising that the first and rather limited attempt to circumscribe union activities, the Taft-Hartley Act of 1947, was fought as a "slave" labor law; and not merely before, but for years after it was passed. To come back to terminology, even with Taft-Hartley, labor's position of power was such that the late Sumner Slichter used to say in the fifties that we lived, not in a capitalistic, but in a *laboristic* economy.

At any rate, if we really hope to establish in these United States a workable free economy, it seems to me that we have to graduate beyond the careless notion that *any* part of society—say, laborers—has the right to act collectively in groups "of their own choosing" *without due regard for the effects of their actions upon others.*

We like to call ourselves a "free society," yet there is a paradox in the very idea of freedom which is at the heart of the whole problem. It is well expressed in a phrase used each year in the commencement exercises at Harvard University in conferring the several degrees in law. And because it is paradoxical, it always brings a light ripple of laughter. The candidates are declared "ready to aid in the shaping and application of those wise restraints which make men free."

We easily forget about these "wise restraints." In fact, economists, and especially economic theorists (of whom I am one), bear a heavy responsibility for helping us to forget about them. It is an old and familiar principle that our economy depends for its proper functioning on self-interest or, more technically, on every unit, whether consumer, la-

borer, or business firm, seeking to maximize something—
satisfaction in the case of the consumer, wages for the laborer and profits for the firm. It is our legacy from classical
individualism, and it will be found in most textbooks—
rarely, I think, today without qualifications, yet I have recently seen it put in extreme form, viz., that it is the *duty*
(no less) of each individual or group to exploit his economic advantage to the full.

Evidently, a philosophical principle as convenient as this
one will not be overlooked by any special interest seeking
to justify its own selfish conduct. Perhaps it is only human
nature, after all, to believe that what is good for one's own
particular group is good for the country. The famous example of Mr. Wilson and General Motors is only one of
many. So we are told by business that profits are essential
and must not be interfered with, by farmers that agriculture prices must be maintained at an artificially high level
so as to keep the whole economy in proper balance, and
by labor that wages must be jacked up steadily every year
so that the economy will not collapse for lack of spending.
In all these cases there is enough partial truth in the proposition to erect a plausible argument in its defense. The trouble is that this harmony of individual and social interest
(with respect to the issues here contemplated) is true only
under certain special assumptions, so that as a *general*
proposition it is simply not true at all. The most important
special assumption is the absence of concentrated economic
power, or, if you will, the absence of power generated by
group action. In other words, that principle of genius, the
famous "invisible hand" of Adam Smith, by which crude
self-interest satisfies social need, depends on an "atomized"
economy, in which, because the individual units are small,
the power problem simply does not arise. Smith never contemplated mass production through large corporate units,
because he never imagined that such complex organizations
could meet the minimum requirements for their internal
co-operative activity, which would make them economically efficient. And of course Smith never even *dreamed* of
modern Big Labor, with its similar problems both of in-

ternal integrity and of power in relation to the rest of the economy.

Economic power is usually *monopoly* power in some form—another word which labor doesn't like (or business either, or anyone, for that matter); and under atomized, so-called "pure" competition no one has any degree of such power. The result is most simply illustrated in the refined "competitive model" of an economy, for which the economic theorist is so much responsible, where attention is focused on price, or in the labor market on a wage. Only by joint action can the price or the wage be increased for the joint benefit of those who have concentrated their power and are acting together. The individual unit, acting alone, cannot raise its price; it "maximizes" its income only by increasing its output, and by so doing it *increases* the national income, which is in the general interest. This simple example, which runs in the limited terms of quantitative output, is capable of indefinite extension into more realistic problems of quality, efficient service, channels of commerce open freely to all, and so forth.

Of course, groups in society exist for many purposes, and some of them, even though mildly restrictive, may be defended if the restrictions are incidental to desirable social gains. But the avowed purpose of *most* collective action, both in industry and among laborers, is precisely to limit or remove competition between members of the group itself. In the case of labor in particular one may add: either to keep others out, or to force them in in order to control them better. Again for both (and of even greater importance) the purpose is to act more effectively as a power in its dealings with the rest of society.

The weak bargaining power of the individual laborer in dealing with his employer has long been recognized, although many elements of weakness in earlier days, arising for instance from extreme immobility and from a total lack of resources in case of a work stoppage, are no longer of the same importance. The chief source of imbalance was always that the individual worker is only one out of a large work force, so that for him to lose his job, although possibly a catastrophe for himself, mattered little to his employer. On this ground collective bargaining between a group of laborers and their employer, and over a wide range of matters beyond merely wages, has been widely defended and is clearly defensible because it deals with the fundamental issue.

But industry-wide bargaining, whatever one may say about it in the end, is another matter. By standardizing practices and wages over a wide area where conditions are actually different, it no doubt plays its part in rendering the whole economy less competitive. And ordinarily it strengthens monopoly power. With minor qualifications, there can be no doubt that higher wage or other costs mean higher prices. Now it seems to be generally recognized that businessmen, acting together over an area of the economy, may extract monopoly profits from it, and we are committed to a policy of trying to prevent them. What is not seen is that labor, acting together over the same area, may do precisely the same thing.

If the potential monopoly income is there, higher wages will force the higher prices through which it is collected and turned over to labor. Or labor may first support the higher prices, as in the soft-coal industry through legislation in the thirties, thereby increasing ability to pay, and collect afterwards. Mr. John L. Lewis and the United Mine Workers affords the classic textbook example of both procedures—as well as of many other things. There seems to be some agreement, for instance that the UMW goes the ordinary monopoly rule one better by maximizing not the total labor income in the field but the *rate* of pay per worker of those fortunate enough to be employed. One wonders how much the difficulties of the railroad industry today may not have the same explanation.

But "collective bargaining," whether in plant, area, or industry, is a misleading phrase by which to describe what really happens. "Economic warfare" is a much better phrase, and it has in fact acquired a thoroughly respectable usage in the literature. It is an especially good term now that we may speak of the cold as well as the hot. As has already been intimated, the rules are at a minimum. According to the New York *Times* of August 31, 1962, the

President of the Flight Engineers acknowledged that he "had had talks, looking towards possible affiliation, with the International Longshoreman's Association, the Transport Workers Union and the Teamsters." So a union is free to seek the most advantageous affiliation, and so bring the collusion of other laborers against their own employer, often with completely destructive force. The threat of potential violence and intimidation through the picket line are powerful factors, so powerful in fact, that nowadays a firm, although it would be within its legal rights, rarely attempts any operations at all if a strike has been called. Boycotts, "hot cargo" rules, refusals to work with non-union labor or on materials produced by non-union labor or by the wrong union, are used with impunity to close the channels of trade and commerce.

While I was in England recently, a British economist of standing who had some familiarity with the work of the McClellan Committee, ventured to hope that it was not too late to bring labor power under some sort of reasonable control in the United States, although he thought England had definitely passed the point of no return. I joined him in the hope. Wise restraints—that is the key. They are necessary for labor, too, in a free society.

FEDERALISM

by Alfred de Grazia

Dr. Alfred de Grazia is Professor of Government at New York University. He has taught political science at various American universities and is the author of numerous books, among them *Public and Republic* (1951), *The American Way of Government* (1961), *The Elements of Political Science* (1952, rev. 1962) and *Politics and Government* (1962).

Modern life is complicated enough. Yet, to every question of social policy, be it outdoor recreation facilities or school lunches for children, we must add the question: should the states or the federal government perform the proposed task? Is there some reason behind this practice, or are we perennially victims of a primeval compromise called federalism, an accident of time and the desire to create a nation?

The reason for the practice, it might be asserted, is implied in the success of American federalism for ninescore years. What has worked, brought wealth and power to the country, and engendered ample liberties can be justified by these facts.

However, the sheer ritualism of that argument will not satisfy the thoughtful person. He may hope that such is the case. He may even take it as a prior article of faith. But finally he must analyze it. If there is an association between a country's success and federalism, it needs to be demonstrated.

Of dozens of historical federations, most have failed. The United States has been the only one to grow to greatness while still a federated nation. Moreover, its successes may have been due both to the original nationalism that was

provided and to a subsequent new nationalism that under-
cut federalism. Furthermore, if it was federalism that un-
derwrote America's successes, that federalism may itself be
fast disappearing, whence we must urgently inquire into its
nature in order to learn how to preserve it.

American federalism was an invention composed of traditional and tested parts. Perhaps nothing save the Electoral College for choosing the President was a new instrumentality in the new Constitution. After the Union was
established, a number of states copied its forms, but originally the Union imitated the forms of the states. Then each
proceeded to work independently with the people and their
social institutions, while the limits of its actions were
watched over by the federal judiciary.

The federal government got its initial force from a brilliant plan and a few tough and versatile leaders. Its early
drive fed upon its direct relation to citizens as individuals,
upon its proprietorship over a vast domain of land (including dominated territorial governments), and upon small
wars. It could probably not have succeeded, furthermore,
if it had been born in an age when the philosophy and
practice of mercantilism or of the welfare state prevailed,
for it would then have been committed to ruling the whole
economy, and, failing that, would have collapsed. That is,
federalism could prosper under the constitutional rules freeing business and creating institutions, such as a uniform
currency, favorable to enterprise; but it could not endure
the centralizing effects of heavy governmental regulation
and ownership of business. In view of the last consideration, the Civil War becomes more understandable: a growing industrial society of the North and Midwest was riding
upon the early forces of federalism but still, because its
policies and those counterposed by the South strove for
ever higher stakes in favorable federal legislation, in effect
failed to gain its objectives within a federal structure. The
war was a blow from which federalism has not yet recovered: the one question, whether it is prohibited to secede,
was finally resolved, but a new set of grave questions arose
that still beg for solution.

The Infrastructure

Whatever the reasons for its original growth, American federalism has provided enough experience to permit its analysis in the light of general federal theory. Federalism is a way of ordering human relations that gives final authority on some questions to governments of areas smaller than the whole union. It contains a division of functions. It guarantees this division and more by a form of pluralism in which autonomous groups are based on geography. It is a form of decentralization with special powers of initiative and veto granted to the decentralized areal units.

The final authority and independence of the parts depends upon their possessing certain critical institutions. To enjoy what may reasonably be called federal authority, a state must have an independent active public, an independent set of officers, an independent legislative power, an independent protective and police power, and an independent judiciary. Without any one of these, the federal nature of the arrangement will disappear in favor of centralization. What is particularly federal about these institutions is that a very powerful political force is required to undermine them; ordinary political and legislative activity leaves them unscathed; they can be damaged only by a shocking concentration of power or by cumulative attrition applied to their "load-bearing" points.

When Madison and Hamilton defended the federal Constitution in the debate over its adoption, they were most impressed by the strength of the states. To them it was obvious that the states carried the aforesaid instruments of independence and also that they would continue to possess them in the face of any foreseeable contingency arising under the proposed Constitution. Thus Hamilton wrote, in Number 28 of *The Federalist*, "It may be safely received as an axiom of our political system, that the State governments will, in all possible contingencies, afford complete security against invasions of the public liberty by the national authority."

The public and elite of the states, he says, will be attentive to such dangers: "Projects of usurpation cannot be masked under pretenses so likely to escape the penetration of select bodies of men, as of the people at large. The legislatures will have better means of information." The states have the power to oppose and know how to use it. "Possessing all the organs of civil power, and the confidence of the people, they can at once adopt a regular plan of opposition, in which they can combine all the resources of the community."

It must be admitted that the two distinguished authors were quite unable to picture the mobilization of forces of which the *national* government would be capable.

They could not know, of course, how the Electoral College would be converted into an instrument for the direct popular election of the President. They could not have foreknowledge of the nationalizing decisions of Chief Justice John Marshall. They might have seen the nationalizing effects of nationally organized political parties. But they could not anticipate the Civil War and its consequent nationalizing amendments, or the amendments of the early twentieth century, permitting a national unapportioned income tax, and requiring the direct election of U.S. senators by the public of the states. They might have taken into account the powers inherent in a President who is chief executive, commander-in-chief, and the expresser of the national will. Furthermore they gave too much credence to the theory that political revolutions occur as conspiracies and to the related converse theory that the states would be so much in touch with one another that they could organize and plan an opposition to centralization. The apparent naïveté of the last two ideas may be partly owing to the authors thinking still of small interconnected groups as running the states and nation. It may be due also to their desire to sell the Constitution to the public then and there; long-range hypotheticals had to wait. In any event, rather than to criticize them, we should do better to criticize those who have failed to draw the appropriate lessons from the century and a half of experience that followed.

Today the position of the states is vastly weaker. The scope, domain, and intensity of state actions relative to national governmental action have greatly diminished. Two basic causes are evident. Popular attention has turned away from the problems of the states, and without a public a rule is weak and undirected. Furthermore, a resignation of authority on the part of state officials is notable, not so much in particular cases and issues as in the lack of drive toward a better life within the state through using the numerous instrumentalities available to the state.

Actually the ability of the states simply to survive as anything beyond administrative subdivisions of a unitary government hinges only upon the structural safeguards accorded the states in the federal Constitution. If one were to write a set of *Federalist* papers today defending the Constitution, he would probably allow the same desperate importance to the defense of the states in the scheme of the union as the original authors gave to the defense of the national interest. To him, public opinion and the leadership must appear just as indifferent, hostile, and skeptical as they did to the original federalists.

A closer examination of those structural bulwarks of federalism is therefore in order. The first is free elections. The elements here are many. They include a free state electorate with an independently established suffrage requirement. They include a freely established republican form of government that cannot be altered by the national government. They include a political party system that, while associated with a national party, operates independently on a local and state level; it can take contrary or minority positions without incurring unbearable reprisals from its national association. A free electoral system also includes a legislature and a governor whose election does not to any great degree depend upon the policies of the central government. So long as these structural features remain, one important condition for federalism exists.

The free legislative power must be granted considerable scope. There must be a reservoir of competence to decide important issues without occasioning massive retaliation by the central government. The scope of these powers, which even originally were never unlimited, must have a boundary at which the total co-ordinated forces of the state can

be lined up for defense and offense. Somewhere there must
be a defensible line in relation to the regulation of commerce, the power to tax, the care of the indigent, and so
forth. There is no perfect or even logical boundary between
central and local authority to legislate. Yet there must be
a battle line. And the territory on each side of the battle
line must be of some value to both sides and to the population of the area.

The definition of the line is the original great compromise
settlement of every federal constitution and from then on a
source of unending contention. What rights of intervention
in society are exclusive, which concurrent, which denied to
both—these are the concepts that come into play over time.
When, however, the legislators and the people are uninter-
ested in the line, then it may be rapidly extinguished, and
the whole apparatus of federalism can become antiquated
and meaningless. When the courts charged with constitutional review become rigidly confident as to where the line
lies, as if it were written in some nationalistic or statist text,
they may deadlock the federal system.

Additional strong points of the system are the independent police and protective power and the independent judiciary. In each case, as in the legislature and principal
executives, the sources of independence lie in the manner
of selection and sustenance. Originally the state militias
were counted upon as a counterpoise to power at the national level and at the same time a national resource; separately constituted, they might be used for the defense of
the state internally and externally except insofar as they
might conflict with the national military authority and as
they might be assimilated to the national forces in conditions of emergency. Today the state militias are a national
guard so tightly bound to the national military establishment that their personnel can carry little force by reason
of their state origins. It was a federalized national guard
unit, it may be remembered, that in Alabama in June of
1963, directed its state Commander-in-Chief, the Governor,
to obey the federal Commander-in-Chief, the President.

On the other hand, the state and local police forces operate free of such built-in pressures. The Federal Bureau

of Investigation and other federal police units provide and receive certain co-operative services from them but are still far from a commanding position. The expansion of the federal enforcement arm has occurred in connection with the extension of federal powers into new areas of social behavior. It has not struck at the principal basis of the state and local enforcement system.

The relations between the state and federal judiciary have changed in the same general way. Independently chosen, the state judiciary has ruled a separate court system. A state judiciary that would have been a branch of the federal, or vice versa, was and is conceivable. But it would probably be less resistant to unifying forces than the present scheme, which was only partially dictated by the Constitution. It results in some overlapping of jurisdiction, but the two structures are independent.

The power of the federal courts, however, to define the meanings of the Constitution, coupled with their national method of appointment and their typically national outlook, has often enabled national executive and legislative authorities to carry out policies that would, if they had been presented to the state court systems for determination, have been constitutionally disputable.

Meshing of Federal and State Machinery

This latter aspect of the judiciary highlights the important question of the machinery used to resolve difficulties in the American federal system. Not only the judiciary but also the political and legislative machinery and the enforcement system of the two governmental levels must come into frequent contact in the course of their activities. From the beginning of the republic there has been a mixture of modes of contact and communication.

In all of them are involved both the need to make federalism possible and the possibility of impairing the system. Thus, it is apparent that the laws of state and federal governments must be meshed to some degree to prevent widespread conflict and injustice. Hence state and federal courts perform many of the same tasks, as well as separate tasks, and do so both as independent and as dependent bodies.

At the same time, for the aforementioned reasons—the power to read the Constitution—a considerable centralization and conceivably a complete centralization might occur by means of federal court opinion. The *Baker* v. *Carr* decision of 1962 on the subject of apportionment is an instance of how the federal courts can not only assume jurisdiction over a subject once almost exclusively that of the states, but also go to the root of determining the structure of another branch of government in the state government, the legislature, by setting rules of "equal" apportionment.

There is presently no institution in American constitutional law to check the Supreme Court in this regard. Assuming a willingness on the part of other federal branches to countenance and exploit such a development, it may proceed apace. The Supreme Court can blast a hole in the federal fence through which another federal authority can drive its truck.

How do the other branches of government stand in this respect? The federal executive may of course follow up initiatives allowed him by the federal courts. For instance, whereas the initial effect of the decision in the case of *Baker* v. *Carr,* referred to above, was, among other things, to enhance the power of the courts, the long-range effect will be to strengthen the "presidential" faction in many states. The chain of causes and effects here is elaborate; it develops, in sum, out of the tendency of reapportionments fostered by the courts to favor the elements in both parties that are most influential and dependent upon the Presidency.

The President may also seek to unite the political parties and public opinion behind his program in order to accomplish politically a unified course of action of the federal and state governments. This is permissible and common behavior. The federal system depends, after all, upon the mutual consultation, co-operation, and alliance of decentralized and federal authority. Federalism should not be a synonym for automatic resistance to state-federal co-operation.

But, going beyond political co-operation of the traditional type, which arises out of common perceived needs and mild mutual sanctions, additional possibilities arise for rigging the political machinery of the country to ensure national predominance. Thus, if presidential patronage is very heavy, as it was in the early New Deal, national political domination can be promoted.

Moreover, to take a case where the causation is more indirect and yet more important, too, whenever the powers of the central executive are strengthened, the powers of the states are weakened. This comes about because the national legislature is more oriented to maintaining state power than the national executive is. Increasing federal executive power reduces the strength of those favorably disposed to federalism and carries right down to the grass roots of state and local politics.

There are really four general political parties in the American Congress: the presidential Republican party, the presidential Democratic party, the congressional Republican party, and the congressional Democratic party. The latter two are more federally rather than nationally oriented.

They would be far stronger than the presidential parties and therefore, one might say, more readily capable of defending states' rights if it were not for the fact that they are chaotically organized, with separate roots in each and every state. Furthermore, for them a number of substantive issues, such as race relations and labor-union rights, are more important than the shape of federalism, so that the interest struck up in the latter is likely to be extinguished by the disputations concerning the former. It would appear, therefore, that an attempt to organize a true federal interest must cut across party lines and embrace compatible substantive positions on social and governmental issues as well. Here as everywhere, the states'-rights interest is feeble politically; despite its ultimate and long-range importance, its protection depends upon being a by-product of a politically more volatile combination.

The beginnings of such a volatile and therefore organizable combination can be closely related to the issue of federalism itself. There is nothing spectacular about a number of structural reforms of state government, but if persistently sought and generally enacted, they can lend stability, intelligence, and long-run effects to the movement toward a new federalism.

Reform of the state representative structure to assimilate the true urban interest is one step to take. By this is meant not reapportionment by equal population districts but representation of metropolitan areas and some degree of functional representation of social and industrial interests in the state legislatures. The need here is for a representation somewhere between sheer lobbying and specific corporate seats.

States may also ease directly the pressure of metropolitan problems, which, along with the problem of race relations, is a threat to our federal system, by helping to organize metropolitan government so as to evade the conflicts of jurisdiction that plague the urban places of many states. This would involve both new general planning and governmental authorities, and also functional authorities operating over specially created districts.

Moreover, the states, whose metropolitan areas converge with those of adjoining states have an urgent obligation to compact under the federal Constitution for the solution of problems common to both. As complex as such interstate compacts may appear to be in prospect, they are probably no more difficult than the problems facing the businessmen and organizations already operating (even if under difficult circumstances) in the same interstate area.

Four Important Federalist Issues

Also basically related to the issue of federalism and yet possessed of considerable political potential are the grant-in-aid programs by which the federal government extends funds and services to the states under a variety of conditions. In a typical year, from 10 to 14 per cent of state and local revenues come from such grants. The range of functions is wide, but of a total of $7.4 billions in 1962 (est.), $3.0 billions went for highways, $3.2 billions for social welfare, $.3 billion for agriculture, and $.3 billion for education.

This relationship has been called "co-operative federalism" to distinguish it from "dual federalism," by this writer and others. Under co-operative federalism, usually, state and federal personnel, funds, and rules of action are jointly approved and administered by the two levels of government. Under "dual federalism" any similar tasks of the two governments are performed independently, exclusively, concurrently, if at all.

At the beginning of the republic, the dual method of conducting federalism was preferred to the co-operative way. "Good fences make good neighbors" was the policy. James Madison wrote once that the national government working on a purely nation-to-state basis would require compulsory procedures that might readily bring "equal calamities to the innocent and the guilty, the necessity of a military force, both obnoxious and dangerous, and in general, a scene much more resembling a civil war than the administration of a regular government. Hence was embraced the alternative of a government which, instead of operating on the States, should operate without their intervention on the individuals composing them."

For a long while this feature of the American federal system was considered a mark of superiority. Then, however, came a period beginning early in this century when national policies began to be imposed through offers of money and assistance to the states. Some of these, such as social welfare programs, were conceived to be probably unconstitutional, given the attitudes of the Supreme Court as then constituted. The grant-voluntarily-received was thought to be a way of evading legal nullification. As it turned out, the Constitution will not "permit" just about every national activity that today is found in the form of co-operative federalism, so that if that were the only reason for grants, they would be unnecessary.

There are other reasons for the programs of grants. One is the fear of state inactivity in areas where an "American standard" is desired by a great many people and is regarded as more important than any issues of state self-rule that may be involved.

The next reason would have to do with finances. It is

widely believed that some states are too poor to pay for their own programs in these areas. Such a judgment is highly subjective. On a scale of capacity to tax, the states vary widely, and a goodly number of the poorest are among those that have tried least to stretch their capacities. By contrast, a few states, such as New York, not only tax their own citizens highly in relation to resources, but also contribute disproportionately to the federal grant programs.

But again, it may be urged that national standards are highly efficient in a society whose members move about so frequently. Uniform state codes might be one answer but not a satisfactory one, since the states have been historically slothful in employing them. A second answer would be to let the national government legislate (in co-operation with the states) the uniformities, while abandoning the grants and the supervision.

What is being suggested here is that the whole set of grant-in-aid programs be examined to determine whether their form any longer serves their function. It may be that they serve negatively a federal system. State governments are notoriously malorganized: the grants-in-aid have not served to better this condition.

Even if they had not rendered state government more chaotic, they have helped to diminish the sharpness of the state image and therefore weakened the sense of accomplishment and personal responsibility that we would wish the leadership of a state to develop, both as an end in itself and as a means to a free society. Here the question is: are "certain American standards" impossible to attain without depressing the more important, if less tangible, "American standards" of initiative, voluntarism, and localism?

Still bearing Madison's words of caution in mind, let us re-examine three major additional problems of contemporary society that have a federal aspect. One is race relations, another is city government, yet a third, education. The race-relations issue is particularly poignant. It enveloped the republic in a disastrous civil war, and it is an agonizing cause for the country today.

If we are to retrace our steps in this case, with a view toward establishing a solution for the future, a policy closer to the idea of dual federalism might be preferred. The national government has for some time lacked very little of the power and means needed to combat racial discrimination in America. Without touching the state governments directly, it might have established a federal electorate, federal elections for federal offices, federal aid to housing, non-discrimination in federal jobs, non-discrimination in the armed forces, and federal schools. In fact, practically everything that the sociological mind might conceive of as calculated to reduce discrimination and increase opportunities among Negroes might have been planned and executed without compelling the states that were directly involved.

The preparation, therefore, of an omnibus legislative program that would use the national government as such, alongside but separate from the state government, in certain states and counties would be an expeditious and relatively conflict-free way of accomplishing the same purposes as stand today back of continual disorders and a probably extended period of continued discrimination.

The case of the government of cities is different. The basic failure of the cities is leadership. Leadership is wanting in the cities, in the states, and in the nation for metropolitan problems. People who have a vision of what city life might be like are singularly absent from the metropolitan political scene. Inasmuch as over 60 per cent of the people of the country and more than that much of the wealth of the country, and most of its educational, cultural, and technological resources are embraced by the metropolises of the country, such a statement might appear astonishing, but one constant fact of all social life must be realized: all the resources of the world do not bring direction or drive.

One of the hardiest illusions of democracy is that leadership springs spontaneously out of the mass of people once they are provided a license to participate fully in politics. The illusion stands and causes a locality, a state, or a nation to act in accordance with it even when the patent facts of life are to the contrary. Perhaps never does a community contain more than 5 per cent of active and informed

citizenry. The average is closer to 3 per cent, or three out
of one hundred adults. And when these are distributed
among the various functions and levels of government, the
number of persons from whom leadership may be obtained
is extremely low.

It should surprise none, but it always does, that a metropolis should be in effect headless under the conditions
of American political life. Over half of the population is
formally disqualified from participation in much of central
city politics by the fact of living in a suburb during the
night. The intricacies of party organization eliminate many
others who have neither the patience nor the time for politics as such.

The fragmentation of metropolitan organization into
independent agencies, towns, committees, commissions,
boards, civic and welfare associations, and educational and
other functional specializations of government, prevent any
sizable group from constituting what might be called the
civic or political community. When both formal requirements and social pressures operate to reduce the number
of leaders, a jurisdiction of any kind must be in deep trouble. It will not continue to operate as an open society and
cannot adopt policies for the whole that are anything but
catch-as-catch-can.

Consequently the metropolis is always on the verge of
intellectual and organizational bankruptcy, if not fiscal
bankruptcy. Thereupon the city group leaders set up a cry
of outside interference, of being strangled in their attempts
to cope with the problems of government and, depending
upon the times, attack either the machine or the state government. They turn to the national government for support, since the national government has never been closely
tied to city government. They see in it a benefactor, a
sympathetic and financially benevolent friend, a disinter-
ested provider of the wherewithal of good government.

It is difficult to justify this view empirically. Why can a
national government provide more solutions to city problems than state government? One argument has it that a
number of metropolitan districts cross over state lines. Yet
interstate compacts are fully competent to handle this type

of situation. The Port of New York Authority, for instance, is the lusty offspring of a compact between New York and New Jersey to control and develop transportation facilities of the region.

That a whole nation should act to solve such a problem is an unprincipled position that says only the policy in itself matters, not how it is done, who does it, or what its consequences are. The argument that national law, by superseding state law, simplifies the situation in comparison with trying to reconcile two bodies of state law, cannot be valid, inasmuch as the national law is in fact a third law jostling the other two systems with just as much conflict.

Supposing the metropolis in question to be contained in one state, a second argument advanced for national intervention is fiscal. The cities, it is said, cannot afford the costs of unification. That they pay the greater costs of non-unification somehow does not seem to enter the picture.

Moreover, the state in many cases does not assume its full obligations to tax its citizens to provide the circumstances that make a city workable and livable. Why should the citizens of other states be taxed for this purpose? And, if they are, will not the typical result be to discourage those metropolises and states that put forward the greater effort to relax and ride along on the promise of national aid? Regrettably, the general response of local leaderships is to seize the opportunity provided by Washington and "ride on it." Those more responsible elements of local leadership who seek to make their own way with local resources are thus sometimes discredited as "do-nothings" or "suckers."

Still another argument for national action is that the services performed are national in effect. But no viable philosophy of individualism or local autonomy ever asserted that national effects are produced only by national initiatives and that all local causes produce local effects. The philosophy of Athens educated the Roman Empire; the Roman Empire reduced Athenian culture to mediocrity; the florins of Florence helped stabilize the bookkeeping of England. The engineers of Glasgow ran the ships of the British Empire. If the proof here is not ample there is the *reductio ad absurdum:* nothing that happens in a city is

without national effect. Should the national government
then do everything?

A related contention is that many activities are national
per se. The government uses the cities for the mails, housing its employees, transporting its personnel, and so on.
Should it not pay for these uses? It should, and can very
easily, by direct assessment on the same bases as other
users of city facilities. Contracts of this kind should cause
no concern except to the few who would use the doctrine
of governmental sovereignty for free-loading.

What then of mass transit programs, city planning, public housing, support of the fine and performing arts; should
they be left to the states and their cities to tend to? They
should. Indeed they must, because such programs are at
best gambles of the public treasury, and the treasury that
gambles should be the one that best knows the odds, the
state and local community. Why the latter should best
know the odds can be explained and will be, but only after
an effort at judging the intervention of the central government into education.

It is of course improper to treat the question of federal
aid to education as if it were something for the future. The
nation aids public education in many ways: by grants to
research, by conducting research itself, by carrying on or
aiding the school systems of the states to carry on education in those areas where federal personnel are numerous.
At least a billion dollars goes to these purposes annually.

It is further proposed that the central government go
directly into the support of education on all levels and for
purposes of constructing physical facilities and improving
the quality of instruction. Such worthy aims cannot be
lightly treated. Yet for several reasons and not alone out
of regard for the structural formalities of federalism, federal aid to education should in most cases be opposed.

General federal aid to education can never be so general
as to prevent injury to the slighted and unaided portions of
education which are bound to consist of some of the most
important kinds of education—civic, religious, humanistic,
and social science.

It must, if it is rather general and extensive, damage the

private school structure of the country—both religious and secular. It must tend to create uniformities in a picture that is already far too uniform in curriculum and administration. It cannot help but produce controls, informal if not legal, and reduce the large body of lay board members around the country and many professional educators to rubber stamps or apathetic imitators.

Certainly here as in other areas, the reliance upon federal funds is a double-edged weapon. It does get money where and when money is temporarily available. (A number of federal aid programs, it is significant to note, have not at all increased since the first flush of generosity that created them.) But then the provision of the money must be referred back to the taxpayers. Again it is difficult to see the inherent virtue in passing money through federal hands: it does not become wise, efficient, and sanctified.

Are we here faced with an element of ideology, just as in the case of our cities? In both areas there is a flight of confidence from the known to the unknown.

Or is the central government known to contain as a permanent feature of its politics some predisposition to good and wisdom that the states and localities do not themselves possess?

Or granted the incredibility of this, may there not be some strong latent desire to transfer, under the guise of democracy, certain functions from the hands of politicians to the hands of experts? "The rationalism born of technological pride," wrote Yves Simon, "hates human liberty both on account of its excellence and on account of its wretchedness." Many a professional educator and antiauthoritarian liberal would like to be rid of the school boards and uncertain popular support that they suffer locally in exchange for a bureaucratic school order managed by their mirror images.

Again it should be insisted that money—in education, for cities, and for other purposes as well—is to be had almost wherever in America the service is being performed. In a few highly limited and specialized areas, activity or aid by the central government is desirable. The great majority of states are at least as competent as the central government to say what makes a city a good place to live in, what makes good racial relations, and of what consists a good education.

It is scarcely understood by the general public that the states have performed creditably in all of these regards in many places. Furthermore, the states are increasing their activity, their taxing, and their spending. General revenues of state and local governments went up 101 per cent between 1952 and 1960, and their direct general expenditures rose 99 per cent. Their debt increased by 132 per cent. These percentages have risen at a faster rate than the Gross National Product in recent years. We need not go into the merits of the new activity at this point, but it certainly cannot be offered as an argument for nationalization of functions that the states are inert.

Unfortunately, the analysis of the problems just treated and of the general topic of federalism are at a rather low level of theory and method. The numerous studies of federalism that emanate from official sources are concerned almost entirely with financial and administrative problems of federal-state relations. At other times, the agencies of reform merely warm up cold chestnuts; they tell the government that the states should and must remain a keystone of our national structure, and let it go at that, hoping for the best. They could use some of what John C. Calhoun once called "those higher faculties of the mind (called metaphysical by those who do not possess them) which decompose and resolve into their elements the complex masses of ideas that exist in the world of mind . . . and without which those deep and hidden causes which are in constant action, and producing such mighty changes in the condition of society, would operate unseen and undetected." In short, we need better philosophy, better sociology, and better political science in dealing with the issues of federalism.

The comparative studies of social customs and institutions as they differ from state to state, where they are available, are generally ignored by the agencies that are responsible for telling us about the effects of federalism. Their own recommendations are all too often of a petty kind and indeed the scope of the action which they carve out for themselves is often of that order. One cannot read, for instance, the record of the Joint Federal-State Action Committee from 1957 to 1959 without some dismay. That group, charged with identifying problems and recommending the shifting of functions and revenue sources from national to state, achieved minor changes in the Atomic Energy Act, disaster relief arrangements, and migratory labor. Most of its other suggestions went unheeded by Congress, the President, and the public, although its birth came about as a suggestion of the President. It must be emphasized that the problems of federalism are basic to American society and must be programmed in that light.

The Advisory Commission on Intergovernmental Relations, which began its work in 1959, has been more active and lends more hope. It carries members from all levels of government, on the whole of a somewhat sanguine frame of mind respecting the problems of federalism. Over half of its resources have gone wisely and necessarily into developing the ramified net of government relations without which research alone is helpless. Its reports have been methodologically more advanced than any others in the field. The commission needs more financial resources to deepen its research into the psychology and social significance of federalism. It needs an ever more forceful presentation of its findings and recommendations before the legislatures and Congress.

Inherent Advantages of Federalism

In the final analysis, the argument against the states on *specific* matters must become an argument against federalism *as a whole*. Ultimately, the case for federalism must rest upon some peculiar advantages possessed by a nation composed of many independent units. There are such advantages.

It is no longer of much use to speak of federalism as preserving a nation as a unity that might otherwise be dissolved into independent and possibly conflicting states. That situation and phase of American federalism are finished. We must look deeper and more generally for its justification.

We can find it in the resistance to majoritarianism. Why should not at least some minorities find a thoroughgoing means of expressing themselves, not alone as dissident voices outside the halls of power, but as locally triumphant activities?

Even if the results of federalism do not produce major local cultures, that is to say, if American life becomes quite standardized by the technological revolution and rapid communications, federalism can supply sources of experiment. Political scientists used to think in "big" terms about the experimental value of federalism; they imagined whole new societies testing under the umbrella of the union. Today one must think in much smaller terms. The scale must be that used in industry, where a given innovation may change a procedure of work, capture many thousands of dollars of profit, and add to human satisfactions and where numerous such innovations justify large effort, a numerous profession of management consultants, and research and development on a broad front.

We do not know the extent to which experts from one state learn from other states unheralded and how the federal government does too. If we could know, we should probably be pleased, but we should also realize the value of continuous and extensive study of comparative procedures and legislation of the states. Like the medieval alchemists, we have been ignoring useful metals while seeking to manufacture gold.

Supposing again that experimentation as well as independent minority cultures were rare, the excitation of initiative that federalism brings to many areas of life is itself a value transmutable into the national advantage and individual welfare. As society becomes increasingly bureaucratized, the sources of initiative have to be preserved and fostered, for they are practical rehearsals for larger things, and they are beneficial and humanizing in themselves.

There would be those who would feel pleasure at the idea that the states might disappear, because some cherished conviction of theirs is being frustrated in some one or another state. It is not enough to tell them to be patient, that some day some equally cherished conviction of their own will survive for the same reason. They must be assured not only of potluck from the federal system but also of some constant basic advantages that accrue continuously. Such are the results of state experimentation, of state initiative, and of the creation of instructed political leadership and citizenry for the nation from training and testing grounds within the states.

They can also be assured that the federal system acts against the concentration of powers in the central government, particularly in the hands of a potential dictator, and spreads power more equally among the people of the land. It inhibits a national single-party system.

At the same time the federal system provides in matters of defense against foreign enemies a resilient, many-headed, socio-political organism with survival value superior to the centralized polity.

The costs of these numerous advantages can be variously calculated. One might add together the charges for maintaining state capitals, of state supervision of localities, of separately organized and supervised police, courts, and elections, and come to some figure that is almost sure to be rather small in relation to all of government spending. If the equivalent operations were nationalized, perhaps $200 million would be saved annually. And this only if the centralized operations did not immediately expand, owing to the looser controls on them.

More significant by far are the indirect costs of federalism. These would include the costs of doing business in various states for truckers, insurance companies, banks, and other groups; the costs of administering separate tax systems; the costs of discovering and following different laws in different states for many purposes of life. How can these be evaluated? At a couple of billions of dollars? Again we presume no areas in which a changeover would increase costs through bureaucratization, lack of experimentation and fruitful comparisons, and so on.

Against these costs are to be matched the possibly very great savings that might occur as localities and states legislate, tax, and administer themselves; the savings from experimentation and initiative; and from all the other advantages. It is manifestly unfair to weigh federalism on a balance of money when direct money advantages are obviously solely on the nationalist side. If it may be concluded that federalism is of some cost to a country, at least in the direct and immediate sense, it is likewise apparent that the cost cannot be heavy and cannot loom large in considering the merits and demerits of a federal system.

With costs, as with other arguments raised against federalism, we are faced more with dangerous illusions than with a matter of fact. Federalism is, when all is said and done, an attitude, and that attitude is more important than any institution in determining the success or failure of federalism. The federal attitude regards due process of law as vitally important in a political order. It has confidence in people and bespeaks it by letting them suffer through their problems. It tolerates differences of many sorts. It tolerates, furthermore, a large measure of ambiguity in society. It does not insist upon the one best solution, though it may fight against the one worst solution. It has a sympathy for local sentiments, customs, and interests.

Many persons may support a federalist position out of many different motives. But unless they possess something resembling this constellation of attitudes, it is unlikely that they will be more than fair-weather friends of the federal system. If, however, such a set of attitudes is possessed by a large number of active citizens, and if they can agree that the principles set forth here are actually operative in society, then a considerable hope may be held out for the continued development of American federalism.

ON THE NATURE OF CIVIL AND RELIGIOUS LIBERTY

REFLECTIONS ON THE CENTENNIAL OF THE GETTYS-
BURG ADDRESS[1]

by Harry V. Jaffa

Dr. Harry V. Jaffa, Professor of Political Science at
Ohio State University, received his B.A. from Yale
and his Ph.D. from the Graduate Faculty of the New
School for Social Research. He has contributed articles
to *American Political Science Review* and other political and social science publications, and has written
two books, *Thomism and Aristotelianism* (1952) and
*Crisis of the House Divided: An Interpretation of the
Issues in the Lincoln-Douglas Debates* (1959).

There is general agreement among Americans that the central political issue of our time is the world-wide conflict
between Communist totalitarianism and political freedom,
that freedom whose principles are affirmed in such docu-
ments as the Declaration of Independence and the Gettysburg Address. All decent Americans repudiate Communism
and recognize their obligation to do what lies in their power
to prevent its ascendancy or triumph. Yet in the field of
civil liberties there is profound confusion as to what, in
crucial cases, decent, freedom-loving citizens may do. With
respect to freedom of speech and the closely related freedoms of assembly, association, and the right of petition,
the question continually arises: can we deny these freedoms
or rights to Communists, or their agents or coadjutors, with-

[1] I would like to dedicate this essay to the memory of my Father, who died on November 19, 1958.—HVJ

out ourselves ceasing, by that denial and to the extent of the denial, to constitute a free society? And, conversely, is it not true that if we do allow Communists the full advantage of these civil liberties we may allow them so to weaken and confuse our resistance that Communism may thereby be enabled to succeed? In short, may it not be true that the indispensable means for denying success to Communism are at the same time the necessary instruments for the self-immolation of freedom? That we may be confronted with such a dilemma has certainly puzzled the will of many conscientious lovers of freedom amongst us. Perhaps even more serious is the sharp conflict which has developed from time to time between those who have grasped one or another horn of the supposed dilemma.

This difficulty is not a new one in the experience of this republic under its present constitution. We should remember that if Thomas Jefferson opposed the Alien and Sedition Acts, George Washington favored them. The Civil War, however, presented the problem in its most acute form. It would perhaps not be inapt to sum up the experience of the years 1861 to 1865 by saying that no American statesman ever violated the ordinary maxims of civil liberties more than did Abraham Lincoln, and few seem to have been more careful of them than Jefferson Davis. Yet the cause for the sake of which the one slighted these maxims was human freedom, while the other, claiming to defend the forms of constitutional government, found in those forms a ground for defending and preserving human slavery. In his message to Congress on July 4, 1861, President Lincoln propounded the universal problem within the particular crisis in these words:

And this issue embraces more than the fate of these United States . . . It forces us to ask: "Is there, in all republics, this inherent and fatal weakness? Must a Government, of necessity, be too *strong* for the liberties of its own people, or too *weak* to maintain its own existence?"

That the liberties Lincoln had in mind were the civil liberties referred to above is shown by his defense, in a major section of that address, of his suspensions of the writ of habeas corpus. All civil liberties depend absolutely upon the privilege of this writ, since no one can exercise his freedom of speech or of association, for example, if he can be detained or imprisoned at the pleasure of any official. It is well then to consider that since the Constitution (Article I, Section 9) provides that the privilege of the writ of habeas corpus may be suspended "when in cases of rebellion or invasion the public safety may require it," the Constitution must contemplate the lawful abridgment under certain circumstances of the freedoms of the First Amendment. It must do so unless the First Amendment is supposed to have cancelled that part of the original Constitution which allows the suspension. No one seriously maintains this, however, because every good thing the people of the United States seek to accomplish in and through their government depends upon the ability of that government to preserve itself. And certainly nothing that led to the adoption of the First Amendment in any way affected the reasons for believing that "in cases of rebellion and invasion" the government might not be able to survive without suspending the writ.

When Lincoln defended his suspensions of the writ of habeas corpus in his Fourth of July message, he was mainly concerned to justify its suspension by the *Executive*. The provision of the Constitution in question is in the article that sets forth the powers (and the limitations upon the powers) of *Congress*. Lincoln's explanation of why the power to suspend cannot be confined to Congress is a masterly example of constitutional construction:

> Now, it is insisted that Congress, and not the Executive, is vested with this power. But the Constitution itself is silent as to which or who is to exercise the power; and as the provision was plainly made for a dangerous emergency, it cannot be believed the framers of the instrument intended that in every case the danger should run its course until Congress could be called together; the very assembling of which might

be prevented, as was intended in this case, by the rebellion.

Earlier in the same message, however, Lincoln had taken much broader ground. Provisions of the Constitution, taken literally, can be in conflict, sometimes in direct contradiction, with each other. As we have seen, the command of the First Amendment that "Congress shall make no law . . . abridging the freedom of speech," is in a certain sense incompatible with the proposition that Congress may, in time of rebellion or invasion, suspend the writ of habeas corpus. And so Lincoln, while denying that he had violated the Constitution maintained nonetheless that, if he had done so he would have been justified. For the Constitution also commanded him to "take care that the laws be faithfully executed," and he had sworn an oath so to execute them. All the laws were being resisted, and failing of execution, in nearly one third of the states, and the whole government faced dissolution if its authority could not be restored. But, he asked, if the Constitution denied him the power to suspend the writ of habeas corpus, should he prefer the total destruction of all the laws, and the government, to the very limited violation of this one law? Lincoln summed the matter up in his usual succinct way:

Are all the laws *but one* to go unexecuted, and the Government itself go to pieces, lest that one be violated?

It is the thesis of this paper that civil liberties are, as their name implies, liberties of men in civil society. As such, they are to be correlated with the duties of men in civil society, and they are therefore subject to that interpretation which is consistent with the duty of men to preserve the polity which incorporates their rights. But the preservation of a civil society does not and cannot mean merely its physical preservation or territorial integrity; nor can it mean merely its freedom from foreign domination or, for that matter, from domestic usurpation. For Lincoln, the preservation of the Union meant all of these things, but it meant above all the preservation of a body whose soul re-

mained *dedicated* to the principles of the Declaration of
Independence. The classic example of a dilemma in interpreting the Constitution, and one whose resolution may
well serve as a guide for resolving the difficulty with which
this paper began, is that afforded by the Fifth Amendment in the decades immediately preceding the Civil War.
Among other things, the amendment charges Congress that
"No person shall be . . . deprived of life, liberty, or property, without due process of law." The pro-slavery South-
erners maintained—and Chief Justice Taney in the Dred
Scott decision upheld the assertion—that a congressional
prohibition of slavery in any United States territory (as in
the Missouri Compromise legislation of 1820) had the effect of freeing slaves that a man had lawfully brought with
him into a territory. This, it was held, constituted an ar-
bitrary deprivation of property. The anti-slavery North-
erners, on the other hand, pointed to the fact that Negroes
were recognized many times by the Constitution as persons (e.g., Article I, Section 2, par. 3.; ibid., Section 9,
par. 1; and Article IV, Section 2, par. 3). They further
insisted that by the terms of the same amendment, no
Negro, being a person, might be held in slavery in a territory. The specific and immediate cause of the Civil War
was precisely this difference over whether the Fifth Amendment made it the duty of Congress to prohibit or to protect slavery in the territories. Every candid student of this
question must come to see, I believe, that the language
of the Constitution admits with nearly perfect impartiality
of either interpretation. In the so-called fugitive-slave
clause of the Constitution—the word slave or slavery never
occurs before the Thirteenth Amendment—a sanction undoubtedly is given to state laws which, in turn, treat certain "persons" as if they were not persons, that is, as if
they were chattels. In short, the word "person" is treated
in the Constitution in such ways that some persons may
be either subjects of rights of their own, or mere objects
of the rights of others. How to resolve this confusion in the
text of the Constitution could not be decided by reference
to the Constitution alone. As in many great matters, the
meaning of the Constitution had and has to be sought

outside the Constitution itself. The great debates that preceded the Civil War, above all the Lincoln-Douglas debates, turned on the question of the authority and meaning of the principles propounded in the Declaration of
Independence, as the guide for interpreting the Constitution. For there could be no doubt that if the Declaration
was authoritative, and if Negroes were included in the
proposition that "all men are created equal," then the free-
soil interpretation of the Fifth Amendment had to prevail, Chief Justice Taney to the contrary notwithstanding
* (Note: On this whole subject, see my *Crisis of the House
Divided: An Interpretation of the Issues in the Lincoln-
Douglas Debates.* New York: Doubleday, 1959, esp. Ch.
XIV, The Universal Meaning of the Declaration of Independence). It is too little realized that the final word
in the greatest of all American controversies is pronounced
in the magisterial opening of the Gettysburg Address.
Stephen A. Douglas had said, and the pro-slavery South-
erners agreed, that we existed as a nation only in virtue
of the Constitution, and the Constitution not only tolerated but gave legal guarantees to the institution of human
slavery. When Lincoln pronounced "Fourscore and seven
years," he forever fixed the year 1776 as the year of the
nation's nativity. In so doing he did not downgrade the
Constitution, he merely affirmed in the most solemn manner what he held to be the essential cause of the dignity
of the Constitution: that it was an instrument for better
securing those human rights affirmed in the Declaration,
that the Union which was to become "more perfect" took
as its standard of perfection, its ends or principles, the
"laws of Nature and of Nature's God" invoked in the earlier document.

The Union was created by its dedication to the equality
of man. Slavery, Lincoln held, might be tolerated as a
necessity, but only so long as it was understood to be a
necessary evil. Douglas sought a middle position, a national "don't care" policy which would allow the settlers
in the territories to decide as they wished in the matter
of slavery. This, Lincoln said with scorn, attempted to treat
as a matter of indifference something to which no human

being could be indifferent. It was, he said, as vain as the
search for a man who should be neither a living man nor
a dead one. Lincoln preferred the candid pro-slavery argument, where the issue could be squarely joined. And he
argued with unbreakable logic that if the slaveowners' interpretation of the Fifth Amendment were correct, and if
the Negroes' humanity were either denied or treated as of
no account, then the moral basis of the authority of the
whole Constitution had to be called into question, and
the American Revolution itself could be regarded as an
expression of mere force without right.

Free government rests upon the consent or opinion of
the governed. Law is an expression of opinion, and the
opinion upon which the law rests is more fundamental
than the law itself. "In this and like communities," Lincoln said in the first of his joint debates with Douglas,
"public sentiment is everything. With public sentiment,
nothing can fail; without it, nothing can succeed. Consequently, he who molds public sentiment, goes deeper than
he who enacts statutes or pronounces decisions. He makes
statutes and decisions possible or impossible to be executed." The Constitution was the creation of a people committed in the Declaration to the idea of human dignity.
Although the people is sovereign, its sovereignty may not
be exercised in a manner inconsistent with the moral
ground of its own authority.

"All men are created equal," is called a self-evident
truth. What does this mean? Not that all men are equal in
intelligence, virtue, strength, or beauty. They are equal in
certain "rights," and the meaning of these rights can perhaps be most easily expressed today in this negative way:
there is no difference between man and man, such as there
is between man and animals of other species, which makes
any man, that is, any normal adult human being, the natural ruler of any man. Man is by nature the master of dog,
horse, cow, or monkey. He is equally the master of the
dangerous wild animals he cannot domesticate, because he
can kill or capture them as a result of his natural superiority, and not because of mere accident. The rights

which men evidently have over other animals, they do not, it is equally evident, have over each other. Men are not angels—who, it may be supposed, would require no government—nor are there angels to govern men. Government, which does not arise directly from *nature*, is then grounded upon *consent*. To repeat, government does not arise *directly* from nature, but it does arise *indirectly*, to the extent that consent, to be the ground of legitimate authority, must itself be based upon a recognition of the essential difference between man and the brutes. If the consent of the governed were given to a regime which treated the rulers as if they were gods or angels, differing essentially in their nature from the ruled, the regime would also be illegitimate. Deception and force are equally incapable of giving rise to legitimate authority. Legitimacy cannot then be claimed for any regime in which the rulers treat the ruled as if they are animals of another species, as if the governed can be used as mere instruments for the advantage of the rulers. Such a regime is illegitimate, we repeat, even if the ruled, for whatever reason, believe that their own highest good consists in gratifying the rulers. The governed, in a civilized regime must, by the principles of our Declaration, be treated as beings with ends of intrinsic worth, which ends the government serves. Cattle may be killed, their flesh eaten, and their skins used to clothe human bodies, because of the indefeasible, objective natural difference between the soul of a man and the soul of a brute.

The Declaration, as we have seen, speaks of the specific nature of man and, inferentially, of its difference from other species, as self-evident. By this it is meant that we cannot demonstrate the essential likeness of men to each other and their difference from other animals. This is because all understanding of the world, all demonstration about the world, proceeds *from* the experience by which we grasp the terms of such propositions as: "This is a man, this is a dog, this is a tree, etc." A self-evident truth is not one which every one necessarily admits to be true; it is one the evidence for which is contained in the terms of the proposition, and which is admitted to be true by everyone *who already grasps the meaning of the terms.* Very young children, lunatics, and savages, are for various reasons deficient in those operations of the mind which issue in the abstractions, man, dog, horse, tree, etc. Hence, until their deficiencies are somehow overcome, they cannot be responsible members of civil society.

The men who founded our system of government were not moral or political relativists, as those terms are understood today. In affirming that all men are created equal, they expressed their conviction that human freedom depends upon the recognition of an order that man himself does not create. Man is not free to disregard the hierarchy of souls in nature. The equality of man flows from and corresponds to the inequality of the human and the subhuman, as it corresponds also to the inequality of the human and the superhuman. For man is part of the order of nature, and his dignity derives from the whole of which he is a part. This whole, being the cause of the dignity of the part which is man, is possessed of a dignity greater than man, for every cause is greater than the effects of which it is the cause. But the whole is not known to us as we and brute creation—the parts—are known. It is a mystery, but a mystery to which man alone in the universe is open. This fact is the ground of freedom of thought, which in turn is the ground of all other freedoms, including civil liberties. Freedom of thought is not freedom to deny that two and two is four. Someone who denies this may be more pitied than censured, but we do not see in his denial a consummation of his freedom. To repeat, all our liberties rest upon the objective fact of the specific difference of the human soul from subhuman souls, and the highest virtue of this difference is the human capacity to confront the mystery of the universe. This is what we mean when we say that the Declaration of Independence affirms the principle of the dignity of man. To call this principle an ideology—which means a mere rationalization of vulgar self-interest—is to demean and debase it. To call it a mere "ideal" is perhaps even worse. An ideal is distinguished from what is real, and the Declaration speaks not of something unreal, but of something real in the highest degree, namely, *truth*. Moreover, there are many ideals, but there is but one truth. To be guided by the laws of Nature and of Nature's God means to be guided not by multiple fantasies but by the unitary ground of actual existence. Present-day skepticism as to the laws of nature mentioned in the Declaration, does not supply us with an alternative ground for justifying civil liberty. Absolute skepticism is a self-devouring monster. Theoretically, it means doubting the ability to doubt. Practically, it teaches that if there is nothing that need be believed as true, neither is there anything that need be disbelieved. Unlimited skepticism quickly transforms itself into unlimited dogmatism. Political freedom exists only upon that wise and tolerant middle ground where men do not treat other men as brutes because they know that they themselves are not gods. But this restraint, this proud humility, is the attribute of those, and only those, who see in the order of nature the ground of the moral and political order.

Let us now turn to the problem with which we began. Does a free society prove false to itself if it denies civil liberties to Communists, Nazis, or anyone else who would use these liberties, if he could, as a means of destroying the free society? The answer, I believe, is now plain that it does not. In saying this I do not counsel, or even justify, any particular measure for dealing with persons of such description. What is right in any case depends upon the facts of that case, and I am here dealing only with principles, not their application. However, those who think that every denial of civil liberties is equally derogatory of the character of a free society, without reference to the character of the persons being denied, make this fundamental error: they confuse means with ends. Free speech is a priceless and indispensable attribute of a free society because it is a necessary means for deliberating upon public policy. But this deliberation does not extend to everything: above all, it does not extend to the question of whether the community shall exchange its freedom for slavery. Certain ends are fixed, and their fixity is the condition of mutability in other respects. The government may deliberate *how* to secure the rights to life and to liberty of all; it may never deliberate *whether* they shall be secured. Certain proposals can never be entertained by a civilized community. The essence of all such proposals would be to kill or enslave someone or some group in the community and distribute their property among the rest. Obviously, in any community in which such a proposal were seriously entertained, even for a moment, those who are proposed for proscription might rightfully consider themselves in a state of war with the rest, and feel justified in using every means to preserve themselves. But the right *not to be proscribed* is inherent in every part of the community, severally, and in the whole community, collectively. Hence *no one* ever has the right to introduce or advocate such a thing. Thus speech calling for the proscription of individuals or classes is inherently wrong, and there is an inherent right in every community to treat it as criminal, wholly apart from any consequences which can be foreseen at the moment.

Just as majority rule is a device for deciding matters of common interest where unanimity is impossible, but can never be rightfully used to destroy the minority, so free speech is a device for deliberating upon the common interest, but can never be rightfully employed to propose the destruction of either a majority or minority. Yet this is precisely what both Nazis and Communists do. Both are creeds calling for the proscription of individuals and groups innocent of any crime. The Nazis believe that one so-called race, the Aryan master race, is so superior to all others that it has the right to treat other men as if they were animals of another species. They do not hesitate to exterminate masses of human beings as if they were plague-bearing rats, or to use their skin as parchment, as if they were cattle. And Communists differ morally from Nazis only in proposing a so-called class, the proletariat, instead of a race, as the sole subject of moral right. For Nazis, morality is an intraracial, for Communists an intraclass phenomenon. Neither believe that faith is to be kept or, indeed, that there are any binding moral rules which extend beyond the barriers of race or class. The Nazis would, and have, proscribed every racial strain beyond the pale of their elite; and the Communists do the same with every class which they do not associate with the dictatorship of the proletariat. An American Communist is one who, if he knows the meaning, and accepts the discipline, of the Party, would use power arbitrarily to deprive his fellow citizens of their property and liberty and, if they resisted, their lives.

Communists and Nazis, I maintain, have no right to the use of free speech in a free society. However, whether it is wise or expedient to deny them its use is another matter. I believe that the United States is a sufficiently civilized and a sufficiently stable community to bear the advocacy of almost anything, whether it be National Socialism, Communism, or Cannibalism. I would take my stand with Jefferson, who in his first inaugural address said, "If there be any among us who would wish to dissolve this Union or to change its republican form, let them stand undisturbed as monuments of the safety with which error of opinion may be tolerated where reason is left free to combat it." But Jefferson only tolerated error; he did not in any way concede a right of the enemies of republican government to change it into a contrary form. As the context of this celebrated passage will show, it was only the impotence of the enemies of republican government which, in Jefferson's view, made it expedient, and right only because expedient, to tolerate them. And thus it was not inconsistent, as some critics have charged, for Jefferson to have instituted prosecutions by state officials for sedition, as he did, if experience revealed that the enemies of republican government were not as impotent as he had supposed. I would accordingly contend that, while it is seldom either expedient or wise to suppress the peaceful advocacy even of inhuman doctrines, in a community like ours, it is not for that reason unjust. But in communities very unlike ours—for example, in a new African nation, constantly threatened by relapse into primitive barbarism on the one hand, and by the barbarism of Communism on the other— the advocacy of many inhuman and indecent things would constantly have to be prohibited.

John Stuart Mill is the most famous of those who have or seem to have demanded absolute freedom of thought and expression. Yet, in the first chapter of his essay *On Liberty*, in the very next paragraph after he proposes his great libertarian principle, he adds a qualification which his present-day followers often overlook or disregard. "It is, perhaps hardly necessary to say," says Mill, quite mistaken as to the necessity, "that this doctrine is meant to apply only to human beings in the maturity of their faculties." The principle of liberty does not apply either to children or to those of less than legal age. Mill is very clear that he presupposes moral characters already formed, and not only able to distinguish right from wrong but disposed toward the right by a decent upbringing. Still further, Mill excludes from the application of his principle "those backward states of society in which the race itself may be considered in its nonage." Barbarians, like children, must be guided for their own good. "Despotism," he says, in a classic passage, "is a legitimate mode of government in dealing with barbarians, provided the end be their improvement, and the means justified by actually effecting that end. Liberty, as a principle, has no application to any state of things anterior to the time when mankind have become capable of being improved by free and equal discussion." I would ask those who today consider themselves followers of John Stuart Mill, what principle would exclude from the enjoyment of civil liberties the subjects of Akbar or Charlemagne, but admit the followers of Hitler or Stalin? Mill's great error was not that of believing moral qualifications were not necessary as a basis for the exercise of liberty. His error lay in his failure to discern that barbarism lurked as a potentiality of modern society no less than that of the Dark Ages. He perceived accurately the depth to which the spirit of modern science had penetrated the Western world, and he was right in believing that scientific progress in that world, and even beyond that world, was essentially irreversible. But he was utterly mistaken, in common with nearly all the thinkers of his time, in believing that the effect of the scientific spirit was to make men more temperate and just. The ability to be guided to improvement by conviction and persuasion, he said, had been "long since reached in all nations with whom we need here concern ourselves." He did not think it possible that a highly civilized modern nation could be persuaded to abandon the principle of persuasion. But we, who have seen Weimar Germany, the freest market place of ideas the world has ever known, give itself up to the Nazis, know differently. And we have also seen modern science flourish both in Hitler's Germany and Stalin's Russia. We know today that there is no necessary correlation between modern physics, chemistry, biology, and mathematics, not to mention the many branches of engineering, and a gentle and tolerant temper. Whatever the intention of the founders of modern science, there is nothing in its method which precludes its appropriation by men who are, in every other respect, barbarians.

There is no passage in the literature dealing with civil liberties more celebrated than the dissenting opinion of Mr. Justice Holmes in the Abrams case of 1919. The super-libertarians of our time quote it endlessly, and recite it as a litany, so much so that one wonders if many of them have not utterly forgotten the Declaration of Independence, with which it is, in many respects, in flagrant contradiction. We will present extensive selections.

Persecution for the expression of opinions seems to me perfectly logical. If you have no doubt of your premises or your power and want a certain result with all your heart you naturally express your wishes in law and sweep away all opposition. To allow opposition by speech seems to indicate that you think the speech is impotent . . . or that you do not care wholeheartedly for the result, or that you doubt either your power or your premises. But when men have realized that time has upset many fighting faiths, they may come to believe even more than they believe the very foundations of their own conduct that the ultimate good desired is better reached by free trade in ideas —that the best test of truth is the power of the

thought to get itself accepted in the competition of
the market, and that truth is the only ground upon
which their wishes safely can be carried out. That, at
any rate, is the theory of our Constitution . . .

. . . I think that we should be eternally vigilant
against attempts to check the expression of opinions
that we loathe and believe to be fraught with death,
unless they so imminently threaten immediate interference with the lawful and pressing purposes of the
law that an immediate check is required to save the
country.

I wholly disagree with the argument of the Government that the First Amendment left the common law
as to seditious libel in force. History seems to me
against the notion.

I should like first to notice Holmes' last point. No one
today doubts that the First Amendment did leave the common law of seditious libel in force in the states in 1791.
Since the publication of Leonard W. Levy's *Legacy of Suppression: Freedom of Speech and Press in Early American
History* (Harvard University Press, 1960) all controversy
on that subject seems to be at an end. Some doubt remains
as to whether the First Amendment, which explicitly laid
a prohibition only on *Congress,* allowed the *federal* courts
to enforce the common law of seditious libel. But that the
states remained free to enforce it, and did enforce it, is
not in dispute. In his draft of the Kentucky Resolutions of
1798, in the third section, Jefferson cited the language of
the Tenth Amendment, and then observed that

no power over freedom of religion, freedom of speech,
or freedom of the press being delegated to the United
States by the Constitution, *nor prohibited by it to the
States,* all lawful powers respecting the same did of
right remain, and were reserved to the States or the
people: that thus was manifested their determination
to retain to themselves the right of judging how far
licentiousness of speech and of the press may be
abridged without lessening their useful freedom . . .
[italics added]

Nothing can be clearer than that, according to Jefferson, the First Amendment laid a prohibition *only* on the federal government. So far was Jefferson from any theoretical views that would prevent the people or their governments from abridging freedom of speech and press, that he insisted that the right of judging when and to what degree they ought to be abridged was a right reserved to them by the Tenth Amendment.

In the same section Jefferson went on to speak of religious freedom in a way that distinguished it profoundly from other civil liberties. In the Constitution, he said, the people "guarded against all abridgment by the United States of the freedom of religious opinions and exercises, and retain to themselves *the right of protecting* the same [italics added] . . ." According to Jefferson the Constitution left to the states and the people the right to judge how far freedom of speech and press might be *abridged,* but left to the same authority the right only of *protecting* freedom of religious opinions. For Jefferson this distinction between religious opinion and other opinions was fundamental. In the *Notes on Virginia,* Query XVII, he says that the legitimate powers of government extend only to those natural rights which we have submitted to government and "The rights of conscience we never submitted, we could not submit." It is in this context that he pronounces the famous dictum, that "Reason and free inquiry are the only effectual agents against error," adding immediately, "Give a loose to them, they will support the true religion by bringing every false one to their tribunal." In the Virginia Statute for Religious Freedom, again referring to religious truth and error, he wrote "that truth is great and will prevail if left to herself . . . errors ceasing to be dangerous when it is permitted freely to contradict them." Dumas Malone, in the latest volume of his Jefferson biography (*Jefferson and the Ordeal of Liberty.* Boston: Little, Brown and Company, 1962) searches the writings of his hero in vain for even a single statement in which Jefferson defends unconditionally any freedom of opinion other than religious opinion. He finally concludes (p. 393), quoting the "reason and free inquiry" passage, that for

Jefferson "freedom of thought was an absolute, and *it may be assumed* that he applied [such maxims] not merely to religious opinion but to all opinion [italics added]." But Malone is wrong. It is no accident that he is forced to make such an assumption. The evidence does not exist because Jefferson did not say what he did not believe.

Freedom of thought was indeed an absolute for Jefferson. "The error seems not sufficiently eradicated, that the operations of the mind, as well as the acts of the body, are subject to the coercion of the laws," he also wrote in Query XVII. "The legitimate powers of government extend to such acts only as are injurious to others. But it does me no injury for my neighbor to say there are twenty gods, or no God. It neither picks my pocket nor breaks my leg." With the purely theoretical question of whether there is no God or twenty, Jefferson says government has no rightful business. But on the practical aspect of the question of whether the mind has a right to entertain such questions, and whether men must be left free by government to entertain them, there was no place in Jefferson's thinking for any neutrality. The error that the mind is not inherently free to speculate, is an error which, Jefferson says, seems not to be "sufficiently eradicated." To deny the power and right of the soul to confront the universe is a denial of human nature. Marxism, for example, by teaching that all opinions on the relation of man to God and to nature are nothing but ideology, that is, devices whereby the mind justifies and thereby co-operates in particular ways of relieving the demands of the body, treats the distinction between body and mind as essentially insignificant. It is no accident that every government professing Marxism therefore attempts to coerce the operations of the mind as well as those of the body. One cannot be equally tolerant then, and certainly Jefferson was not, of opinions destructive, and of opinions not destructive, of the regime of liberty itself. The sphere comprehended by what Jefferson called religious opinions, was essentially the sphere of theory. In his pungent phrase, it was the sphere in which a man's opinion, one way or another, neither picked Jefferson's pocket nor broke his leg. But political opinions, as

they bore on the security of the government which preserved men's absolute liberty of theoretical opinion, were
not matters of similar indifference. These Jefferson did not
entrust to the mere hazard of any "market" of ideas. In
his second inaugural address he wrote:

> No inference is here intended, that the laws, provided
> by the State against false and defamatory publica-
> tions, should not be enforced; he who has time, ren-
> ders a service to public morals and public tranquillity,
> in reforming these abuses by the salutary coercions
> of the law . . .

Mr. Justice Holmes has written that persecution is perfectly logical if you do not doubt your premises or your
power. But there are different kinds of "persecution." Jefferson was sick of the long, melancholy record of human
government by superstition and terror. To be blunt, he had
no doubt of the premises from which he deduced their il-
legitimacy, and he recorded his confidence when he proclaimed these premises to be self-evident truths. It was to
end persecution that he and his partisans drew the sword
of what was indeed a fighting faith. To persecute perse-
cutors, or to be intolerant of intolerance is then not the
contradiction that dilettantes of political philosophy sometimes affect.

As the crisis of the Civil War approached, many frenzied
efforts were made to placate Southern opinion. In 1860, in
the wake of John Brown's raid, Senator Douglas of Illinois
proposed a sedition law to punish abolitionist propaganda
as an incitement to crime. In the Cooper Union speech,
Lincoln argued against any such legislation. But he never
even suggested that it would be wrong to pass such a law
because it violated freedom of speech or of the press. "If
slavery is right," said Lincoln, "all words, acts, laws, and
constitutions against it, are themselves wrong, and should
be silenced, and swept away . . . All they ask, we could
readily grant, if we thought slavery right; all we ask, they
could as readily grant, if they thought it wrong. Their
thinking it right, and our thinking it wrong, is the precise
fact upon which depends the whole controversy." Freedom

of speech was logically subordinate to personal freedom, because a man who was a slave could not demand the right to speak. Lincoln argued over and over, with a logic which no one can now deny, that there was no principle by which the enslavement of Negroes could be justified, which could not also justify the enslavement of white men. The sheet-anchor of our liberties was not the Constitution but the principle of the Declaration of Independence, which alone gave life and meaning to the Constitution. To say that the Constitution protects the right to deny that all men are created equal, is as much as to say that it protects the right to deny any obligations to obey its law.

Lincoln and Jefferson both believed that a free government is the slowest and most reluctant to restrict the liberties even of its most dangerous and fanatical enemies. It is the one which least needs to protect itself by such distasteful means, because it is the one which commands the loyalty of the mass of the citizens by the benefits they feel in their daily lives. Still, it is necessary that our loyalty be enlightened, and to that end we must ever possess ourselves of the true standard by which to measure our blessings. If we fail to see the sanity and nobility of the charter of our own freedom, we will fail to recognize the barbarism of totalitarian doctrines. And it is much better if we repudiate the foul and perverted reasonings that would justify the bestiality of a Hitler or a Stalin, and all their regimes have spawned, by the force of opinion among us. For the more we accomplish by opinion, the less we will have to do by law.